W9-BZR-427

24 TESTED, READY-TO-RUN GAME PROGRAMS IN BASIC

Other TAB books by the author:

No.	771	*Integrated Circuits Guidebook*
No.	861	*Display Electronics*
No.	960	*IC Function Locator*
No.	1000	*57 Practical Programs & Games in BASIC*
No.	1055	*The BASIC Cookbook*
No.	1095	*Programs in BASIC for Electronic Engineers, Technicians & Experimenters*

Dedication

dedicated to all those incredible home computers

24 TESTED, READY-TO-RUN GAME PROGRAMS IN BASIC

BY KEN TRACTON

TAB BOOKS Inc.

BLUE RIDGE SUMMIT, PA. 17214

FIRST EDITION

FIRST PRINTING—NOVEMBER 1978
SECOND PRINTING—DECEMBER 1979
THIRD PRINTING—AUGUST 1980

Printed in the United States of America

Reproduction or publication of the content in any manner, without express permission of the publisher, is prohibited. No liability is assumed with respect to the use of the information herein.

Copyright © 1978 by TAB BOOKS Inc.

Library of Congress Cataloging in Publication Data

Tracton, Ken.
    24 tested, ready-to-run game programs in Basic.

    Includes index.
    1. Games—Computer programs. 2. Games—Data processing. 3. Basic (Computer program language) I. Title.
GV1469.2.T72   793.9   78-11779
ISBN 0-8306-9876-0
ISBN 0-8306-1085-5 pbk.

Cover illustration courtesy Atari Inc.

Preface

Many people look at game playing on a computer as a waste of time; unfortunately, they do not realize that this type of activity stimulates the user's interest in computers and program writing and helps him better understand computers.

Games should never be considered a waste of time because if they do nothing else, they teach the user something within the realm of the game whether it be reaction, calculation, logical reasoning or use of mathematical ideas.

Of course, the easiest way to learn about BASIC or about computers is to play with them, and games provide an excellent channel for this type of expression.

I would like to thank Peter for all his help and advice, and especially thank Bill and Dan for their infinite patience with me.

Ken Tracton

Contents

Section I
Computer Games In BASIC

This section contains 24 games in BASIC for your home computer. These games serve as exercises to increase your knowledge of programming in BASIC language and your working knowledge of what your computer can do.

Some games are word games. Others are combat or chase games where you're on search and destroy missions. Number games include guessing games and plotting routines. Some games show graphics displays while others are designed to be of practical use.

All games include a flowchart, sample run and program listing. All programs will run in 8K of memory (not including BASIC) except for Star Warp which requires 20K.

Information is included on which programs can be used on a Radio Shack TRS-80 computer. Section II contains actual program listings for some of the games for a TRS-80 or PET®.

WUMPUS

The wumpus is asleep somewhere in his cave of 20 rooms. You must track him down and shoot him with one of your five arrows. The trick is in not getting eaten by the wumpus, being taken to another room by a super bat, or falling into a bottomless pit during the hunt. Also, be sure to avoid shooting yourself with an arrow!

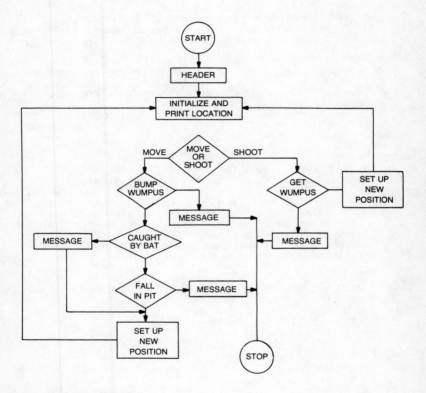

Flowchart for Wumpus

Sample Run

```
INSTRUCTIONS? (Y-N)
? Y
WELCOME TO 'HUNT THE WUMPUS'
   THE WUMPUS LIVES IN A CAVE OF 20 ROOMS. EACH ROOM
HAS 3 TUNNELS LEADING INTO OTHER ROOMS.(LOOK AT A
DUODECAHEDRON TO SEE HOW THIS WORKS --IF YOU DON'T KNOW
WHAT A DUODECAHEDRON IS, ASK SOMEONE)

      HAZARDS
BOTTOMLESS PITS, THERE ARE 2 OF THESE
FALL INTO ONE, AND YOU WILL LAND IN CHINA
   SUPER BATS - TWO OTHER ROOMS HAVE SUPER BATS. IF YOU
      GO THERE, A BAT GRABS YOU AND TAKES YOU TO SOME OTHER
      ROOM AT RANDOM. (WHICH MIGHT BE TROUBLESOME)

      WUMPUS
THE WUMPUS IS NOT BOTHERED BY THE HAZARDS (HE HAS SUCKER
FEET AND IS TOO BIG FOR A BAT TO LIFT).  USUALLY
HE IS ASLEEP. TWO THINGS WAKE HIM UP, YOUR ENTERING
HIS ROOM OR YOUR SHOOTING AN ARROW.
   IF THE WUMPUS WAKES, HE MOVES (P=.75) ONE ROOM
OR STAYS STILL (P=.25). AFTER THAT, IF HE IS WHERE YOU
ARE, HE EATS YOU UP ( & YOU LOSE!)

      YOU
EACH TURN YOU MAY MOVE OR SHOOT A CROOKED ARROW
   MOVING: YOU CAN GO ONE ROOM (THRU ONE TUNNEL)
   ARROWS: YOU HAVE 5 ARROWS. YOU LOSE WHEN YOU RUN OUT.
   EACH ARROW CAN GO FROM 1 TO 5 ROOMS. YOU AIM BY TELLING
   THE COMPUTER THE ROOM/S TOU WANT THE ARROW TO GO TO.
   IF THE ARROW CAN'T GO THAT WAY (IE NO TUNNEL) IT MOVES
   AT RANDOM TO THE NEXT ROOM.
   IF THE ARROW HITS THE WUMPUS, YOU WIN.
   IF THE ARROW HITS YOU, YOU LOSE.

      WARNINGS
   WHEN YOU ARE ONE ROOMS AWAY FROM THE WUMPUS OR HAZARD,
   THE COMPUTER SAYS
   WUMPUS  --   'I SMELL A WUMPUS'
   BAT     --   'BATS NEARBY'
   PIT     --   'I FEEL A DRAFT'

HUNT THE WUMPUS
--- --- --- --- --- --- --- --- ---

YOU ARE IN ROOM  2
TUNNELS LEAD TO 1              3                    10

SHOOT OR MOVE ? (S-M)
? M
OKAY, WHERE TO NOW?
? 3


I FEEL A DRAFT!
YOU ARE IN ROOM  3
TUNNELS LEAD TO 2             4                    12
```

```
SHOOT OR MOVE ? (S-M)
? M
OKAY, WHERE TO NOW?
? 4
A FIT, CHINA HERE I COME !!!!!!!
DUMMY, YOU LOSE, WUMPII JUST LOVE YOU!!!
SAME SET UP? (Y-N)
? YES
HUNT THE WUMPUS
-------------------------------

I SMELL A WUMPUS!
YOU ARE IN ROOM  15
TUNNELS LEAD TO  6             14              16


SHOOT OR MOVE ? (S-M)
? M
OKAY, WHERE TO NOW?
? 16

YOU ARE IN ROOM  16
TUNNELS LEAD TO  15            17              20

SHOOT OR MOVE ? (S-M)
? M
OKAY, WHERE TO NOW?
? 15
I SMELL A WUMPUS!
YOU ARE IN ROOM  15
TUNNELS LEAD TO  6             14              16


SHOOT OR MOVE ? (S-M)
? 14
SHOOT OR MOVE ? (S-M)
? M
OKAY, WHERE TO NOW?
? 14
DUMMY, YOU BUMPED INTO A WUMPUS!!
I SMELL A WUMPUS!
BATS NEARBY
YOU ARE IN ROOM  14
TUNNELS LEAD TO  4             13              15

SHOOT OR MOVE ? (S-M)
? S
NUMBER OF ROOMS? (1-5)
? 2
ROOM #? 4
ROOM #? 13
AHA! YOU GOT THE WUMPUS!
OKAY HOT SHOT, THE WUMPII WILL GET THEIR REVENGE
WUMPII SPIRITS WILL HAUNT YOU 'TILL THEN
SAME SET UP? (Y-N)
? NO
HUNT THE WUMPUS
-------------------------------

I SMELL A WUMPUS!
YOU ARE IN ROOM  18
TUNNELS LEAD TO  9             17              19

SHOOT OR MOVE ? (S-M)
? S
NUMBER OF ROOMS? (1-5)
```

Program Listing

```
10 REM HUNT THE WUMPUS

30 PRINT "INSTRUCTIONS? (Y-N)"
40 INPUT I$
50 IF I$="N" THEN      70
60 GOSUB    670
70 DIM S(20,3)
80 FOR J=1 TO 20
90 FOR K=1 TO 3
100 READ S(J,K)
110 NEXT K
120 NEXT J
130 DATA 2,5,8,1,3,10,2,4,12,3,5,14,1,4,6
140 DATA 5,7,15,6,8,17,1,7,9,8,10,18,2,9,11
150 DATA 10,12,19,3,11,13,12,14,20,4,13,15,6,14,16
160 DATA 15,17,20,7,16,18,9,17,19,11,18,20,13,16,19
170 DEF FNA(X)=INT(20*RND(0)+1)
180 DEF FNB(X)=INT(3*RND(0)+1)
190 DEF FNC(X)=INT(4*RND(0)+1)
200 REM LOCATE L ARRAY ITEMS
210 REM 1=YOU,2=WUMPUS,3&4=PITS,5&6=BATS
220 DIM L(6)
230 DIM M(6)
240 FOR J= 1 TO 6
250 L(J) =FNA(0)
260 M(J) = L(J)
270 NEXT J
280 REM CHECK FOR CROSSOVERS
290 FOR J=1 TO 6
300 FOR K=J TO 6
310 IF J=K THEN      330
320 IF L(J) = L(K) THEN      240
330 NEXT K
340 NEXT J
350 REM SET ARROWS
360 A=5
370 L=L(1)
380 REM RUN THE GAME
390 PRINT "HUNT THE WUMPUS"
400 PRINT"------------------"
410 REM HAZARD WARNINGS AND LOCATIONS
420 GO SUB  1090
430 REM MOVE OR SHOOT
440 GO SUB  1280
450 IF O = 1 THEN      470
460 IF O = 2 THEN      510
470 GO SUB  1370
480 IF F=0 THEN   420
490 GO TO  530
500 REM MOVE
510 GO SUB  1880
520 IF F=0 THEN      420
530 IF F>0 THEN      580
540 REM LOSE
550 PRINT"DUMMY, YOU LOSE, WUMPII JUST LOVE YOU!!!"
560 GO TO   600
570 REM WIN
580 PRINT"OKAY HOT SHOT, THE WUMPII WILL GET THEIR REVENGE"
590 PRINT"WUMPII SPIRITS WILL HAUNT YOU 'TILL THEN"
600 FOR J=1 TO 6
610 L(J)=M(J)
620 NEXT J
630 PRINT "SAME SET UP? (Y-N)"
640 INPUT I$
650 IF I$<>"Y" THEN      240
660 GO TO   360
670 REM INSTRUCTIONS
680 PRINT "WELCOME TO 'HUNT THE WUMPUS'"
690 PRINT " THE WUMPUS LIVES IN A CAVE OF 20 ROOMS. EACH ROOM"
700 PRINT "HAS 3 TUNNELS LEADING INTO OTHER ROOMS.(LOOK AT A"
710 PRINT"DUODECAHEDRON TO SEE HOW THIS WORKS -IF YOU DON'T KNOW"
720 PRINT "WHAT A DUODECAHEDRON IS, ASK SOMEONE)"
```

```
 730 PRINT
 740 PRINT"     HAZARDS "
 750 PRINT"BOTTOMLESS PITS, THERE ARE 2 OF THESE"
 760 PRINT"FALL INTO ONE, AND YOU WILL LAND IN CHINA"
 770 PRINT" SUPER BATS - TWO OTHER ROOMS HAVE SUPER BATS. IF YOU"
 780 PRINT "   GO THERE, A BAT GRABS YOU AND TAKES YOU TO SOME OTHER"
 790 PRINT "   ROOM AT RANDOM. (WHICH MIGHT BE TROUBLESOME)"
 800 PRINT
 810 PRINT"    WUMPUS "
 820 PRINT " THE WUMPUS IS NOT BOTHERED BY THE HAZARDS (HE HAS SUCKER"
 830 PRINT " FEET AND IS TOO BIG FOR A BAT TO LIFT).  USUALLY"
 840 PRINT " HE IS ASLEEP. TWO THINGS WAKE HIM UP, YOUR ENTERING"
 850 PRINT " HIS ROOM OR YOUR SHOOTING AN ARROW."
 860 PRINT "    IF THE WUMPUS WAKES, HE MOVES (P=.75) ONE ROOM"
 870 PRINT " OR STAYS STILL (P=.25). AFTER THAT, IF HE IS WHERE YOU"
 880 PRINT " ARE, HE EATS YOU UP ( & YOU LOSE!)"
 890 PRINT
 900 PRINT "    YOU "
 910 PRINT " EACH TURN YOU MAY MOVE OR SHOOT A CROOKED ARROW"
 920 PRINT "    MOVING  YOU CAN GO ONE ROOM (THRU ONE TUNNEL)"
 930 PRINT "    ARROWS  YOU HAVE 5 ARROWS. YOU LOSE WHEN YOU RUN OUT."
 940 PRINT "    EACH ARROW CAN GO FROM 1 TO 5 ROOMS. YOU AIM BY TELLING"
 950 PRINT "    THE COMPUTER THE ROOM/S YOU WANT THE ARROW TO GO TO."
 960 PRINT "    IF THE ARROW CAN'T GO THAT WAY (IE NO TUNNEL) IT MOVES"
 970 PRINT "    AT RANDOM TO THE NEXT ROOM."
 980 PRINT "    IF THE ARROW HITS THE WUMPUS, YOU WIN."
 990 PRINT "    IF THE ARROW HITS YOU, YOU LOSE."
1000 PRINT
1010 PRINT "    WARNINGS "
1020 PRINT "    WHEN YOU ARE ONE ROOMS AWAY FROM THE WUMPUS OR HAZARD,"
1030 PRINT "    THE COMPUTER SAYS "
1040 PRINT "    WUMPUS -  'I SMELL A WUMPUS'"
1050 PRINT "    BAT    -  'BATS NEARBY'"
1060 PRINT "    PIT    -  'I FEEL A DRAFT'"
1070 PRINT " "
1080 RETURN
1090 REM PRINT LOCATION AND HAZARD WARNINGS
1100 PRINT
1110 FOR J=2 TO 6
1120 FOR K=1 TO 3
1130 IF S(L(1),K) <>L(J) THEN  1220
1140 IF J=2 THEN  1170
1150 IF J=3 OR J=4 THEN  1190
1160 IF J=5 OR J=6 THEN  1210
1170 PRINT "I SMELL A WUMPUS!"
1180 GO TO 1220
1190 PRINT "I FEEL A DRAFT!"
1200 GO TO 1220
1210 PRINT"BATS NEARBY"
1220 NEXT K
1230 NEXT J
1240 PRINT "YOU ARE IN ROOM ";L(1)
1250 PRINT "TUNNELS LEAD TO ";S(L,1),S(L,2),S(L,3)
1260 PRINT
1270 RETURN
1280 REM  CHOOSE OPTION
1290 PRINT "SHOOT OR MOVE ? (S-M)"
1300 INPUT I$
1310 IF I$<>"S" THEN  1340
1320 O=1
1330 RETURN
1340 IF I$<>"M" THEN  1290
1350 O=2
1360 RETURN
1370 REM ARROW ROUTINE
1380 F=0
1390 REM PATH OF ARROW
1400 DIM P(5)
1410 PRINT "NUMBER OF ROOMS? (1-5)"
1420 INPUT J9
1430 IF J9<1 OR J9>5 THEN  1410
1440 FOR K=1 TO J9
1450 PRINT "ROOM #";
1460 INPUT P(K)
1470 IF K<=2 THEN  1510
1480 IF P(K)<> P(K-2) THEN 01510
```

15

```
1490 PRINT"ARROWS ARE NOT SUPER MAGIC, BE REALISTIC"
1500 GO TO  1450
1510 NEXT K
1520 REM SHOOT ARROW
1530 L=L(1)
1540 FOR K=1 TO J9
1550 FOR K1 = 1 TO 3
1560 IF S(L,K1)=P(K) THEN  1720
1570 NEXT K1
1580 REM NO TUNNEL FOR ARROW
1590 L=S(L,FNB(1))
1600 GO TO  1730
1610 NEXT K
1620 PRINT "MISSED"
1630 L=L(1)
1640 REM MOVE WUMPUS
1650 GO SUB  1800
1660 REM AMMO CHECK
1670 A = A-1
1680 IF A>0 THEN  1700
1690 F=-1
1700 RETURN
1710 REM SEE IF ARROW IS AT L(1) OR L(2)
1720 L=P(K)
1730 IF L<>L(2) THEN  1770
1740 PRINT "AHA! YOU GOT THE WUMPUS!"
1750 F = 1
1760 RETURN
1770 IF L<>L(1) THEN  1610
1780 PRINT "OUCH!!! ARROW GOT YOU!"
1790 GO TO  1690
1800 REM - MOVE WUMPUS ROUTINE
1810 K=FNC(1)
1820 IF K=4 THEN  1840
1830 L(2)=S(L(2),K)
1840 IF L(2)<>L THEN  1870
1850 PRINT"WUMPUS GOT YA!!!, DUMMY!!!"
1860 F = -1
1870 RETURN
1880 REM MOVE ROUTINE
1890 F=0
1900 PRINT"OKAY, WHERE TO NOW?"
1910 INPUT L
1920 IF L<1 OR L>20 THEN  1900
1930 FOR K=1 TO 3
1940 REM   CHECK IF LEGAL MOVE
1950 IF S(L(1),K)=L THEN  2010
1960 NEXT K
1970 IF L=L(1) THEN  2010
1980 PRINT"ARE YOU FOR REAL, THAT'S NOT POSSIBLE"
1990 GO TO  1900
2000 REM CHECK FOR HAZARDS
2010 L(1)=L
2020 REM WUMPUS
2030 IF L<>L(2) THEN  2100
2040 PRINT"DUMMY, YOU BUMPED INTO A WUMPUS!!"
2050 REM - MOVE WUMPUS
2060 GO SUB  1810
2070 IF F=0 THEN  2100
2080 RETURN
2090 REM - PIT
2100 IF L<>L(3) AND L<>L(4) THEN  2150
2110 PRINT"A PIT, CHINA HERE I COME !!!!!!!"
2120 F=-1
2130 RETURN
2140 REM - BATS
2150 IF L<>L(5) AND L<>L(6) THEN  2190
2160 PRINT"SUPER-BATS!!! GOOD-LUCK!!!!!!!"
2170 L=FNA(1)
2180 GO TO  2010
2190 RETURN
2200 END
```

An adaptation of this program designed specifically for the Radio Shack TRS-80 computer using Level II BASIC can be found on page 183 in Section II.

SUB HUNT

This game pits you against a nuclear enemy sub lurking in nearby seas. The area of conflict is a 10 × 10 unit grid, and the enemy can dive down to a depth of 10 units. Figure 1-1 helps you visualize the playing area.

Your mission is to destroy the sub. You have a limited number of depth charges. This number changes from game to game, but you always will have at least 16.

To destroy the sub, you must place the charge not only on the right coordinate but also fused for the right depth.

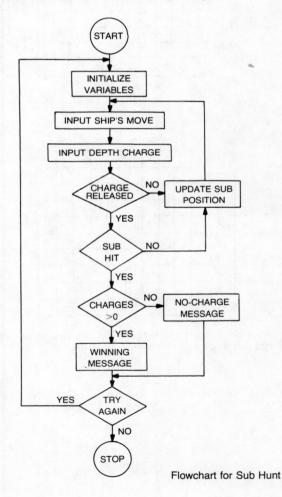

Flowchart for Sub Hunt

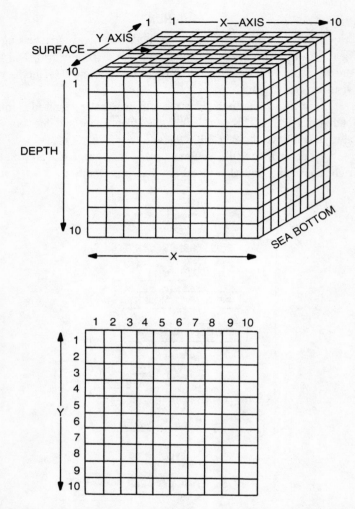

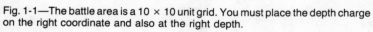

Fig. 1-1—The battle area is a 10 × 10 unit grid. You must place the depth charge on the right coordinate and also at the right depth.

18

Sample Run

```
RUN
SUB HUNT
WELCOME TO THE GAME OF SUB HUNT
THE ENEMY SUB MAY BE LURKING
ANYWHERE WITHIN THE GRID.

TO COMPLICATE FINDING IT AND

DESTROYING IT WITH DEPTH CHARGES,

THE SUB CAN ALSO DIVE.

DEPTH CHARGES MAY BE DROPPED

ANYWHERE ON THE GRID, BUT

THEY ARE NOT EFFECTIVE UNLESS

THEY HAVE BEEN SET FOR THE RIGHT

DEPTH.

SINCE THE SUB CAN DIVE TO THE SEA

BOTTOM, SO CAN DEPTH CHARGES BE

SET FOR THIS DEPTH, 10 IS THE SEA

BOTTOM, WHILE 1 IS THE SURFACE OF

THE SEA.

THE SUB'S POSITION WILL BE UPDATED

AFTER EACH MOVE, AS IT WAITS TO SEE

WHAT YOUR MOVE IS.

THE SUB, BEING NUCLEAR POWERED CAN

STAY AT ANY DEPTH, FOR ANY PERIOD OF

TIME.

TO DESTROY THE SUB, YOU MUST

DROP THE DEPTH CHARGE NOT ONLY AT

THE RIGHT COORDINATE, BUT IT MUST

BE FUSED FOR THE RIGHT DEPTH.

IF NOT, YOU HAVE WASTED A DEPTH

CHARGE.

YOU HAVE A DISADVANTAGE AND AN
```

ADVANTAGE OVER THE SUB.

THE DISADVANTAGE IS YOU'RE LIMITED
TO THE NUMBER OF DEPTH CHARGES
YOU HAVE, SINCE YOU HAVE BEEN AT
SEA SO LONG.

THE ADVANTAGE IS THAT THE SUB CAN MOVE
ONLY ONE SQUARE AT A TIME, AND ALSO
IT CAN MOVE ONLY UP OR DOWN IN DEPTH
ONE COORDINATE AT A TIME.

GOOD LUCK, COMMANDER.

YOU, COMMANDER, ARE AT COORDINATES 1,1

COMMANDER, WHERE DO WE SAIL FOR

? 5,5

COMMANDER, WHAT SETTING FOR DEPTH
CHARGES A SETTING OF 0 RELEASES NO
CHARGES

? 5

NELSON WOULD BE PROUD OF YOU

YOU GOT THE DEVIL SUB...

YOU STILL HAVE 9 DEPTH CHARGES

TO PLAY AGAIN TYPE 1, OTHERWISE 0

?0

THE COMPUTER KNEW YOU WERE A LANDLUB-
BER.

RUN COMPLETE.

Program Listing

```
10    REM THE GAME OF SUB HUNT

20    REM THE SUB HUNT IS PLAYED

30    REM ON A 10 X 10 GRID WITH

40    REM THE ORIGIN ON THE LEFT

50    REM TOP CORNER.

60    REM THE X AXIS READS FROM

70    REM 1 TO 10 GOING LEFT TO

80    REM RIGHT, THE Y AXIS READS

90    REM FROM 1 TO 10 GOING

100   REM TOP TO BOTTOM, THEREFORE

110   REM COORDINATE 10,10 IS THE RIGHT

120   REM LOWER CORNER OF THE GRID

130   REM SUBS ARE CRAFTY, WATCH THEM

140   REM CAREFULLY

150   PRINT

160   PRINT ''SUB HUNT''

170   PRINT

180   PRINT

190   PRINT ''WELCOME TO THE GAME OF
      SUB HUNT''

200   PRINT

210   PRINT ''THE ENEMY SUB MAY BE
      LURKING''

220   PRINT ''ANYWHERE WITHIN THE GRID.''

230   PRINT ''TO COMPLICATE FINDING IT
      AND''

240   PRINT ''DESTROYING IT WITH DEPTH
      CHARGES,''
```

```
250   PRINT ''THE SUB CAN ALSO DIVE.''
260   PRINT ''DEPTH CHARGES MAY BE
      DROPPED''
270   PRINT ''ANYWHERE ON THE GRID,
      BUT''
280   PRINT ''THEY ARE NOT EFFECTIVE
      UNLESS''
290   PRINT ''THEY HAVE BEEN SET FOR
      THE RIGHT''
300   PRINT ''DEPTH.''
310   PRINT ''SINCE THE SUB CAN DIVE TO
      THE SEA''
320   PRINT ''BOTTOM, SO CAN DEPTH
      CHARGES BE''
330   PRINT ''SET FOR THIS DEPTH, 10 IS
      THE SEA''
340   PRINT ''BOTTOM, WHILE 1 IS THE
      SURFACE OF''
350   PRINT ''THE SEA.''
360   PRINT ''THE SUB'S POSITION WILL
      BE UPDATED''
370   PRINT ''AFTER EACH MOVE, AS IT
      WAITS TO SEE''
380   PRINT ''WHAT YOUR MOVE IS.''
390   PRINT ''THE SUB, BEING NUCLEAR
      POWERED, CAN''
400   PRINT ''STAY AT ANY DEPTH, FOR
      ANY PERIOD OF''
410   PRINT ''TIME.''
420   PRINT ''TO DESTROY THE SUB, YOU
      MUST''
```

```
430   PRINT ''DROP THE DEPTH CHARGE NOT
      ONLY AT''
440   PRINT ''THE RIGHT COORDINATES,
      BUT IT MUST''
450   PRINT ''BE FUSED FOR THE RIGHT
      DEPTH.''
460   PRINT ''IF NOT, YOU HAVE WASTED A
      DEPTH.''
470   PRINT ''CHARGE.''
480   PRINT ''YOU HAVE A DISADVANTAGE
      AND AN''
490   PRINT ''ADVANTAGE OVER THE SUB.''
500   PRINT ''THE DISADVANTAGE IS
      YOU'RE LIMITED''
510   PRINT ''TO THE NUMBER OF DEPTH
      CHARGES''
520   PRINT ''YOU HAVE, SINCE YOU HAVE
      BEEN AT''
530   PRINT ''SEA SO LONG.''
540   PRINT ''THE ADVANTAGE IS THAT THE
      SUB CAN MOVE''
550   PRINT ''ONLY ONE SQUARE AT A TIME,
      AND ALSO''
560   PRINT ''IT CAN MOVE ONLY UP OR
      DOWN IN DEPTH''
570   PRINT ''ONE COORDINATE AT A TIME.''
580   REM AMOUNT OF DEPTH CHARGES
590   C1 = INT(RND(0) * 11) + 16
600   PRINT ''GOOD LUCK, COMMANDER.''
610   PRINT
```

```
620    PRINT ''YOU, COMMANDER, ARE AT
       COORDINATES 1,1''
630    PRINT
640    REM SET UP POSITION FOR SUB
650    A = INT{RND{O} * 10} + 1
660    B = INT{RND{O} * 10} + 1
670    D = INT{RND{O} * 10} + 1
680    REM A IS THE X AXIS
690    REM B IS THE Y AXIS
700    REM D IS THE DEPTH
710    REM SHIP'S STARTING COORDINATES
720    X1 = 1
730    Y1 = 1
740    REM GET SHIP'S MOVE
750    PRINT
760    PRINT ''COMMANDER, WHERE DO WE
       SAIL FOR''
770    INPUT X,Y
780    REM TEST THAT X,Y ARE NOT OUT OF
       BOUNDS
790    IF X > 10 OR X < 1 THEN 820
800    IF Y > 10 OR Y < 1 THEN 820
810    GOTO 840
820    PRINT ''COMMANDER, STAY WITHIN
       THE GRID''
830    GOTO 750
840    X1 = X
850    Y1 = Y
860    PRINT
870    PRINT ''COMMANDER, WHAT SETTING
       FOR DEPTH CHARGES''
```

```
880   PRINT ''A SETTING OF 0 RELEASES
      NO CHARGES.''
890   INPUT C
900   IF C = 0 THEN 960
910   IF C > 10 OR C < 1 THEN 930
920   GOTO 1430
930   PRINT ''COMMANDER, THE SUB IS IN
      THE WATER''
940   PRINT ''NEITHER ABOVE THE SURFACE,
      NOR BELOW THE BOTTOM''
950   GOTO 860
960   PRINT
970   PRINT ''THE SUB IS AT CO-
      ORDINATES:—''
980   PRINT ''X = ''; A; ''Y = ''; B
990   PRINT ''AND AT A DEPTH OF ''; D
1000  REM NEW SUB POSITION
1010  A1 = INT(RND(0) * 2)
1020  B1 = INT(RND(0) * 2)
1030  D1 = INT(RND(0) * 2)
1040  REM CHECK FOR PROPER MOVE
1050  REM GET NEGATIVE OR POSITIVE
      MOVE
1060  Q1 = INT(RND(0) * 2)
1070  Q2 = INT(RND(0) * 2)
1080  Q3 = INT(RND(0) * 2)
1090  IF Q1 = 1 THEN 1120
1100  Q1 = -1
1110  GOTO 1130
1120  Q1 = 1
```

```
1130   IF Q2 = 1 THEN 1160
1140   Q2 = -1
1150   GOTO 1170
1160   Q2 = 1
1170   IF Q3 = 1 THEN 1200
1180   Q3 = -1
1190   GOTO 1210
1200   Q3 = 1
1210   IF A + {A1 * Q1} > 10 OR A + {A1
       * Q1} < 1 THEN 1240
1220   A = A + {A1 * Q1}
1230   GOTO 1280
1240   IF A + {A1 * Q1} > 10 THEN 1270
1250   A = 1
1260   GOTO 1280
1270   A = 9
1280   IF B + {B1 * Q2} > 10 OR B + {B1
       * Q1} < 1 THEN 1310
1290   B = B + {B1 * Q2}
1300   GOTO 1350
1310   IF B + {B1 * Q2} > 10 THEN 1340
1320   B = 1
1330   GOTO 1350
1340   B = 9
1350   IF D + {D1 * Q3} > 10 OR D + D
       {D1 * Q3} < 1 THEN 1380
1360   D = D + {D1 * Q3}
1370   GOTO 1420
1380   IF D + {D1 * Q3} > 10 THEN 1410
1390   D = 1
```

```
1400    GOTO 1420
1410    D = 9
1420    GOTO 750
1430    IF X = A AND Y = B AND C = D
        THEN 1630
1440    PRINT
1450    PRINT ''SORRY, COMMANDER, WE
        HAVE MISSED''
1460    C1 = C1 - 1
1490    IF C1 > 0 THEN 960
1500    PRINT
1510    PRINT ''SORRY, COMMANDER, NO
        MORE DEPTH CHARGES''
1520    PRINT ''WE CANNOT GET HIM WITH-
        OUT CHARGES''
1530    PRINT
1540    PRINT ''TO PLAY AGAIN TYPE 1,
        OTHERWISE 0''
1550    INPUT L
1560    IF L = 1 THEN 1610
1570    PRINT
1580    PRINT ''THE COMPUTER KNEW YOU
        WERE A''
1590    PRINT ''LANDLUBBER...''
1600    STOP
1610    PRINT
1620    GOTO 580
1630    PRINT
1640    PRINT ''NELSON WOULD BE PROUD
        OF YOU''
```

```
1650   PRINT ''YOU GOT THE DEVIL SUB.''
1660   PRINT ''YOU STILL HAVE ''; C1;
       ''DEPTH CHARGES''
1670   GOTO 1530
1680   END
```

An adaptation of this program designed specifically for the Radio Shack TRS-80 computer using Level II BASIC can be found on page 188 in Section II.

SINK THE BISMARK

This is an exciting chase game with many messages from the computer to the captain.

Both vessels can fire at each other. Your mission is to sink the enemy before the enemy sinks you. As you get closer, the damage done by the high explosive shells becomes more pronounced.

Caution: the number of shells available for either ship is limited. The number of shells is picked at random by the computer, yet there is always a minimum of 20 shells initially available to each ship.

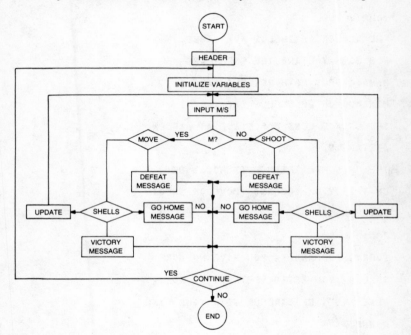

Flowchart for Sink the Bismark

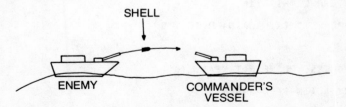

Fig. 1-2—As the distance between vessels becomes closer, the effectiveness of the high-explosive shells increases.

Sample Run

```
INSTRUCTIONS ARE:—

THIS IS THE GAME OF SINK THE BISMARK
BOTH YOUR VESSEL AND THAT
OF THE ENEMY HAVE HIGH
EXPLOSIVE SHELLS.
YOUR MISSION IS TO SINK THE ENEMY
VESSEL BEFORE IT CAN SINK
YOUR VESSEL.
THE NUMBER OF SHELLS AVAILABLE
FOR BOTH YOU AND THE ENEMY ARE
RANDOM, BUT BOTH VESSELS HAVE A
MINIMUM OF 20 SHELLS EACH.
SHELLS ARE LESS EFFECTIVE AT LARGER
DISTANCES.
THE PRESENT DISTANCE IS NOW 1500
WHAT IS YOUR COMMAND, MOVE OR SHOOT
ENTER M OR S
? M
SORRY, COMMANDER, YOU HAVE NO MORE
SHELLS, YOU BETTER RETREAT TO PORT,
NEXT TIME, BE CAREFUL WITH YOUR FIRE
POWER..
TO TRY AGAIN AND BE MORE
WATCHFUL THIS TIME
TYPE L TO TRY AGAIN, 0 TO STOP
?0
I GUESS YOU'RE NOT READY TO
TRY AGAIN, COMMANDER..
WELL MAYBE NEXT TIME..
RUN COMPLETE.
```

Program Listing

```
10   REM THIS PROGRAM PITS TWO
     DESTROYERS
20   REM AGAINST EACH OTHER
30   REM ONE VESSEL IS UNDER YOUR
     COMMAND
40   REM THE OTHER IS UNDER COMPUTER
     CONTROL
50   REM TO EVEN THE ODDS, THE COMPUTER
     MUST
60   REM USE RANDOM VARIABLES OR ELSE
     THE CONTEST
70   REM WOULD DEFINITELY BE BIASED TO-
     WARDS THE
80   REM COMPUTER.
90   REM INITIALIZE VARIABLES
100  REM ESTABLISH DISTANCE AT START
     OF GAME
110  D = 1000 + INT(RND(0) * 2000)
120  REM ESTABLISH NUMBER OF SHOTS
     AVAILABLE
130  REM TO THE ENEMY
140  S = INT(RND(0) * 25) + 20
150  REM ESTABLISH NUMBER OF SHOTS
     AVAILABLE TO
160  REM TO YOUR VESSEL
170  S1 = INT(RND(0) * 25) + 20
180  V = 0
190  E = 0
200  PRINT
```

```
210   PRINT TAB {7}; ''DESTROYER''
220   PRINT TAB {7}; ''_____''
230   PRINT
240   PRINT
250   PRINT ''INSTRUCTIONS ARE:— ''
260   PRINT
270   PRINT ''THIS IS THE GAME OF SINK
      THE BISMARK''
280   PRINT ''BOTH YOUR VESSEL AND
      THAT''
290   PRINT ''OF THE ENEMY HAVE HIGH''
300   PRINT ''EXPLOSIVE SHELLS.''
310   PRINT ''YOUR MISSION IS TO SINK
      THE ENEMY''
320   PRINT ''VESSEL BEFORE IT CAN
      SINK''
330   PRINT ''YOUR VESSEL.''
340   PRINT ''THE NUMBER OF SHELLS
      AVAILABLE''
350   PRINT ''FOR BOTH YOU AND THE
      ENEMY ARE''
360   PRINT ''RANDOM, BUT BOTH VESSELS
      HAVE A''
370   PRINT ''MINIMUM OF 20 SHELLS
      EACH''
380   PRINT ''SHELLS ARE LESS EFFECTIVE
      AT LARGE DISTANCES.''
390   PRINT
400   PRINT ''THE PRESENT DISTANCE IS
      NOW'';D
```

```
410   PRINT
420   PRINT ''WHAT IS YOUR COMMAND,
      MOVE OR SHOOT''
430   PRINT ''ENTER M OR S''
440   INPUT C$
450   IF C$ = ''M'' THEN 500
460   IF C$ = ''S'' THEN 1830
470   PRINT
480   PRINT ''YOUR COMMAND MUST BE
      EITHER S OR M''
490   GOTO 410
500   PRINT
510   PRINT ''HOW FAR { - = TOWARDS, +
      = AWAY}''
520   INPUT D1
530   IF D1/ABS{D1} = 1 THEN 560
540   D = D - ABS{D1}
550   GOTO 570
560   D = D + D1
570   REM GET ENEMY SHOT
580   S = S - 1
590   IF S < 0 THEN 1290
600   REM Q IS TEMPORARY VARIABLE
610   Q = RND{10}
620   Q = Q - {D / 500}
630   Q = ABS{Q}
640   V = Q + V
650   IF V > = 100 THEN 1510
660   IF V > 10 AND V < 21 THEN 790
670   IF V > 20 AND V < 31 THEN 830
```

```
680   IF V > 30 AND V < 41 THEN 870
690   IF V > 40 AND V < 51 THEN 920
700   IF V > 60 AND V < 71 THEN 960
710   IF V > 60 AND V < 71 THEN 1010
720   IF V > 70 AND V < 81 THEN 1060
730   IF V > 80 AND V < 91 THEN 1200
740   IF V > 90 AND V < 100 THEN 1250
750   PRINT
760   PRINT ''THE ENEMY HAS NOW ONLY'';
      S; ''SHELLS''
770   PRINT ''YOUR VESSEL HAS NOW ONLY
      ''; S1; ''SHELLS''
780   GOTO 390
790   PRINT
800   PRINT ''CAUTION, YOU'RE TAKING ON
      WATER''
810   PRINT ''NO SERIOUS DAMAGE YET''
820   GOTO 750
830   PRINT
840   PRINT ''THERE ARE A FEW SMALL
      FIRES''
850   PRINT ''BUT THEY ARE UNDER
      CONTROL''
860   GOTO 750
870   PRINT
880   PRINT ''YOU ARE LISTING TO PORT
      5 DEGREES''
890   PRINT ''WATER LEVEL IS STILL NOT
      DANGEROUS''
900   PRINT ''CAUTION, FIRES ARE
      SPREADING''
```

```
910   GOTO 750
920   PRINT
930   PRINT ''ENGINES ARE OVERHEATING
      AND''
940   PRINT ''THE BILGE PUMPS ARE ACT-
      ING UP''
950   GOT 750
960   PRINT
970   PRINT ''MOST OF YOUR CREW IS''
980   PRINT ''SERIOUSLY HURT, THE FIRES
      ARE''
990   PRINT ''APPROACHING THE POWDER
      ROOM''
1000  GOTO 750
1010  PRINT
1020  PRINT ''THE LIFE BOATS ARE BEING
      READIED''
1030  PRINT ''SMOKE FILLS MOST OF THE
      CORRIDORS''
1040  PRINT ''BILGE PUMPS ARE NEAR
      FAILURE''
1050  GOTO 750
1060  PRINT
1070  PRINT ''YOUR CREW IS ABANDONING
      SHIP''
1080  PRINT ''THE BILGE PUMPS HAVE
      STOPPED''
1090  PRINT ''ONE ENGINE HAS BURNED
      OUT''
1100  GOTO 750
```

```
1200   PRINT
1210   PRINT ''THE SHIP IS BURNING,
       YOU HAVE''
1220   PRINT ''PLACED THE SHIP ON
       AUTOMATIC''
1230   PRINT ''YOU ARE LOSING
       STABILITY, COMMANDER''
1240   GOTO 750
1250   PRINT
1260   PRINT ''YOUR SHIP IS BADLY
       DESTROYED, THERE''
1270   PRINT ''IS LITTLE HOPE,
       COMMANDER..''
1280   GOTO 750
1290   PRINT
1300   PRINT ''THE ENEMY IS RETREAT-
       ING..''
1310   PRINT ''YOU HAVE WON THIS
       BATTLE''
1320   PRINT
1330   PRINT ''COMMANDER, YOU HAVE
       WON WITH''; S1
1340   PRINT ''SHELLS LEFT ON YOUR
       VESSEL''
1350   PRINT
1360   PRINT ''SINCE YOU ARE SUCH
       A GREAT COMMANDER''
1370   PRINT ''THE COMPUTER WANTS TO
       KNOW IF YOU''
1380 PRINT ''WANT TO FIGHT AGAIN.''
1390   PRINT
```

```
1400    PRINT ''TO HAVE ANOTHER BATTLE
        TYPE 1''
1410    PRINT ''IF NOT TYPE 0''
1420    INPUT L
1430    IF L = 1 THEN 110
1440    PRINT
1450    PRINT ''OKAY GIVE UP WHILE YOU
        ARE AHEAD''
1460    PRINT
1470    PRINT ''THE COMPUTER SAYS
        GOODBYE''
1480    PRINT ''THE ENEMY SAYS GOODBYE
        FROM''
1490    PRINT ''DAVY JONES LOCKER''
1500    STOP
1510    PRINT
1520    PRINT ''YOUR VESSEL IS GOING
        DOWN''
1530    PRINT ''YOU BETTER GET INTO THE
        LIFE BOAT''
1540    PRINT ''HURRY, CAPTAIN, IF YOU
        ARE''
1550    PRINT ''GOING TO MAKE IT..''
1560    PRINT
1570    PRINT ''YOU LOST THIS TIME, DO
        YOU WANT''
1580    PRINT ''TO TRY AGAIN,
        COMMANDER?''
1590    PRINT
1600    PRINT ''TYPE 1 TO TRY AGAIN, 0
        TO STOP''
```

```
1700    INPUT L

1710    IF L = 1 THEN 1770

1720    PRINT

1730    PRINT ''I GUESS YOU ARE NOT
        WILLING..''

1740    PRINT ''WHO KNOWS, PERHAPS YOU
        COULD HAVE''

1750    PRINT ''WON IF YOU HAD TRIED..''

1760    STOP

1770    PRINT

1780    PRINT ''THE COMPUTER IS HAPPY,
        YOU ARE''

1790    PRINT ''OF THE FIGHTING TYPE''

1800    PRINT ''BETTER LUCK NEXT TIME,
        COMMANDER.''

1810    PRINT

1820    GOTO 110

1830    S1 = S1 - 1

1840    IF S 1 < 0 THEN 1860

1850    GOTO 2040

1860    PRINT

1870    PRINT ''STORY, COMMANDER, YOU
        HAVE NO MORE''

1880    PRINT ''SHELLS, YOU BETTER RE-
        TREAT TO PORT,''

1890    PRINT ''NEXT TIME, BE CAREFUL
        WITH YOUR FIRE''

1900    PRINT ''POWER..''

1910    PRINT

1920    PRINT ''TO TRY AGAIN, AND BE
        MORE''
```

```
1930    PRINT ''WATCHFUL THIS TIME.''
1940    PRINT ''TYPE 1 TO TRY AGAIN, 0
        TO STOP''
1940    INPUT L
1950    IF L = 1 THEN 2010
1960    PRINT
1970    PRINT ''I GUESS YOU'RE NOT
        READY TO''
1980    PRINT ''TRY AGAIN, COMMANDER..''
1990    PRINT ''WELL, MAYBE NEXT TIME..''
2000    STOP
2010    PRINT
2020    PRINT ''TRY HARDER THIS TIME
        COMMANDER.''
2030    GOTO 110
2040    REM Q IS A TEMPORARY VARIABLE
2050    Q = RND{10}
2060    Q = Q - {D / 500}
2070    Q = ABS{Q}
2080    E = Q + E
2090    IF E > = 100 THEN 2230
2100    IF E > 10 AND E < 21 THEN 2390
2110    IF E > 20 AND E < 31 THEN 2430
2120    IF E > 30 AND E < 41 THEN 2480
2130    IF E > 40 AND E < 51 THEN 2540
2140    IF E > 50 AND E < 61 THEN 2580
2150    IF E > 60 AND E < 71 THEN 2630
2160    IF E > 70 AND E < 81 THEN 2680
2170    IF E > 80 AND E < 91 THEN 2740
2180    IF E > 90 AND E < 100 THEN 2800
```

```
2190   PRINT
2200   PRINT ''THE ENEMY IS TAKING ON
       WATER''
2210   PRINT ''THERE SEEMS TO BE SOME
       SMOKE''
2220   GOTO 570
2230   PRINT
2240   PRINT ''YOU HAVE DESTROYED THE
       ENEMY''
2250   PRINT ''VESSEL..''
2260   PRINT
2270   PRINT ''SINCE YOU ARE SO GOOD AT
       THIS''
2280   PRINT ''WHY DONT YOU TRY AGAIN''
2290   PRINT ''TYPE 1 TO CONTINUE, 0
       TO STOP''
2300   INPUT L
2310   IF L = 1 THEN 2360
2320   PRINT
2330   PRINT ''GUESS YOU ARE TIRED
       FROM THE''
2340   PRINT ''BATTLE, COMMANDER''
2350   STOP
2360   PRINT
2370   PRINT ''HOPE YOUR LUCK HOLDS
       OUT''
2380   GOTO 110
2390   PRINT
2400   PRINT ''THE ENEMY SHIP IS LOSING
       GROUND..''
```

```
2410   PRINT ''ALREADY THERE ARE SMALL
       FIRES''
2420   GOTO 570
2430   PRINT
2440   PRINT ''LOOKS LIKE SOME OF THE
       OTHER''
2450   PRINT ''VESSEL'S CREW ARE
       LEAVING''
2460   PRINT ''IN LIFE BOATS,
       COMMANDER''
2470   GOTO 570
2480   PRINT
2490   PRINT ''COMMANDER, THE RADIO
       ROOM HAS''
2500   PRINT ''PICKED UP COMMUNICATIONS
       FROM''
2510   PRINT ''THE ENEMY, RADIOING TO
       SAY IT IS''
2520   PRINT ''TAKING ON WATER
       QUICKLY.''
2530   GOTO 570
2540   PRINT
2550   PRINT ''THE ENEMY STILL HAS NO
       SERIOUS DAMAGE''
2560   PRINT ''BUT SHE SURE IS TAKING
       ON WATER.''
2570   GOTO 570
2580   PRINT
2590   PRINT ''THE OTHER SHIP SEEMS TO
       HAVE SOME''
```

```
2600   PRINT ''FIRES NOW, BUT THEY
       SEEM TO BE''
2610   PRINT ''UNDER CONTROL.''
2620   GOTO 570
2630   PRINT
2640   PRINT ''THE ENEMY IS LISTING
       SERIOUSLY''
2650   PRINT ''IT CANNOT LAST MUCH
       LONGER.''
2660   PRINT ''KEEP IT UP, COMMANDER.''
2670   GOTO 570
2680   PRINT
2690   PRINT ''COMMANDER, THE ENEMY
       HAS LOST''
2700   PRINT ''ALL MOTIVE POWER''
2710   PRINT ''IF WE KEEP ON SHOOTING
       WE'LL''
2720   PRINT ''GET HER.''
2730   GOTO 570
2740   PRINT
2750   PRINT ''MOST OF THE ENEMY'S
       CREW''
2760   PRINT ''HAS LEFT ON LIFE BOATS.''
2770   PRINT ''A FEW MORE ACCURATE
       SHOTS''
2780   PRINT ''AND WE'LL GET HER SUNK.''
2790   GOTO 570
2800   PRINT
2810   PRINT ''SHE CAN'T TAKE MUCH
       MORE,''
```

```
2820   PRINT ''COMMANDER, IT LOOKS
       LIKE THE''
2830   PRINT ''ENEMY IS GOING DOWN,
       PROBABLY''
2940   PRINT ''TO JOIN DAVY JONES
       LOCKER''
2850   GOTO 570
2860   END
```

An adaptation of this program designed specifically for the Radio Shack TRS-80 computer using Level II BASIC can be found on page 191 in Section II.

MOUSE HUNT

Your object is to squash the obnoxious mouse. You do this by hops, but the mouse also can hop away. The size of the hop is random, but you can choose the direction.

The computer also will tell you where the mouse is in relation to your initial point on a graph where x and y = ϕ. If you catch him—SPLATT!!! goes the mouse.

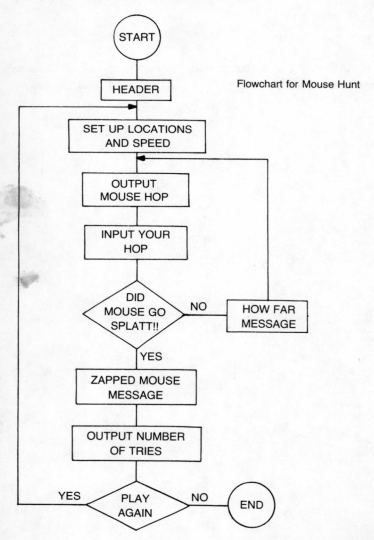

Flowchart for Mouse Hunt

Sample Run

```
THIS PROGRAM ALLOWS YOU TO GO ON A MOUSE HUNT
FOR A VERY OBNOXIOUS MOUSE
THE MOUSE TRIES TO DO DGE YOU BY HOPPING
RANDOMLY
YOU CAN CATCH IT BY BEING WHERE THE MOUSE LANDS
YOU CAN CHANGE DIRECTION TOO

YOU HAVE TO GET WITHIN  67  FEET OF THE MOUSE TO 'KETCH' IT
HOP SIZES       DA MOUSE  90   YOUSE  270

THE COMPUTER SAYS: I WISH YOU GREAT FORTUNE IN YOUR ENDEAVOR
FROM THE MOUSE: DROP DEAD - TURKEY
FROM THE COMPUTER: KEEP IT CLEAN BOYS


TRY #            1
THE MOUSE IS  583.216  FEET AWAY
AT LOCATION    -450  BY   -371
AND TOOK OFF AT AN ANGLE OF    157  DEGREES
YOU ARE
AT LOCATION  0  BY  0
OWWW THAT HURTS - YOURE NOT EVEN CLOSE
WHAT DIRECTION DO YOU WISH TO JUMP? 225

TRY #            2
THE MOUSE IS  371.368  FEET AWAY
AT LOCATION   -532.845  BY   -335.834
AND TOOK OFF AT AN ANGLE OF    353  DEGREES
YOU ARE
AT LOCATION -190.919  BY -190.919
OWWW THAT HURTS - YOURE NOT EVEN CLOSE
WHAT DIRECTION DO YOU WISH TO JUMP? 270

TRY #            3
THE MOUSE IS  277.179  FEET AWAY
AT LOCATION   -443.516  BY   -346.802
AND TOOK OFF AT AN ANGLE OF    185  DEGREES
YOU ARE
AT LOCATION -190.919  BY -460.919
OWWW THAT HURTS - YOURE NOT EVEN CLOSE
WHAT DIRECTION DO YOU WISH TO JUMP? 135

TRY #            4
THE MOUSE IS  173.4  FEET AWAY
AT LOCATION    -533.174  BY   -354.646
AND TOOK OFF AT AN ANGLE OF    158  DEGREES
YOU ARE
AT LOCATION -381.838  BY -270.
OWWW THAT HURTS - YOURE NOT EVEN CLOSE
WHAT DIRECTION DO YOU WISH TO JUMP? 170


TRY #            5
THE MOUSE IS  102.647  FEET AWAY
AT LOCATION    -616.62  BY   -320.932
AND TOOK OFF AT AN ANGLE OF    285  DEGREES
YOU ARE
AT LOCATION -647.736  BY -223.115
```

```
OWWW THAT HURTS - YOURE NOT EVEN CLOSE
WHAT DIRECTION DO YOU WISH TO JUMP? 270
SPLAT!!!!
YOU GOT IT
BOY WHAT A MESS - SQUASHED MOUSE EVERYWHERE
YOU TOOK    5   TRIES TO 'KETCH(UP)' THE MOUSE
WANT TO TRY AGAIN?(YES/NO)  ? YES
YOU HAVE TO GET WITHIN  314  FEET OF THE MOUSE TO 'KETCH' IT
HOP SIZES        DA MOUSE  130  YOUSE  260


THE COMPUTER SAYS: I WISH YOU GREAT FORTUNE IN YOUR ENDEAVOR
FROM THE MOUSE: DROP DEAD - TURKEY
FROM THE COMPUTER: KEEP IT CLEAN BOYS



TRY #            1
THE MOUSE IS  614.357  FEET AWAY
AT LOCATION   -453  BY    415
AND TOOK OFF AT AN ANGLE OF    3   DEGREES
YOU ARE
AT LOCATION  0   BY   0
OWWW THAT HURTS - YOURE NOT EVEN CLOSE
WHAT DIRECTION DO YOU WISH TO JUMP? 135
SPLAT!!!!
YOU GOT IT
BOY WHAT A MESS - SQUASHED MOUSE EVERYWHERE
YOU TOOK    1   TRIES TO 'KETCH(UP)' THE MOUSE
WANT TO TRY AGAIN?(YES/NO)  ? YES
YOU HAVE TO GET WITHIN  238  FEET OF THE MOUSE TO 'KETCH' IT
HOP SIZES        DA MOUSE  130  YOUSE  260


THE COMPUTER SAYS: I WISH YOU GREAT FORTUNE IN YOUR ENDEAVOR
FROM THE MOUSE: DROP DEAD - TURKEY
FROM THE COMPUTER: KEEP IT CLEAN BOYS



TRY #            1
THE MOUSE IS  670.343  FEET AWAY
AT LOCATION   -472  BY    476
AND TOOK OFF AT AN ANGLE OF   160   DEGREES
YOU ARE
AT LOCATION  0   BY   0
OWWW THAT HURTS - YOURE NOT EVEN CLOSE
WHAT DIRECTION DO YOU WISH TO JUMP? 135



TRY #            2
THE MOUSE IS  530.722  FEET AWAY
AT LOCATION   -594.16  BY    520.463
AND TOOK OFF AT AN ANGLE OF   144   DEGREES
YOU ARE
AT LOCATION -183.848  BY  183.848
OWWW THAT HURTS - YOURE NOT EVEN CLOSE
WHAT DIRECTION DO YOU WISH TO JUMP? 150
```

46

```
TRY #           3
THE MOUSE IS   405.449   FEET AWAY
AT LOCATION    -699.332  BY       596.875
AND TOOK OFF AT AN ANGLE OF     204   DEGREES
YOU ARE
AT LOCATION -409.014  BY   313.848
OWWW THAT HURTS - YOURE NOT EVEN CLOSE
WHAT DIRECTION DO YOU WISH TO JUMP? 180

TRY #           4
THE MOUSE IS   274.215   FEET AWAY
AT LOCATION    -818.093  BY       543.999
AND TOOK OFF AT AN ANGLE OF     119   DEGREES
YOU ARE
AT LOCATION -669.014  BY   313.848
MISSED AGAIN- BUT PRETTY CLOSE
WHAT DIRECTION DO YOU WISH TO JUMP? 135
SPLAT!!!!
YOU GOT IT
BOY WHAT A MESS - SQUASHED MOUSE EVERYWHERE
YOU TOOK    4   TRIES TO 'KETCH(UP)' THE MOUSE
WANT TO TRY AGAIN?(YES/NO)   ? NO


RUN COMPLETE.
```

Program Listing

```
100  REM CHANGE A MOUSE
200  PRINT  "THIS PROGRAM ALLOWS YOU TO GO ON A MOUSE HUNT "
300  PRINT  "FOR A VERY OBNOXIOUS MOUSE "
400  PRINT  "THE MOUSE TRIES TO DODGE YOU BY HOPPING "
500  PRINT  "RANDOMLY "
600  PRINT  "YOU CAN CATCH IT BY BEING WHERE THE MOUSE LANDS "
700  PRINT  "YOU CAN CHANGE DIRECTION TOO "
800  PRINT
900  T=RND(0)*1000
1000 T=INT(T)
1100 PRINT  "YOU HAVE TO GET WITHIN "$T$  " FEET OF THE MOUSE
     TO 'KETCH' IT "
1200 T=T*T
1300 REM SET UP THE LOCATIONS AND SPEEDS
1400 REM 10  "KETCH " THE MOUSE
1500 REM YOU ARE THE FOX
1600 R1=INT(RND(0)*10+.5)*10+50
1700 R2=(INT(RND(0)*2+.5)+1)*R1
1800 K1=RND(0)
1900 K2=RND(0)
2000 IF K1>.5 THEN  2300
2100 K1=-1
2200 GOTO  2400
2300 K1=1
2400 IF K2>.5 THEN  2700
2500 K2=1
2600 GOTO  2800
2700 K2=-1
2800 Q1=INT(RND(0)*400+100)
2900 Q1=Q1*K1
3000 Q2=INT(RND(0)*400+100)
3100 Q2=Q2*K2
3200 IF Q2=0 OR Q1=0 THEN  1800
3300 Q3=0
3400 Q4=0
3500 PRINT  "HOP SIZES ", "DA MOUSE "$R1, "YOUSE "$R2
3600 PRINT
3700 PRINT  "THE COMPUTER SAYS  I WISH YOU GREAT FORTUNE IN
     YOUR ENDEAVOR "
3800 PRINT  "FROM THE MOUSE  DROP DEAD - TURKEY "
3900 PRINT  "FROM THE COMPUTER  KEEP IT CLEAN BOYS "
4000 PRINT
4100 P1=3.14159254/180
4200 K3=1
4300 Z1=(Q3-Q1)*(Q3-Q1)+(Q4-Q2)*(Q4-Q2)
4400 REM
4500 REM PRINT A CYCLE
4600 REM
4700 PRINT
4800 PRINT  "TRY # ",K3
4900 PRINT  "THE MOUSE IS "$SQR(Z1)$  " FEET AWAY "
5000 PRINT  "AT LOCATION   "$Q1$  " BY  "$Q2
5100 D1=INT(RND(0)*359)
5200 IF Z1<=T THEN  5400
5300 PRINT  "AND TOOK OFF AT AN ANGLE OF   "$D1$  " DEGREES "
5400 PRINT  "YOU ARE "
5500 PRINT  "AT LOCATION "$Q3$  " BY "$Q4
5600 IF Z1>2*T THEN  6200
```

```
5700 IF Z1>T THEN   6400
5800 PRINT   "SPLAT!!!!  "
5900 PRINT   "YOU GOT IT "
6000 PRINT   "BOY WHAT A MESS - SQUASHED MOUSE EVERYWHERE "
6100 GOTO   8800
6200 PRINT   "OWWW THAT HURTS - YOURE NOT EVEN CLOSE "
6300 GOTO   6500
6400 PRINT   "MISSED AGAIN- BUT PRETTY CLOSE "
6500 PRINT   "WHAT DIRECTION DO YOU WISH TO JUMP";
6600 INPUT D2
6700 IF D2>=0 AND D2<=360 THEN   7000
6800 PRINT   "BETWEEN 0 AND 360 DEGREES ONLY "
6900 GOTO   6500
7000 Q5=R1*COS(D1*P1)/100
7100 Q6=R1*SIN(D1*P1)/100
7200 Q7=R2*COS(D2*P1)/100
7300 Q8=R2*SIN(D2*P1)/100
7400 C1=Z1
7500 C2=Z1
7600 FOR I=1 TO 100
7700 Q1=Q1+Q5
7800 Q2=Q2+Q6
7900 Q3=Q3+Q7
8000 Q4=Q4+Q8
8100 C2=(Q3-Q1)*(Q3-Q1)+(Q4-Q2)*(Q4-Q2)
8200 IF C2>C1 THEN 08400
8300 C1=C2
8400 NEXT I
8500 IF C1<=T THEN   5800
8600 K3=K3+1
8700 GOTO   4300
8800 PRINT   "YOU TOOK   ";K3;  " TRIES TO 'KETCH(UP)'
     THE MOUSE "
8900 PRINT   "WANT TO TRY AGAIN?(YES/NO)   ";
9000 INPUT A$
9100 IF A$="YES" THEN    900
9200 IF A$<>"NO" THEN   8900
9300 STOP
9400 END
```

An adaptation of this program designed specifically for the Radio Shack TRS-80 computer using Level II BASIC can be found on page 194 in Section II.

CAPTURE THE ALIEN

Capture the Alien is a slightly different version of the famous Star Trek games. Instead of killing off the baddies, we capture them. To capture the enemy vessel, you must destroy all the regions around it, using phaser power. The Battle Computer will keep you up to date on how you are doing.

There is a protected area where the alien first enters your sphere of influence, namely the x axis = 1 and the y axis = 1. Firing in there is like firing at an already destroyed region. But remember, your mission is to capture the enemy vessel. If you zap the alien by mistake, watch out. The computer gets mad.

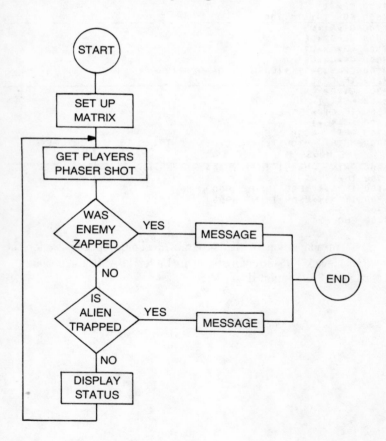

Flowchart for Capture the Alien

Sample Run

```
ENTER YOUR NAME FOR THE GALACTIC RECORDS
? KEN

INSTRUCTIONS KEN (1=YES, 2=NO)
? 1


YOUR MISSION COMMANDER KEN IS TO CAPTURE
AN ENEMY BATTLE VESSEL. YOU MUST NOT DESTROY
THE ENEMY, YOU MUST TAKE HIM ALIVE.
TO EFFECT A CAPTURE, YOU MUST DESTROY ALL
REGIONS AROUND IT. THE INBOARD BATTLE-DEFENSE
COMPUTER WILL KEEP YOU UP-TO-DATE ON THE
ENEMY'S LAST POSITION
THERE IS ALSO A PROTECTED AREA USING THE
AXES X=1 AND Y=1, SO THAT THE ALIEN HAS A CHANCE
YOU FIRE INTO THIS REGION ,IT IS THE SAME AS FIRING
INTO A PREVIOUSLY DESTROYED AREA!!!!!!!!!


GOOD-LUCK COMMANDER KEN


COMMANDER KEN YOU HAVE   25   SHOTS

ENEMY'S LAST KNOWN POSITION
SECTOR  3 ,  1

                    1
    * * * * * * *   2
    * * * * * * *   3
    * * * * * * *   4
    * * * * * * *   5
    * * * * * * *   6
    * * * * * * *   7
    * * * * * * *   8
  1 2 3 4 5 6 7 8


ENTER YOUR PHASER SHOT (X,Y)? 2,2

ENEMY'S LAST KNOWN POSITION
SECTOR  4 ,  2

                    1
      * * * * * *   2
    * * * * * * *   3
    * * * * * * *   4
    * * * * * * *   5
    * * * * * *· * *   6
    * * * * * * *   7
    * * * * * * *   8
  1 2 3 4 5 6 7 8
```

COMMANDER KEN YOU HAVE BEEN ATTACKED
ENERGY USED TO REPLENISH SHIELDS
COMMANDER KEN ONLY   23   SHOTS REMAIN

ENTER YOUR PHASER SHOT (X,Y)? 4,3

ENEMY'S LAST KNOWN POSITION
SECTOR   5 ,   3

```
                     1
      * * * * * *    2
    * * * * * * *    3
    *   * * * * *    4
    * * * * * * *    5
    * * * * * * *    6
    * * * * * * *    7
    * * * * * * *    8
  1 2 3 4 5 6 7 8
```

COMMANDER KEN YOU HAVE BEEN ATTACKED
ENERGY USED TO REPLENISH SHIELDS
COMMANDER KEN ONLY   21   SHOTS REMAIN

ENTER YOUR PHASER SHOT (X,Y)? 6,3

ENEMY'S LAST KNOWN POSITION
SECTOR   4 ,   4

```
                     1
      * * * * * *    2
    * * * * * * *    3
    *   * * * * *    4
    * * * * * * *    5
    *   * * * * *    6
    * * * * * * *    7
    * * * * * * *    8
  1 2 3 4 5 6 7 8
```

ENTER YOUR PHASER SHOT (X,Y)? 4,5

ENEMY'S LAST KNOWN POSITION
SECTOR   3 ,   5

```
                     1
      * * * * * *    2
    * * * * * * *    3
    *   *   * * *    4
    * * * * * * *    5
    *   * * * * *    6
    * * * * * * *    7
    * * * * * * *    8
  1 2 3 4 5 6 7 8
```

ENTER YOUR PHASER SHOT (X,Y)? 2,5

52

```
ENEMY'S LAST KNOWN POSITION
SECTOR  2 , 6

                      1
      * *    * * *     2
  * * * * * * *       3
  *   *    * * *       4
  * * * * * * *       5
  *    * * * *        6
  * * * * * * *       7
  * * * * * * *       8
  1 2 3 4 5 6 7 8


ENTER YOUR PHASER SHOT (X,Y)? 2,7
COMMANDER KEN
DID YOU EVER BLOW IT THIS TIME
YOU ZAPPED THE ALIEN!!!!!!!!!!
YOUR MISSION WAS A TOTAL WASTE OF TIME
FOR YOU AND THE EMPIRE



RUN COMPLETE.
```

Program Listing

```
10 REM LETS CAPTURE A ENEMY VESSEL
20 REM INSTEAD OF DESTROYING HIM
30
40 DIM Q(9,9)
50 PRINT
60 PRINT"ENTER YOUR NAME FOR THE GALACTIC RECORDS"
70 INPUT A$
80 S=25
90 PRINT
100 PRINT"INSTRUCTIONS "$A$$" (1=YES, 2=NO)"
110 INPUT C
120 IF C<>1 THEN     290
130 PRINT
140 PRINT"YOUR MISSION COMMANDER "$A$$" IS TO CAPTURE"
150 PRINT"AN ENEMY BATTLE VESSEL. YOU MUST NOT DESTROY"
160 PRINT"THE ENEMY, YOU MUST TAKE HIM ALIVE."
170 PRINT"TO EFFECT A CAPTURE, YOU MUST DESTROY ALL"
180 PRINT"REGIONS AROUND IT. THE INBOARD BATTLE-DEFENSE"
190 PRINT"COMPUTER WILL KEEP YOU UP-TO-DATE ON THE"
200 PRINT"ENEMY'S LAST POSITION"
210 PRINT"THERE IS ALSO A PROTECTED AREA USING THE"
220 PRINT"AXES X=1 AND Y=1, SO THAT THE ALIEN HAS A CHANCE"
230 PRINT"YOU FIRE INTO THIS REGION ,IT IS THE SAME AS FIRING"
240 PRINT"INTO A PREVIOUSLY DESTROYED AREA!!!!!!!!!!"
250 PRINT
260 PRINT"GOOD-LUCK COMMANDER "$A$
270 PRINT
280 PRINT
290 PRINT"COMMANDER "$A$$" YOU HAVE "$S$" SHOTS"
300 FOR X=1 TO 9
310 FOR Y=1 TO 9
320 Q(Y,X)=0
```

```
330 Q(1,X)=-1
340 Q(9,X)=-1
350 Q(Y,1)=-1
360 Q(Y,9)=-1
370 NEXT Y
380 NEXT X
390 X=INT(10*RND(0))
400 IF X<1 THEN     390
410 IF X>8 THEN     390
420 Y=INT(10*RND(0))
430 IF Y<1 THEN     420
440 IF Y>8 THEN     420
450 PRINT
460 PRINT"ENEMY'S LAST KNOWN POSITION"
470 PRINT"SECTOR ";X;" , ";Y
480 PRINT
490 IF S<=0 THEN    1310
500 C=X
510 D=Y
520 A=INT(10*RND(0))
530 IF A<C THEN     .550
540 GOTO     560
550 X=X-1
560 IF A>C THEN     580
570 GOTO     590
580 X=X+1
590 IF X<1 THEN     610
600 GOTO     620
610 X=1
620 IF X>8 THEN     640
630 GOTO     650
640 X=8
650 A=INT(10*RND(0))
660 IF A<D THEN     680
670 GOTO     690
680 Y=Y-1
690 IF A>D THEN     710
700 GOTO     720
710 Y=Y+1
720 IF Y<1 THEN     740
730 GOTO     750
740 Y=1
750 IF Y>8 THEN     770
760 GOTO     780
770 Y=8
780 IF Q(Y,X)<>-1 THEN 00820
790 X=C
800 Y=D
810 GOTO     520
820 FOR A=1 TO 8
830 FOR B=1 TO 8
840 IF Q(B,A)=0 THEN     860
850 GOTO 00870
860 PRINT" ";"*";
870 IF Q(B,A)=-1 THEN    890
880 GOTO     900
890 PRINT" ";" ";
900 NEXT B
910 PRINT" ";A
920 NEXT A
930 PRINT" 1 2 3 4 5 6 7 8"
940 PRINT
950 A=INT(10*RND(0))
960 IF A>4 THEN 01020
```

```
 970  PRINT"COMMANDER ";A$;" YOU HAVE BEEN ATTACKED"
 980  PRINT"ENERGY USED TO REPLENISH SHIELDS "
,990  S=S-1
1000  PRINT"COMMANDER ";A$;" ONLY ";S;" SHOTS REMAIN"
1010  PRINT
1020  A=INT(10*RND(0))
1030  IF A<9 THEN 01150
1040  A=INT(10*RND(0))
1050  IF A=X THEN  1040
1060  IF A<1 THEN  1040
1070  IF A>8 THEN  1040
1080  B=INT(10*RND(0))
1090  IF B=Y THEN  1080
1100  IF B<1 THEN  1080
1110  IF B>8 THEN  1080
1120  Q(B,A)=-1
1130  PRINT"NOVA IN SECTOR ";A;" , ";B
1140  PRINT
1150  PRINT"ENTER YOUR PHASER SHOT (X,Y)";
1160  INPUT A,B
1170  S=S-1
1180  IF A=X AND B=Y THEN  1340
1190  IF Q(B,A)=-1 THEN  1400
1200  Q(B,A)=-1
1210  FOR A=X-1 TO X+1
1220  FOR B=Y-1 TO Y+1
1230  IF A=X AND B=Y THEN  1250
1240  IF Q(B,A)<>-1 THEN  450
1250  NEXT B
1260  NEXT A
1270  PRINT"GOOD SHOW COMMANDER ";A$
1280  PRINT"YOU HAVE CAPTURED THE ALIEN ENEMY"
1290  PRINT"AND YOU HAVE ";S;" SHOTS REMAINING"
1300  STOP
1310  PRINT"COMMANDER ";A$
1320  PRINT"YOU HAVE NO MORE ENERGY FOR PHASERS"
1330  GOTO  1370
1340  PRINT"COMMANDER ";A$
1350  PRINT"DID YOU EVER BLOW IT THIS TIME"
1360  PRINT"YOU ZAPPED THE ALIEN!!!!!!!!!!!"
1370  PRINT"YOUR MISSION WAS A TOTAL WASTE OF TIME "
1380  PRINT"FOR YOU AND THE EMPIRE"
1390  STOP
1400  PRINT"COMMANDER ";A$
1410  PRINT"GOOD-SHOT, YOU FIRED ON A PREVIOUSLY DESTROYED
      AREA"
1420  PRINT"TURKEY"
1430  GOTO   450
1440  END
```

An adaptation of this program designed specifically for the Radio Shack TRS-80 computer using Level II BASIC can be found on page 196 in Section II.

STAR WARP

Star Warp is an interactive program like Star Trek, except that instead of graphs being drawn, dialogue goes on between crew members. This type of program requires less memory and no graphics capabilities. The game sometimes can go on for over one hour!

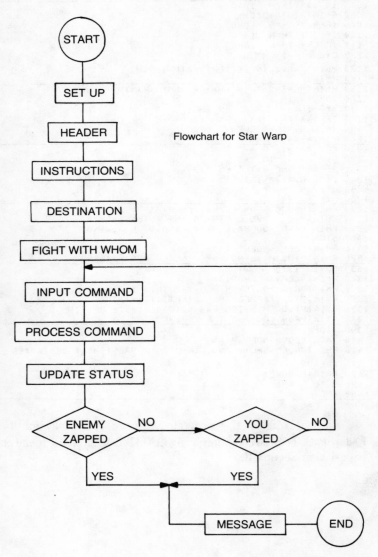

Flowchart for Star Warp

Sample Run

PROGRAM STAR WARP

SPACE, THE FINAL FRONTIER,
THIS IS THE VOYAGE OF THE STARSHIP PROMETHEUS.
IT S FIVE YEAR MISSION, TO EXPLORE STRANGE NEW WORLDS,
TO SEEK OUT NEW LIFE AND NEW CIVILIZATIONS,
TO BOLDLY GO WHERE NO MAN HAS GONE BEFORE.

YEOMAN: SIR ENTER YOUR NAME FOR THE LOG ? KEN
SPOCK YOU ARE IN COMMAND OF THE PROMETHEUS, CAPTAIN KEN.
  DO YOU WISH A LIST OF THE POSSIBLE COMMANDS, SIR? YES

SPOCK THE POSSIBLE COMMANDS ARE DESIGNATED BY
  THE FOLLOWING NUMBERS OF CODE WORDS

CODE	COMMAND
RANGE	REPEAT RANGE AND BEARING OF ENEMY
PHASEF	FIRE PHASERS FORWARD BANK
PHASER	FIRE PHASERS REAR BANK
TORPF	FIRE PHOTON TORPEDOES FORWARD
TORPR	FIRE PHOTON TORPEDOES REAR
PROBE	LAUNCH ANTIMATTER PROBE (ONLY 10)
CLOSE	APPROACH ENEMY (IMPULSE DRIVE)
AWAY	RETREAT FROM ENEMY (IMPULSE DRIVE)
PURSE	APPROACH ENEMY (WARP DRIVE)
ESCAPE	RETREAT USING WARP DRIVE
SHIELDS	USE OPTIMUM SHIELD
ROTATE	ROTATE THE SHIP
CHANCES	FIRING CHANCES
COMMANDS	REPEAT COMMANDS
DAMAGE	FULL DAMAGE REPORT
BLUFF	CORBOMITE MANEUVER
WAIT	ENEMY MOVES NEXT
SUICIDE	SELF-DESTRUCTION
SURRENDER	GIVE-UP TO ENEMY
LVEER	TURN 90 DEGREES LEFT
RVEER	TURN 90 DEGREES RIGHT

NOTE WEAPON RANGES ARE
       PHASERS   0-400 MGM (OPTIMUM 200 MGM)
       TORPEDOES 300-700 MGM (OPTIMUM 500 MGM)
       PROBES   ALL RANGES

PHASERS ARE MORE DEADLY THAN TORPEDOES.
PROBES CAUSE TOTAL DESTRUCTION BUT ARE EFFECTIVE
ONLY 7 PERCENT OF THE TIME (APPROXIMATELY).
TORPEDOES AND PHASERS ARE MORE DEADLY WHEN THE
BEARING OF THE ENEMY IS CLOSE TO 0,180,AND-180
DEGREES.

KEN CAPTAIN'S LOG, STAR DATE 517.657 .
  WE ARE PRESENTLY ON COURSE FOR BETEGEUSE 7
  TO RESCUE MINERS UNDER THE ATTACK
  BY OUTSIDER BATTLE CRUISERS.
SULU SIR. I'M PICKING UP A VESSEL ON AN ATTACK VECTOR
  WITH THE PROMETHEUS.
SPOCK SHIP'S COMPUTERS INDICATE THAT IT IS THE OUTSIDER VESSEL
  CTHULU UNDER THE COMMAND OF CAPTAIN TWEEL.
KEN SOUND RED ALERT, LIEUTENANT UHURA.

```
UHURA   AYE, SIR.
SPOCK: CTHULU IS AT RANGE   925.163  MGM, BEARING -100.204 DEGREES.
SULU   WHAT ARE YOUR ORDERS, SIR ? LVEER
KEN    TURN 90 DEGREES LEFT MR. CHEKOV
SPOCK: CTHULU IS AT RANGE   390.304  MGM, BEARING -140.399 DEGREES.
SULU   WHAT ARE YOUR ORDERS, SIR ? TORPR
KEN    FIRE REAR PHOTON TORPEDOES
CHEKOV  MISSED HIM, SIR.
SPOCK: CTHULU IS AT RANGE   56.3293  MGM, BEARING -14.0924 DEGREES.
SULU   WHAT ARE YOUR ORDERS, SIR ? PHASER
KEN    FIRE REAR PHASER BANK
CHEKOV  INCORRECT VECTOR, SIR.
SPOCK: CTHULU IS AT RANGE   448.67   MGM, BEARING -116.54 DEGREES.
SULU   WHAT ARE YOUR ORDERS, SIR ? TORPR
KEN    FIRE REAR PHOTON TORPEDOES
CHEKOV  DIRECT HIT, SIR.
SPOCK   A HIT ON SHIELD # 1 .
SPOCK: CTHULU IS AT RANGE   796.981  MGM, BEARING  42.2506 DEGREES.
SULU   WHAT ARE YOUR ORDERS, SIR ? TORPR
KEN    FIRE REAR PHOTON TORPEDOES
CHEKOV  INCORRECT VECTOR, SIR.
SPOCK: CTHULU IS AT RANGE   205.356  MGM, BEARING -150.974 DEGREES.
SULU   WHAT ARE YOUR ORDERS, SIR ? WAIT
KEN    LET'S WAIT, WHAT WILL THE ENEMY DO NEXT
SPOCK: CTHULU IS AT RANGE   811.958  MGM, BEARING -132.879 DEGREES.
SULU   WHAT ARE YOUR ORDERS, SIR ? BLUFF
KEN    LIEUTENANT, OPEN A VOICE CHANNEL TO STAR FLEET
KEN    USE CODE 2.
UHURA   CODE 2, SIR? THE OUTSIDERS BROKE CODE 2 YESTERDAY, SIR.
KEN    CODE 2, LIEUTENANT, IMMEDIATELY.
UHURA   AYE, SIR. GO AHEAD, SIR.
KEN    THIS IS CAPTAIN KEN OF THE STARSHIP PROMETHEUS.
  WE ARE UNDER ATTACK BY THE OUTSIDER SHIP CTHULU
  AND, IN ORDER TO PREVENT THE PROMETHEUS FROM FALLING
  INTO ENEMY HANDS, WE ARE ACTIVATING THE CORBOMITE
  DEVICE.  SINCE THIS WILL RESULT IN THE COMPLETE
  ANNIHILATION OF ALL MATTER WITHIN A RANGE OF 5000
  MEGAMETERS, ALL VESSELS SHOULD BE WARNED TO STAY
  CLEAR OF THIS AREA FOR THE NEXT  3
  SOLAR YEARS.
  I WISH TO RECORD COMMENDATIONS FOR THE ENTIRE CREW
  AND ESPECIALLY COMMANDER SPOCK, LIEUTENANT
  COMMANDER SCOTT, DOCTOR MCCOY, LIEUTENANT UHURA,
  LIEUTENANT SULU, AND ENSIGN CHEKOV.
SULU   NO IMMEDIATE CHANGE IN OUTSIDER COURSE AND SPEED, SIR.

SPOCK   IT WOULD SEEM THAT THEY HAVE, AS YOU HUMANS PUT IT,
  'CALLED OUR BLUFF', CAPTAIN.
SPOCK: CTHULU IS AT RANGE   568.429  MGM, BEARING  122.279 DEGREES.
SULU   WHAT ARE YOUR ORDERS, SIR ? PURSE
KEN    APPROACH ENEMY AT WARP SPEED
SPOCK: CTHULU IS AT RANGE   722.898  MGM, BEARING  113.52 DEGREES.
SULU   WHAT ARE YOUR ORDERS, SIR ? CLOSE
KEN    COME UP ON THE ENEMY VESSEL
SPOCK: CTHULU IS AT RANGE   159.005  MGM, BEARING -88.9298 DEGREES.
SULU   WHAT ARE YOUR ORDERS, SIR ? PHASER
KEN    FIRE REAR PHASER BANK
CHEKOV  INCORRECT VECTOR, SIR.
SPOCK: CTHULU IS AT RANGE   648.824  MGM, BEARING  131.995 DEGREES.
SULU   WHAT ARE YOUR ORDERS, SIR ? PHASER
KEN    FIRE REAR PHASER BANK
CHEKOV  PHASERS FIRING, SIR.
CHEKOV  MISSED HIM, SIR.
SPOCK: THE OUTSIDER IS FIRING PHOTON TORPEDOES AT US
A DIRECT HIT ON SHIELD # 3 .
SULU   WHAT ARE YOUR ORDERS, SIR ? WAIT
KEN    LET'S WAIT, WHAT WILL THE ENEMY DO NEXT
SPOCK: THE OUTSIDER IS FIRING PHOTON TORPEDOES AT US
 EVASIVE MANEUVERS WERE EFFECTED,NO DAMAGE.
SULU   WHAT ARE YOUR ORDERS, SIR ? ROTATE
```

```
KEN    TURN US ABOUT 180 DEGREES, MR.SULU
SPOCK; THE OUTSIDER IS FIRING PHOTON TORPEDOES AT US
 EVASIVE MANEUVERS WERE EFFECTED,NO DAMAGE.
SPOCK: CTHULU IS AT RANGE  648.824  MGM, BEARING -48.0051 DEGREES.
SULU   WHAT ARE YOUR ORDERS, SIR ? WAWY
SULU TROUBLE HEARING YOU CAPTAIN KEN
SULU   WHAT ARE YOUR ORDERS, SIR ? AWAY
KEN    RETREAT FROM THE ENEMY
SPOCK: CTHULU IS AT RANGE  478.55  MGM, BEARING -69.5286 DEGREES.
SULU   WHAT ARE YOUR ORDERS, SIR ? ESCAPE
KEN    RETREAT AT TOP WARP SPEED
SPOCK: CTHULU IS AT RANGE  472.399  MGM, BEARING  108.811 DEGREES.
SULU   WHAT ARE YOUR ORDERS, SIR ? SURRENDER
KEN    LIEUTENANT, OPEN A VOICE CHANNEL TO THE ENEMY
KEN    THIS IS CAPTAIN KEN OF THE STARSHIP PROMETHEUS.
 WILL YOU ACCEPT OUR UNCONDITIONAL SURRENDER?
TWEEL  ON BEHALF OF THE OUTSIDER EMPIRE, I ACCEPT YOUR
 UNCONDITIONAL SURRENDER, PREPARE FOR IMMEDIATE BOARDING.

COMPUTER, DO YOU WISH TO ATTEMPT ANOTHER BATTLE
 IN COMMAND OF THE PROMETHEUS ? NO
COMPUTER DO YOU WISH TO CHANGE SHIP ? NO



RUN COMPLETE.
```

Program Listing

```
 30 REM SET RANDOM NUMBER
 40 LET R6=TIM(0)
 50 LET R5=INT(R6)
 60 LET R5=R6-R5
 70 LET R5=RND(R5)
 80 DIM N$(16), O$(21), Z$(21)
 90 DEF FND(B)=INT(ABS(B/90))
100 DEF FNX(B)=3.1415926*ABS(90-ABS(B))/180
110 FOR I=1 TO 8
120 READ L$(I)
130 NEXT I
140 REM PLACES TO GO
150 DATA GAMMA 7,ALPHA CENTAURI
160 DATA SIRIUS 12,BETEGEUSE 7
170 DATA SOL 3,SOL 9
180 DATA ALDERBARAN 5,ANDROMENDA
190 FOR I= 1 TO 16
200 READ N$(I)
210 NEXT I
220 REM THE GOOD GUY'S SHIPS
230 DATA ENTERPRISE, SOL-KEEPER,BRAVE,EXETER
240 DATA ACTURUS,SONG-BIRD,DRAGON,LION
250 DATA EXCALIBER,TIGER,REPUBLIC,DEFIANT
260 DATA PROMETHEUS,SIBERIA,LENIN,MARX
270 FOR I=1 TO 3
280 READ K$(I)
290 NEXT I
300 REM TYPE OF BADDIES
310 DATA KLINGON,ROMULAN,OUTSIDER
320 FOR I=1 TO 5
330 READ R$(I)
340 NEXT I
350 REM BADDIES' SHIPS
360 DATA CTHULU,QUARK,KLIXSNIP,XOTOP,KLEEP
```

```
370 FOR I=1 TO 5
380 READ T$(I)
390 NEXT I
400 REM LETS NAME THE CAPTAIN OF THE BADDIES
410 DATA KLEEK,RYJKA,DYSNIP,JOJLM,TWFEL
420 FOR I=1 TO 21
430 READ O$(I)
440 NEXT I
450 DATA RANGE AND BEARING OF THE ENEMY
460 DATA FIRE FORWARD PHASER BANK
470 DATA FIRE REAR PHASER BANK
480 DATA FIRE FORWARD PHOTON TORPEDOES
490 DATA FIRE REAR PHOTON TORPEDOES
500 DATA LAUNCH ANTIMATTER PROBE
510 DATA COME UP ON THE ENEMY VESSEL
520 DATA RETREAT FROM THE ENEMY
530 DATA APPROACH ENEMY AT WARP SPEED
540 DATA RETREAT AT TOP WARP SPEED
550 DATA "USE OPTIMUM SHIELD DEPLOYMENT MR.SULU"
560 DATA "TURN US ABOUT 180 DEGREES, MR.SULU"
570 DATA "MR.SPOCK, WHAT ARE OUR CHANCES AT A HIT"
580 DATA "MR. SPOCK, WHAT OPTIONS ARE AVAILABLE"
590 DATA "MR.SPOCK, FULL DAMAGE REPORT"
600 DATA "LIEUTENANT, OPEN A VOICE CHANNEL TO STAR FLEET"
610 DATA "LET'S WAIT, WHAT WILL THE ENEMY DO NEXT"
620 DATA "ACTIVATE COMPUTER DESTRUCT SEQUENCE"
630 DATA "LIEUTENANT, OPEN A VOICE CHANNEL TO THE ENEMY"
640 DATA "TURN 90 DEGREES LEFT MR. CHEKOV"
650 DATA "TURN 90 DEGREES RIGHT MR. CHEKOV"
660 FOR I=1 TO 21
670 READ Z$(I)
680 NEXT I
690 DATA RANGE,PHASEF,PHASER,TORPF
700 DATA TORPR,PROBE,CLOSE,AWAY
710 DATA PURSF,ESCAPE,SHIELDS
720 DATA ROTATE,CHANCES,COMMANDS
730 DATA DAMAGE,BLUFF,WAIT,SUICIDE
740 DATA SURRENDER,LVEER,RVEER,H
750 PRINT
760 LET S$=N$(RND(0)*16+1)
770 PRINT "SPACE, THE FINAL FRONTIER."
780 PRINT "THIS IS THE VOYAGE OF THE STARSHIP ";S$;"."
790 PRINT "IT S FIVE YEAR MISSION, TO EXPLORE STRANGE NEW WORLDS,"
800 PRINT "TO SEEK OUT NEW LIFE AND NEW CIVILIZATIONS,"
810 PRINT "TO BOLDLY GO WHERE NO MAN HAS GONE BEFORE."
820 PRINT
830 PRINT
840 PRINT TAB(20);"S T A R    WARP "
850 PRINT TAB(20);"------------------"
860 PRINT
870 PRINT"YEOMAN   SIR ENTER YOUR NAME FOR THE LOG";
880 INPUT C$
890 PRINT "SPOCK   YOU ARE IN COMMAND OF THE ";S$;", CAPTAIN ";C$;"."
900 PRINT "  DO YOU WISH A LIST OF THE POSSIBLE COMMANDS, SIR";
910 INPUT A$
920 IF A$<>"YES" THEN    950
930 GOSUB  5530
940 GOSUB  5950
950 PRINT
960 LET E$=K$(RND(0)*3+1)
970 LET F$=R$(RND(0)*5+1)
980 LET U$=T$(RND(0)*5+1)
990 LET D$=L$(RND(0)*8+1)
1000 LET Y=50*(RND(0)-.5)
1010 PRINT C$;"  CAPTAIN'S LOG, STAR DATE "999*RND(0);"."
1020 PRINT "  WE ARE PRESENTLY ON COURSE FOR ";D$
1030 ON INT(RND(0)*5)+1 GOTO 1040,  1070,  1100,  1120,  1140
1040 PRINT"  TO RESCUE MINERS UNDER THE ATTACK"
1050 PRINT "  BY ";E$;" BATTLE CRUISERS."
1060 GOTO  1150
```

```
1070 PRINT" WITH A CARGO OF DILITHIUM CRYSTALS TO "
1080 PRINT" POWER THE COLONISTS STATION"
1090 GOTO 1150
1100 PRINT" TO SEARCH FOR NEW MINERALS FOR THE FEDERATION"
1110 GOTO 1150
1120 PRINT" WITH MARTIAN FLU-CURE"
1130 GOTO 1150
1140 PRINT" FOR OBSERVATION OF BLACK HOLES"
1150 PRINT "SULU  SIR. I'M PICKING UP A VESSEL ON AN ATTACK VECTOR"
1160 PRINT " WITH THE ";S$;"."
1170 PRINT "SPOCK  SHIP'S COMPUTERS INDICATE THAT IT IS THE ";
1180 PRINT E$;" VESSEL "
1190 PRINT " ";F$;" UNDER THE COMMAND OF CAPTAIN ";C$;"."
1200 PRINT C$;"  SOUND RED ALERT, LIEUTENANT UHURA"
1210 PRINT "UHURA  AYE, SIR."
1220 IF RND(0)>.5 THEN 1250
1230 LET X$="SULU"
1240 GOTO 1260
1250 LET X$="CHEKOV"
1260 LET H1=H2=G=X=S=0
1270 LET P=0
1280 FOR I=1 TO 4
1290 LET Z(I)=100
1300 LET S(I)=100
1310 NEXT I
1320 LET R=1000-100*RND(0)
1330 LET B=360*(RND(0)-.5)
1340 LET B1=360*(RND(0)-.5)
1350 GOTO 01380
1360 IF I<7 THEN 01390
1370 IF I>12 THEN 01390
1380 GOSUB 05810
1390 PRINT X$" WHAT ARE YOUR ORDERS, SIR";
1400 INPUT M$
1410 FOR I=1 TO 21
1420 IF Z$(I)=M$ THEN 1480
1430 NEXT I
1440 CHANGE M$ TO M
1450 LET I=M(1)-27
1460 IF M(1)=1 THEN 1480
1470 LET I=10*I+M(2)-27
1480 IF I<1 THEN 1500
1490 IF I22 THEN 1520
1500 PRINT X$;" TROUBLE HEARING YOU CAPTAIN ";C$
1510 GOTO 01390
1520 PRINT C$;"  "O$(I)
1530 IF I>12 THEN 1570
1540 IF I>6 THEN 1560
1550 ON I GOTO '1380, 1580, 1610, 1640, 1670, '1700
1560 ON (I-6) GOTO 1730, 1730, 1760, 1760, 2670, 1730
1570 ON (I-12) GOTO 2780, 2900, 2920, 1790, 3710, 3540, 3630,
     6180, 6210
1580 IF H1<7 THEN 1900
1590 PRINT "CHEKOV  FORWARD PHASERS ARE DEAD, SIR."
1600 GOTO 3710
1610 IF H1<6 THEN 02320
1620 PRINT "CHEKOV  REAR PHASER IS DEAD, SIR."
1630 GOTO 3710
1640 IF H1<9 THEN 2340
1650 PRINT "CHEKOV  FORWARD PHOTON TORPEDOES ARE DEAD, SIR."
1660 GOTO 3710
1670 IF H1<8 THEN 2410
1680 PRINT "CHEKOV  REAR PHOTON TORPEDO IS DEAD, SIR."
1690 GOTO 3710
1700 IF H1<11 THEN 2430
1710 PRINT "CHEKOV  PROBE LAUNCHER IS DEAD, SIR."
1720 GOTO 3710
1730 IF H1<14 THEN 2520
1740 PRINT "SULU  IMPULSE ENGINES ARE DEAD, SIR."
```

61

```
1750 GOTO 3710
1760 IF H1<11 THEN 2520
1770 PRINT "SULU  WARP DRIVE IS DEAD, SIR."
1780 GOTO 3710
1790 IF H2<11 THEN 1820
1800 PRINT "SPOCK  THE ";E$;" HAS NO ENGINES, SIR."
1810 GOTO 3710
1820 IF G=0 THEN 3270
1830 PRINT "SPOCK  I DO NOT THAT THE ";E$;"S WILL BE FOOLED"
1840 PRINT "  BY THAT MANEUVER AGAIN, SIR."
1850 GOTO 3710
1860 IF ABS(B)<90 THEN 1890
1870 PRINT "CHEKOV  INCORRECT VECTOR, SIR."
1880 GOTO 3710
1890 PRINT "CHEKOV  PHASERS FIRING, SIR."
1900 LET R9=R
1910 LET B9=B
1920 GOSUB 6130
1930 IF RND(0)<F8 THEN 1960
1940 PRINT "CHEKOV  MISSED HIM, SIR."
1950 GOTO 3710
1960 IF RND(0)<.2 THEN 2140
1970 LET V=.5
1980 LET K=1
1990 FOR K1=2 TO 4
2000 IF S(K)>=S(K1) THEN 2020
2010 LET K=K1
2020 NEXT K1
2030 IF S(K)>50 THEN 2050
2040 LET K=INT(RND(0)*4+1)
2050 LET H2=H2+V
2060 PRINT "SPOCK  A HIT ON SHIELD #";K;"."
2070 IF S(K)=0 THEN 2170
2080 LET S(K)=S(K)-30*V*(RND(0)+.1)
2090 GOTO 2100
2100 IF S(K)>0 THEN 2130
2110 PRINT "  WHICH IS NOW GONE."
2120 LET S(K)=0
2130 GOTO 3710
2140 LET V=1
2150 PRINT "CHEKOV  DIRECT HIT, SIR."
2160 GOTO 1980
2170 PRINT "CHEKOV  GOT HIM, SIR."
2180 IF RND(0)<.5 THEN 5440
2190 PRINT "SPOCK  THE ";E$;" VESSEL REMAINS INTACT, CAPTAIN."
2200 PRINT C$;"  OPEN A HAILING FREQUENCY, LIEUTENANT."
2210 PRINT "UHURA  HAILING FREQUENCY OPEN, SIR."
2220 PRINT C$;"  THIS IS CAPTAIN ";C$;" OF THE STARSHIP ";S$;"."
2230 PRINT "  PREPARE TO COMMENCE BEAMING OVER SURVIVORS."
2240 IF RND(0)<.5 THEN 2300
2250 PRINT U$;"  I AM AFRAID THAT WILL BE QUITE IMPOSSIBLE."
2260 PRINT "  CAPTAIN, SINCE WE HAVE JUST INITIATED OUR AUTO-DESTRUCT."
2270 PRINT "  10 9 8 7 6 5 4 3 2 1"
2280 PRINT
2290 GOTO 5440
2300 PRINT U$;"  VERY WELL, CAPTAIN. OUR SHIELDS HAVE BEEN DEACTIVATED."
2310 GOTO 05840
2320 IF ABS(B)<90 THEN 1870
2330 GOTO 1890
2340 IF ABS(B)>=90 THEN 1870
2350 LET R9=R
2360 LET B9=B
2370 GOSUB 6080
2380 IF RND(0)>F9 THEN 1940
2390 IF RND(0)<.25 THEN 1970
2400 GOTO 02140
2410 IF ABS(B)<90 THEN 1870
2420 GOTO 2350
2430 IF X<10 THEN 2460
2440 PRINT "CHEOV  WE HAVE NO MORE PROBES, SIR."
```

62

```
2450 GOTO  3720
2460 LET X=X+1
2470 IF RND(0)<.07135 THEN  2500
2480 PRINT "SPOCK   PROBE LOST, CAPTAIN."
2490 GOTO  3710
2500 PRINT "SPOCK   PROBE IS HOMING ON THE ";F$;" , SIR."
2510 GOTO  5440
2520 ON (I-6) GOTO 2530,  2560,  2600,  2630,  2670,  2740
2530 GOSUB  4880
2540 LET R=ABS(R-Y)
2550 GOTO  3710
2560 GOSUB  4940
2570 LET R=ABS(R+Y)
2580 IF R>5000 THEN  4780
2590 GOTO  3710
2600 GOSUB  .4980
2610 LET R=ABS(R-2*Y)
2620 GOTO  3710
2630 GOSUB  5040
2640 LET R=ABS(R+2*Y)
2650 IF R>5000 THEN  4780
2660 GOTO  3710
2670 LET S=1
2680 FOR J=2 TO 4
2690 IF Z(J)<=Z(S) THEN  2710
2700 LET S=J
2710 NEXT J
2720 PRINT "SULU   SHIELD #";S;" IS IN POSITION."
2730 GOTO  1390
2740 LET B=B+180
2750 IF B<=180 THEN  3710
2760 LET B=B-360
2770 GOTO  3710
2780 PRINT "SPOCK   AT RANGE ";R;" I WOULD ESTIMATE THE PROBABILITY"
2790 LET R9=R
2800 LET B9=B
2810 GOSUB  6130
2820 LET F8=F8*100
2830 PRINT "  OF A PHASER HIT AT ";F8;" AND THE PROBABLILITY"
2840 LET R9=R
2850 LET B9=B
2860 GOSUB  6080
2870 LET F9=F9*100
2880 PRINT "  OF A PHOTON TORPEDO AT ";F9;"."
2890 GOTO  1390
2900 GOSUB  5530
2910 GOTO  1390
2920 PRINT "SPOCK   DAMAGES ARE AS FOLLOWS,"
2930 PRINT TAB(10);"OF SHIELDS REMAINING"
2940 PRINT TAB(6);"SHIELD #";TAB(16);S$;TAB(30);F$
2950 FOR J=1 TO 4
2960 PRINT TAB(9);J;TAB(16);Z(J);TAB(30);S(J)
2970 NEXT J
2980 PRINT S$;" DAMAGE";
2990 IF H1>5.5 THEN 03020
3000 PRINT TAB(20);"NONE"
3010 GOTO  3140
3020 PRINT TAB(20);"REAR PHASER DEAD"
3030 IF H1<7 THEN  3140
3040 PRINT TAB(20);"FORWARD PHASERS DEAD"
3050 IF H1<8 THEN  3140
3060 PRINT TAB(20);"REAR PHOTON TORPEDOES DEAD"
3070 IF H1<9 THEN  3140
3080 PRINT TAB(20);"FORWARD PHOTON TORPEDOES DEAD"
3090 IF H1<11 THEN  3140
3100 PRINT TAB(20);"PROBE LAUNCHER DESTROYED"
3110 PRINT TAB(20);"WARP DRIVE LOST"
3120 IF H1<14 THEN  3140
3130 PRINT TAB(20);"IMPULSE POWER LOST"
3140 PRINT F$;" DAMAGE";
```

```
3150 IF H2>5.5 THEN  3180
3160 PRINT TAB(20);"NONE"
3170 GOTO  3250
3180 PRINT TAB(20);"ALL PHASERS DEAD"
3190 IF H2<9 THEN  3250
3200 PRINT TAB(20);"ALL TORPEDOES DEAD"
3210 IF H2<11 THEN  3250
3220 PRINT TAB(20);"WARP DRIVE DEAD"
3230 IF H2<14 THEN  3250
3240 PRINT TAB(20);"IMPULSE ENGINES DEAD"
3250 PRINT
3260 GOTO  1390
3270 PRINT C$"  USE CODE 2."
3280 PRINT "UHURA   CODE 2, SIR? THE ";E$;"'S BROKE CODE 2 YESTERDAY,
     SIR."
3290 PRINT C$"   CODE 2, LIEUTENANT, IMMEDIATELY."
3300 PRINT "UHURA  AYE, SIR, GO AHEAD, SIR."
3310 PRINT C$"   THIS IS CAPTAIN ";C$;" OF THE STARSHIP ";S$;"."
3320 PRINT "   WE ARE UNDER ATTACK BY THE ";E$;" SHIP ";F$
3330 PRINT "   AND, IN ORDER TO PREVENT THE ";S$;" FROM FALLING"
3340 PRINT "   INTO ENEMY HANDS, WE ARE ACTIVATING THE CORBOMITE"
3350 PRINT "   DEVICE.  SINCE THIS WILL RESULT IN THE COMPLETE"
3360 PRINT "   ANNIHILATION OF ALL MATTER WITHIN A RANGE OF 5000"
3370 PRINT "   MEGAMETERS, ALL VESSELS SHOULD BE WARNED TO STAY"
3380 PRINT "   CLEAR OF THIS AREA FOR THE NEXT ";INT(RND(0)*4)+2
3390 PRINT "   SOLAR YEARS."
3400 PRINT "   I WISH TO RECORD COMMENDATIONS FOR THE ENTIRE CREW"
3410 PRINT "   AND ESPECIALLY COMMANDER SPOCK, LIEUTENANT"
3420 PRINT "   COMMANDER SCOTT, DOCTOR MCCOY, LIEUTENANT UHURA,"
3430 PRINT "   LIEUTENANT SULU, AND ENSIGN CHEKOV."
3440 LET G=1
3450 IF RND(0)>.2 THEN  3500
3460 PRINT "SULU  ";E$;" IS MOVING AWAY AT WARP10, SIR."
3470 PRINT "SPOCK  THE TACTIC APPEARS TO HAVE BEEN EFFECTIVE, SIR."
3480 PRINT "   THE ";E$;" HAS BEEN REPULSED."
3490 GOTO 05840
3500 PRINT "SULU  NO IMMEDIATE CHANGE IN ";E$;" COURSE AND SPEED, SIR."
3510 PRINT "SPOCK  IT WOULD SEEM THAT THEY HAVE, AS YOU HUMANS PUT IT,"
3520 PRINT "   'CALLED OUR BLUFF', CAPTAIN."
3530 GOTO  3710
3540 PRINT "COMPUTER  10 9 8 7 6 5 4 3 2 1"
3550 PRINT "   THE ";S$;" HAS BEEN DESTROYED."
3560 LET W=200*RND(0)
3570 PRINT "   RADIUS OF EXPLOSION ";Q;" MGM."
3580 IF G>=R THEN  3610
3590 PRINT "   ";E$;" VESSEL REMAINS INTACT."
3600 GOTO  5840
3610 PRINT "   ";E$;" VESSEL DESTROYED."
3620 GOTO  5840
3630 IF E$<>"ROMULAN" THEN 03660
3640 PRINT "UHURA  NO ANSWER FROM THE ";F$;", SIR."
3650 GOTO  3710
3660 PRINT C$"   THIS IS CAPTAIN ";C$;" OF THE STARSHIP ";S$;"."
3670 PRINT "   WILL YOU ACCEPT OUR UNCONDITIONAL SURRENDER?"
3680 PRINT U$;"   ON BEHALF OF THE ";E$;" EMPIRE, I ACCEPT YOUR"
3690 PRINT "   UNCONDITIONAL SURRENDER, PREPARE FOR IMMEDIATE BOARDING."
3700 GOTO  5840
3710 REM  ENEMY MOVE DECISION SECTION
3720 IF H2<9 THEN  4030
3730 IF H2<11 THEN  3870
3740 IF H2>13.9 THEN  4670
3750 IF H1>10.9 THEN  4780
3760 IF H1>8.9 THEN  3820
3770 IF R<200*RND(0) THEN  4830
3780 GOSUB  4880
3790 LET R=ABS(R+Y)
3800 IF R>5000 THEN  4780
3810 GOTO  1380
3820 IF RND(0)<.5 THEN  3780
```

64

```
3830 GOSUB  4940
3840 LET R=ABS(R-Y)
3850 IF R>5000 THEN  4780
3860 GOTO  1380
3870 IF H1<7 THEN  4000
3880 IF H1<9 THEN  3770
3890 IF H1>10.9 THEN  4780
3900 IF RND(0)<.5 THEN  3820
3910 IF RND(0)<.5 THEN  3540
3920 GOSUB  4980

3930 LET R=ABS(R+2*Y)
3940 IF R>5000 THEN  4780
3950 GOTO  1380
3960 GOSUB  5040
3970 LET R=ABS(R-2*Y)
3980 IF R>5000 THEN  4780
3990 GOTO  1380
4000 IF R>700 THEN  3960
4010 IF R>200 THEN  3920
4020 GOTO  3770
4030 IF H<6 THEN  4200
4040 IF H1<7 THEN  4120
4050 IF R<300 THEN  3960
4060 IF R>700 THEN  3920
4070 IF H1>7.9 THEN  4090
4080 IF FND(B1)>FND(B) THEN  3960
4090 IF ABS(B1-90)>=ABS(B-90)-20 THEN  5080
4100 IF RND(0)<.5 THEN  3960
4110 GOTO  3920
4120 LET R9=R
4130 LET B9=B1
4140 GOSUB  6130
4150 LET R9=R
4160 LET B9=B1
4170 GOSUB  5080
4180 IF F8>F9 THEN  3960
4190 GOTO  4050
4200 IF H1<7 THEN  4290
4210 IF R>150 THEN  4240
4220 IF RND(0)<.5 THEN  3830
4230 GOTO  3960
4240 IF R>=400 THEN  04270
4250 IF ABS(B1)<30 THEN  5150
4260 GOTO  3830
4270 IF R>700 THEN  3920
4280 GOTO  4080
4290 IF R>700 THEN  3920
4300 LET R9=R
4310 LET B9=B1
4320 GOSUB  6080
4330 LET R9=R
4340 LET B9=B1
4350 GOSUB  6130
4360 IF F9>F8 THEN  4080
4370 IF H1>6.9 THEN  4390
4380 IF FND(B1)>FND(B) THEN  3960
4390 IF ABS(B1-90)>=ABS(B-90)-20 THEN  5150
4400 GOTO  3960
4410 IF H1<6 THEN  4660
4420 LET T=H1-V
4430 IF ABS(T-6)<.1 THEN  4470
4440 IF ABS(H1-6.26)>.3 THEN  4470
4450 PRINT "CHEKOV  REAR PHASER DEAD, SIR."
4460 GOTO  4660
4470 IF ABS(T-7)<.1 THEN  4510
4480 IF ABS(H1-7.25)>.3 THEN  4510

4490 PRINT "CHEKOV  FORWARD PHASERS DEAD, SIR."
4500 GOTO  4660
```

```
4510 IF ABS(T-8)<.1 THEN  4550
4520 IF ABS(H1-8.25)>.3 THEN  4550
4530 PRINT "CHEKOV  REAR PHOTON TORPEDOES DEAD, SIR."
4540 GOTO  4660
4550 IF ABS(T-9)<.1 THEN  4590
4560 IF ABS(H1-9.25)>.3 THEN  4590
4570 PRINT "CHEKOV  FORWARD PHOTON TORPEDOES DEAD, SIR."
4580 GOTO  4660
4590 IF ABS(T-11)<.1 THEN  4630
4600 IF ABS(H1-11.25)>.3 THEN  4630
4610 PRINT "CHEKOV  PROBE LAUNCHER AND WARP DRIVE GONE, SIR."
4620 GOTO  4660
4630 IF ABS(T-14)<.1 THEN  4660
4640 IF ABS(H1-14.25)>.3 THEN  4660
4650 PRINT "CHEKOV  IMPULSE ENGINES DEAD, SIR."
4660 RETURN
4670 IF P>0 THEN  1360
4680 LET P=1
4690 PRINT "SPOCK  THE ";E$;" SHIP IS COMPLETELY CRIPPLED, SIR."
4700 PRINT "  DO YOU WANT TO SURRENDER";
4710 INPUT A$
4720 IF A$="YES" THEN  2200
4730 PRINT "SPOCK  DO YOU WANT TO DESTROY THE ";F$;", CAPTAIN";
4740 INPUT A$
4750 IF A$="YES" THEN  1390
4760 GOTO  4790
4770 REM  LOSS OF CONTACT SECTION
4780 PRINT "SULU  CONTACT WITH THE ";F$;" VESSEL HAS BEEN BROKEN, SIR."
4790 PRINT C$;"  RESUME COURSE FOR ";D$;", MR.SULU."
4800 PRINT "CHEKOV  AYE,SIR."
4810 GOTO  5840
4820 REM  ENEMY SUICIDE SECTION
4830 PRINT "SPOCK  SENSORS INDICATE THAT THE ";F$;" IS OVERLOADING"
4840 PRINT "  WHAT REMAINS OF ITS ANTIMATTER PODS, UNDOUBTEDLY"
4850 PRINT "  ASUICIDAL MOVE,CAPTAIN. PODS WILL DETONATE"
4860 PRINT "  IN 12 SECONDS -10 9 8 7 6 5 4 3 2 1"
4870 GOTO  5440
4880 LET R=R-200*(RND(0)*.5)
4890 LET B=360 *(RND(0)-.5)
4900 LET B1=360*(RND(0)-.5)
4910 IF R>0 THEN  4930
4920 LET R=-R
4930 RETURN
4940 LET R=R+200*(RND(0)+.5)
4950 LET B=360*(RND(0)-.5)
4960 LET B1=360*(RND(0)-.5)
4970 RETURN
4980 LET R=R-400*(RND(0)+.5)
4990 LET B=360*(RND(0)-.5)
5000 LET B1=360*(RND(0)-.5)
5010 IF R>0 THEN  5030
5020 LET R=-R
5030 RETURN
5040 LET R=R+400*(RND(0)+.5)
5050 LET B=360*(RND(0)-.5)
5060 LET B1=360*(RND(0)-.5)
5070 RETURN
5080 PRINT "SPOCK; THE ";E$;" IS FIRING PHOTON TORPEDOES AT US"
5090 LET R9=R
5100 LET B9=B1
5110 GOSUB  6080
5120 IF RND(0)>F9 THEN  5420
5130 IF RND(0)<.4 THEN  5360
5140 GOTO 05210
5150 PRINT "SPOCK THE ";E$;" IS FIRING PHASERS AT US,SIR."
5160 LET R9=R
5170 LET B9=B1
5180 GOSUB  6130
5190 IF RND(0)>F8 THEN  5420
5200 IF RND(0)<.2 THEN  5360
```

```
5210 LET V=.5
5220 LET K=INT(RND(0)*4)+1
5230 IF S=0 THEN  5250
5240 LET K=S
5250 PRINT " A HIT ON SHIELD #";K;"."
5260 IF Z(K)<=0 THEN  5340
5270 LET Z(K)=Z(K)-30*V*(RND(0)+.1)
5280 LET H1=H1+V
5290 GOSUB  4410
5300 IF Z(K)>0 THEN  1360
5310 LET Z(K)=0
5320 PRINT "  SHIELD #";K;" IS GONE."
5330 GOTO 1360
5340 PRINT "COMPUTER THE ";S$;" HAS BEEN DESTROYED."
5350 GOTO  5840
5360 LET V=1
5370 LET K=INT(RND(0)*4)+1
5380 IF S=0 THEN  5400
5390 LET K=S
5400 PRINT "A DIRECT HIT ON SHIELD #";K;"."
5410 GOTO  5260
5420 PRINT " EVASIVE MANEUVERS WERE EFFECTED,NO DAMAGE."
5430 GOTO  1360
5440 PRINT
5450 LET Q=200*RND(0)
5460 IF Q<R THEN  05500
5470 PRINT "COMPUTER RADIUS OF EXPLOSION ";Q;" MGM."
5480 PRINT " ";S$;" HAS BEEN DESTRUCTED."
5490 GOTO  5840
5500 PRINT "SPOCK ";E$;" VESSEL DESTROYED."
5510 PRINT " RADIUS OF EXPLOSION ";Q;" MGM."
5520 GOTO  5840
5530 PRINT
5540 PRINT "SPOCK THE POSSIBLE COMMANDS ARE DESIGNATED BY"
5550 PRINT " THE FOLLOWING NUMBERS OF CODE WORDS "
5560 PRINT
5570 PRINT"CODE                    COMMAND"
5580 PRINT
5590 PRINT"RANGE                   REPEAT RANGE AND BEARING OF ENEMY"
5600 PRINT"PHASEF                  FIRE PHASERS FORWARD BANK"
5610 PRINT"PHASER                  FIRE PHASERS REAR BANK"
5620 PRINT"TORPF                   FIRE PHOTON TORPEDOES FORWARD"
5630 PRINT"TORPR                   FIRE PHOTON TORPEDOES REAR"
5640 PRINT"PROBE                   LAUNCH ANTIMATTER PROBE (ONLY 10)"
5650 PRINT"CLOSE                   APPROACH ENEMY (IMPULSE DRIVE)"
5660 PRINT"AWAY                    RETREAT FROM ENEMY (IMPULSE DRIVE)"
5670 PRINT"PURSE                   APPROACH ENEMY (WARP DRIVE)"
5680 PRINT"ESCAPE                  RETREAT USING WARP DRIVE"
5690 PRINT"SHIELDS                 USE OPTIMUM SHIELD"
5700 PRINT"ROTATE                  ROTATE THE SHIP"
5710 PRINT"CHANCES                 FIRING CHANCES"
5720 PRINT"COMMANDS                REPEAT COMMANDS"
5730 PRINT"DAMAGE                  FULL DAMAGE REPORT"
5740 PRINT"BLUFF                   CORBOMITE MANEUVER"
5750 PRINT"WAIT                    ENEMY MOVES NEXT"
5760 PRINT"SUICIDE                 SELF-DESTRUCTION"
5770 PRINT"SURRENDER               GIVE-UP TO ENEMY"
5780 PRINT"LVEER                   TURN 90 DEGREES LEFT"
5790 PRINT"RVEER                   TURN 90 DEGREES RIGHT"
5800 RETURN
5810 PRINT"SPOCK ";F$;" IS AT RANGE ";R;" MGM, BEARING ";B;
5820 PRINT "DEGREES."
5830 RETURN
5840 PRINT
5850 PRINT "COMPUTER, DO YOU WISH TO ATTEMPT ANOTHER BATTLE"
5860 PRINT " IN COMMAND OF THE ";S$;
5870 INPUT A$
5880 IF A$<>"YES" THEN  5900
5890 GOTO   960
```

```
5900 PRINT "COMPUTER DO YOU WISH TO CHANGE SHIP";
5910 INPUT A$
5920 IF A$<>"YES" THEN  6260
5930 LET S$=N$(RND(0)*16+1)
5940 GOTO  890
5950 PRINT
5960 PRINT "NOTE WEAPON RANGES ARE"
5970 PRINT"    PHASERS      0-400 MGM (OPTIMUM 200 MGM)"
5980 PRINT"    TORPEDOES   300-700 MGM (OPTIMUM 500 MGM)"
5990 PRINT "    PROBES      ALL RANGES"
6000 PRINT
6010 PRINT "PHASERS ARE MORE DEADLY THAN TORPEDOES."
6020 PRINT "PROBES CAUSE TOTAL DESTRUCTION BUT ARE EFFECTIVE"
6030 PRINT "ONLY 7 PERCENT OF THE TIME (APPROXIMATELY)."
6040 PRINT "TORPEDOES AND PHASERS ARE MORE DEADLY WHEN THE"
6050 PRINT "BEARING OF THE ENEMY IS CLOSE TO 0,180,AND-180"
6060 PRINT "DEGREES."
6070 RETURN
6080 LET F9=0
6090 IF ABS(R9-500)>200 THEN  6120
6100 LET F9=1-(R9-500)^2/40000
6110 LET F9=F9*SIN(FNX(B9))*(3-FND(B9))/3
6120 RETURN
6130 LET F8=0
6140 IF R9>400 THEN  .6170
6150 LET F8=1-(R9-200)^2/40000
6160 LET F8=F8*SIN(FNX(B9))*(5-FND(B9))/5
6170 RETURN
6180 IF H1>=14 THEN  1740
6190 LET B=B+90
6200 GOTO  2750
6210 IF H1>=14 THEN  1740
6220 LET B=B-90
6230 IF B>=0 THEN  2750
6240 LET B=360-B
6250 GOTO  2750
6260 END
```

An adaptation of this program designed specifically for the Radio Shack TRS-80 computer using Level II BASIC can be found on page 198 in Section II.

BOMB DISPOSAL SQUAD

There is a time bomb with 10 wires. You must cut the wires to defuse the bomb. Unfortunately, because of the way the bomb was made, two of the wires will cause immediate explosion if they are cut. Out of the remaining eight wires, four are absolutely harmless. And you only have six moves to defuse the bomb.

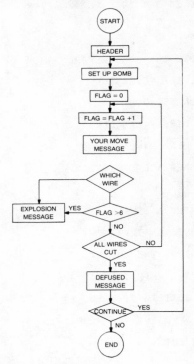

Flowchart for Bomb Disposal Squad

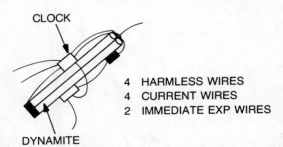

Fig. 1-3—There are 4 harmless wires, 4 current wires, and 2 immediate explosion wires.

Sample Run

```
RUN

BOMB DISPOSAL SQUAD

---------

INSTRUCTIONS ARE AS FOLLOWS

THE TIME BOMB IS SET TO EXPLODE AFTER

AFTER 6 MOVES

YOU MUST DEFUSE THE BOMB BEFORE

THEN, OR ELSE THE RESULTING

EXPLOSION WILL GET YOU...

THERE ARE 10 WIRES, LABELLED 1

TO 10, 2 OF THESE WIRES

WILL CAUSE IMMEDIATE EXPLOSION

IF CUT..

OF THE REMAINING 8 WIRES

4 ARE NOT CONNECTED TO ANY

SENSOR, INCLUDING THE CLOCK.

THE BOMB MAKER PLANTS THESE

FALSE WIRES, JUST TO GIVE YOU A

HARD TIME IN DEFUSING THE BOMB.

WHICH WIRE TO CUT

?2

SILLY GOOSE, YOU HAVE EXPLODED

THE BOMB...

                    BANG..

TO PLAY AGAIN TYPE 1,

IF NOT TYPE 0

?1

WHICH WIRE TO CUT

?3
```

WHICH WIRE TO CUT

?7

SORRY, THAT WAS A HARMLESS WIRE

WHICH WIRE TO CUT

?9

WHICH WIRE TO CUT

?1

WHICH WIRE TO CUT

?6

YOU SHOULD BE WITH THE BOMB SQUAD

YOU HAVE SUCCESSFULLY DEFUSED THE

DEVICE IN ONLY 5 MOVES

TO PLAY AGAIN TYPE 1

IF NOT TYPE 0

?0

NEVER DID LIKE EXPLOSIONS, DID YOU?

RUN COMPLETE

Program Listing

```
10    REM THIS IS THE PROGRAM OF BOMB
      DISPOSAL SQUAD
20    REM THE BOMB CONSISTS OF 4 STICKS
      OF
30    REM DYNAMITE AND IS CONNECTED TO A
40    REM DIGITAL CLOCK AND OTHER SENS-
      ORS.
50    REM UNFORTUNATELY YOU CANNOT JUST
60    REM CUT THE WIRES FROM THE CLOCK
70    REM IF THE WIRES ARE NOT CUT
      ACCORDING
80    REM TO SEQUENCE, BANG. YOU BLOW UP
90    PRINT
100   PRINT
110   PRINT
120   PRINT ''TIME BOMB''
130   PRINT ''---------''
140   PRINT
150   PRINT ''INSTRUCTIONS ARE AS
      FOLLOWS''
160   PRINT
170   PRINT
180   PRINT ''THE TIME BOMB IS SET TO
      EXPLODE''
190   PRINT ''AFTER 6 MOVES.''
200   PRINT ''YOU MUST DEFUSE THE BOMB
      BEFORE''
210   PRINT ''THEN, OR ELSE THE RESULT-
      ING''
```

```
220  PRINT ''EXPLOSION WILL GET YOU..''
230  PRINT
240  PRINT ''THERE ARE 10 WIRES,
     LABELLED 1''
250  PRINT ''TO 10, 2 OF THESE WIRES''
260  PRINT ''WILL CAUSE IMMEDIATE
     EXPLOSION,''
270  PRINT ''IF CUT..''
280  PRINT ''OF THE REMAINING 8 WIRES''
290  PRINT ''4 ARE NOT CONNECTED TO
     ANY''
300  PRINT ''SENSOR, INCLUDING THE
     CLOCK.''
310  PRINT ''THE BOMB MAKER PLANTS
     THESE''
320  PRINT ''FALSE WIRES, JUST TO GIVE
     YOU A''
330  PRINT ''HARD TIME IN DEFUSING THE
     BOMB.''
340  PRINT
350  REM SET UP WIRE CONNECTIONS
360  DIM W{10}
370  REM THE WIRES ARE
380  A = INT{RND{0} * 10} + 1
390  B = INT{RND{0} * 10} + 1
400  IF B = A THEN 390
410  W{A} = 3
420  W{B} = 3
430  REM THE ABOVE TWO WIRES CAUSE
     EXPLOSION
```

```
440  T = 0
450  REM THE HARMLESS WIRES, W{X} = 1
460  C = INT{RND{0} * 10} + 1
470  IF C = A OR C = B THEN 460
480  W{C} = 1
490  D = INT{RND{0} * 10} + 1
500  IF D = C OR D = B OR D = A THEN
     490
510  W{D} = 1
520  E = INT{RND{0} * 10} + 1
530  IF E = D OR E = C OR E = B OR E
     = A THEN 520
540  W{E} = 1
550  F = INT{RND{0} * 10} + 1
560  IF F = E OR F = D OR F = C OR F =
     B OR F = A THEN 550
570  W{F} = 1
580  REM SET UP LIVE WIRES W{X} = 2
590  G = INT{RND{0} * 10} + 1
600  IF G = F OR G = E OR G = D THEN
     590
610  IF G = C OR G = B OR G = A THEN
     590
620  W{G} = 2
630  H = INT{RND{0} * 10} + 1
640  IF H = G OR H = F OR H = E OR H
     = D THEN 630
650  IF H = C OR H = B OR H = A THEN
     630
660  W{H} = 2
```

```
670    I = INT{RND{0} * 10} + 1
680    IF I = H OR I = G OR I = F OR I
       = D THEN 670
690    IF I = E OR I = C OR I = B OR I
       = A THEN 670
700    W{I} = 2
710    REM SET UP LAST WIRE W{X} = 2
720    FOR J = 1 TO 10
730    IF W{J} = 3 OR W{J} = 1 THEN 760
740    IF W{J} = 2 THEN 760
750    W{J} = 2
760    NEXT J
770    REM ALL WIRES ARE NOT CONNECTED
780    M = 0
790    M = M + 1

800    PRINT ''WHICH WIRE TO CUT''
810    INPUT L
820    IF L< >INT {L} THEN 800
830    IF L < 1 OR L > 10 THEN 800
840    IF W{L} = 3 THEN 870
850    IF W{L} = 1 THEN 1030
860    GOTO 1060
870    PRINT
880    PRINT ''SILLY GOOSE, YOU HAVE
       EXPLODED''
890    PRINT ''THE BOMB...''
900    PRINT
910    PRINT''                    BANG..''
920    PRINT
930    PRINT
```

```
940    PRINT ''TO PLAY AGAIN TYPE 1,''
950    PRINT ''IF NOT TYPE 0''
960    INPUT C
970    IF C = 1 THEN 1010
980    PRINT
990    PRINT ''NEVER DID LIKE EXPLOSIONS,
       DID YOU?''
1000   STOP
1010   PRINT
1020   GOTO 380
1030   IF M > 6 THEN 870
1040   PRINT ''SORRY, THAT WAS A HARM-
       LESS WIRE.''
1050   GOTO 790
1060   IF M > 6 THEN 870
1070   W{L} = 1
1080   T = T + 1
1090   IF T = 4 THEN 1110
1100   GOTO 790
1120   PRINT ''YOU SHOULD BE WITH THE
       BOMB SQUAD''
1130   PRINT ''YOU HAVE SUCCESSFULLY
       DEFUSED THE''
1140   PRINT ''DEVICE IN ONLY''; M;
       ''MOVES''
1150   GOTO 930
```

An adaptation of this program designed specifically for the
Radio Shack TRS-80 computer using Level II BASIC can be found on
page 204 in Section II.

BIORHYTHM

This program computes your biorhythm for either a month or a year starting with the month and year you desire. All it needs is your birth date.

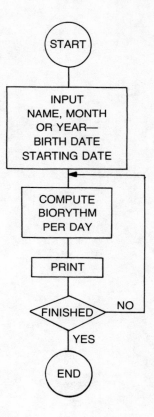

Flowchart for Biorhythm

Sample Run

```
ENTER YOUR NAME ? KEN TRACTON
ENTER EITHER M FOR MONTH OR
Y FOR YEAR, FOR YOUR PLOT
? M
ENTER YOUR BIRTH DATE
MONTH,DAY,YEAR =   ? 10,30,1949
ENTER STARTING MONTH AND YEAR ? 4,1978



BIORYTHM CHART FOR KEN TRACTON
BIRTHDATE  30 OCTOBER  1949

*=COGNITIVE OR INTELLECT
+=PHYSICAL STATE
$=SENSITIVITY OR EMOTIONAL


BIORYTHM CHART FOR APRIL  1978
      KEN TRACTON
          (-)                                  (+)

APRIL   1   $                 *      !                    +
APRIL   2   $              *         !                 +
APRIL   3   $         *              !              +
APRIL   4    $   *                   !          +
APRIL   5       *$                   ! +
APRIL   6   *        $          +    !
APRIL   7   *             $+         !
APRIL   8   *        +         $     !
APRIL   9   *   +                    $
APRIL  10   #                        !    $
APRIL  11   +   *                    !        $
APRIL  12   +       *                !          $
APRIL  13     +       *              !            $
APRIL  14        +      *            !             $
APRIL  15            +     *   !               $
APRIL  16                  +   *               $
APRIL  17                      +  *            $
APRIL  18                    !     + *        $
APRIL  19                    !        #    $
APRIL  20                    !        $*+
APRIL  21                    !     $    *+
APRIL  22                    !  $           *+
APRIL  23                    $              #
APRIL  24             $   !              +*
APRIL  25         $       !            +   *
APRIL  26      $          !         +    *
APRIL  27    $            !      +      *
APRIL  28   $            !  +        *
APRIL  29   $            + !       *
APRIL  30   $          +    !      *

SRU     1.002 UNTS.

RUN COMPLETE.
```

Program Listing

```
 10 REM BIORHYTHM PROGRAM

 30 M$="DAY"
 40 DIM A$(31)
 50 DIM M$(12)
 60 M$(1)="JANUARY"
 70 M$(2)="FEBRUARY"
 80 M$(3)="MARCH"
 90 M$(4)="APRIL"
100 M$(5)="MAY"
110 M$(6)="JUNE"
120 M$(7)="JULY"
130 M$(8)="AUGUST"
140 M$(9)="SEPTEMBER"
150 M$(10)="OCTOBER"
160 M$(11)="NOVEMBER"
170 M$(12)="DECEMBER"
180 P9=6.283185
190 P1=23
200 P2=28
210 P3=33
220 D1=P9/P1
230 D2=P9/P2
240 D3=P9/P3
250 DATA 31,28,31,30
260 DATA 31,30,31,31
270 DATA 30,31,30,31
280 PRINT"ENTER YOUR NAME";
290 INPUT N$
300 PRINT"ENTER EITHER M FOR MONTH OR"
310 PRINT"Y FOR YEAR, FOR YOUR PLOT"
320 INPUT X$
330 N1=0
340 PRINT"ENTER YOUR BIRTH DATE"
350 PRINT"MONTH,DAY,YEAR = ";
360 INPUT B1,B2,B3
370 IF B3<1900 THEN  470
380 IF B1>2 THEN  420
390 IF B1=2 AND B2=29 THEN  420
400 IF INT((B3-1900)/4)<>(B3-1900)/4 THEN  420
410 N1=1
420 PRINT"ENTER STARTING MONTH AND YEAR";
430 INPUT C1,C3
440 IF B3>=C3 THEN  1500
450 FOR J=1 TO B1
460 READ X
470 NEXT J
480 N1=N1+X-B2
490 IF B1=12 THEN  540
500 FOR J=B1+1 TO 12
510 READ X
520 N1=N1+X
530 NEXT J
540 REM MORE CALCULATIONS
550 IF C3-B3<2 THEN  620
560 FOR J=B3-1899 TO C3-1901
```

79

```
570 IF INT(J/4)=J/4 THEN      590
580 GOTO     600
590 N1=N1+1
600 N1=N1+365
610 NEXT J
620 RESTORE
630 IF C1=1 THEN     680
640 FOR J=1 TO C1-1
650 READ X
660 N1=N1+X
670 NEXT J
680 IF INT((C3-1900)/4)<>(C3/4) THEN      720
690 IF C1>2 THEN     710
700 GOTO     720
710 N1=N1+1
720 I1=N1
730 I2=N1
740 I3=N1
750 READ X
760 FOR J=1 TO 5
770 PRINT
780 NEXT J
790 PRINT"BIORYTHM CHART FOR ";N$
800 PRINT"BIRTHDATE ";B2;M$(B1);" ";B3
810 PRINT
820 PRINT"*=COGNITIVE OR INTELLECT"
830 PRINT"+=PHYSICAL STATE"
840 PRINT"$=SENSITIVITY OR EMOTIONAL"
850 FOR J=1 TO 5
860 PRINT
870 NEXT J
880 L=0
890 GOSUB   1330
900 D=0
910 L=L+1
920 FOR I=1 TO 31
930 X$(I)=" "
940 NEXT I
950 X$(16)="!"
960 Y1=INT(15*SIN((L+I1)*D1)+16.5)
970 Y2=INT(15*SIN((L+I2)*D2)+16.5)
980 Y3=INT(15*SIN((L+I3)*D3)+16.5)
990 X$(Y1)="+"
1000 X$(Y2)="$"
1010 X$(Y3)="*"
1020 IF Y1=Y2 THEN     1040
1030 GOTO    1050
1040 X$(Y1)="#"
1050 IF Y1=Y3 THEN     1070
1060 GOTO    1080
1070 X$(Y1)="#"
1080 IF Y2=Y3 THEN     1100
1090 GOTO    1110
1100 X$(Y3)="#"
1110 D=D+1
1120 IF D<X+1 THEN     1240
1130 S1=S1+1
1140 IF S1=12 THEN     1530
1150 C1=C1+1
```

```
1160 IF C1>12 THEN    1200
1170 READ X
1180 GOSUB .1330
1190 GOTO  1240
1200 RESTORE
1210 C1=1
1220 C3=C3+1
1230 GOTO  1170
1240 IF D>9 THEN  1270
1250 PRINT MS(C1);" ";D;" ";TAB(9);
1260 GOTO 01280
1270 PRINT MS(C1);" ";D;TAB(9);
1280 FOR J=1 TO 31
1290 PRINT XS(J);
1300 NEXT J
1310 PRINT
1320 GOTO  .910
1330 REM PRINT MONTH
1340 IF X9=1 THEN  1530
1350 IF XS="M" THEN   1370
1360 GOTO  1380
1370 X9=1
1380 FOR J=1 TO 5
1390 PRINT
1400 NEXT J
1410 PRINT"BIORYTHM CHART FOR ";MS(C1);" ";C3
1420 PRINT TAB(5);NS
1430 PRINT TAB(10);"(-)";TAB(34);"(+)"
1440 PRINT
1450 D=1
1460 RETURN
1470 PRINT
1480 PRINT"YEAR MUST BE 1900 OR LATER"
1490 GOTO   .340
1500 PRINT
1510 PRINT"STARTING YEAR MUST BE GREATER THAN BIRTH YEAR"
1520 GOTO   .420
1530 REM NOW WE STOP
1540 END
```

An adaptation of this program designed specifically for the Radio Shack TRS-80 computer using Level II BASIC can be found on page 206 in Section II.

GUESS

The friendly computer picks a number at random and you must guess it. If you are too low or too high, it will tell you with the appropriate message. At the end, it will tell you how many tries you took.

The best way is to guess quickly by using the binary search method shown in Fig. 1-4. Basically, you pick a point halfway between the last known too high point and too low point.

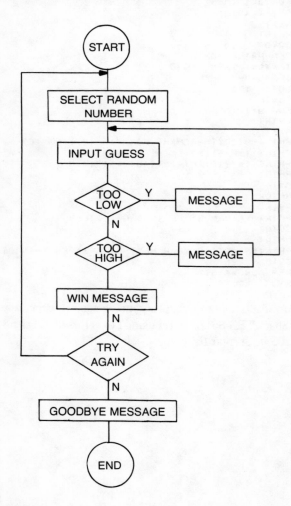

Flowchart for Guess

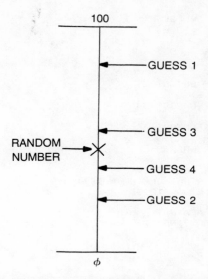

Fig. 1-4—1. If guess 1 was too high, try halfway between it and 0. 2. Since guess 2 was too low, try halfway between guess 1 and guess 2. 3. Since guess 3 is too high, try halfway between it and guess 2. You are narrowing the range each time by ½ (binary) until you reach the desired number.

Sample Run

```
PROGRAM   GUESS

ARE INSTRUCTIONS REQUIRED(1=YES, 2=NO)
? 1

AT RANDOM YOUR FRIENDLY COMPUTER WILL
CHOOSE A NUMBER BETWEEN 1 AND 100
YOU WILL TRY TO GUESS THE RANDOM NUMBER
HINT!!THE BINARY SEARCH METHOD!!


          GOOD-LUCK
          ---- ---- ---- ---- ---- ----

          GUESS
          ---- ---- ---- ----

WHAT IS YOUR GUESS? 50
YOU ARE HIGH
WHAT IS YOUR GUESS? 25
YOU ARE HIGH
WHAT IS YOUR GUESS? 12
YOU ARE HIGH
WHAT IS YOUR GUESS? 6
YOU GOT IT, RIGHT ON THE NOSE!!!!
YOU ONLY TOOK  4  TRIES

WANT TO TRY AGAIN
TYPE 1=YES OR 2=NO? 1
```

```
                GUESS
                -----


WHAT IS YOUR GUESS:
? 50
YOU ARE HIGH
WHAT IS YOUR GUESS? 25
YOU ARE LOW
WHAT IS YOUR GUESS? 34
YOU ARE LOW
WHAT IS YOUR GUESS? 46
YOU ARE HIGH
WHAT IS YOUR GUESS? 36
YOU ARE LOW
WHAT IS YOUR GUESS? 39
YOU GOT IT, RIGHT ON THE NOSE!!!!
YOU ONLY TOOK  6  TRIES

WANT TO TRY AGAIN
TYPE 1=YES OR 2=NO? 1

                GUESS
                -----


WHAT IS YOUR GUESS:
? 50
YOU ARE LOW
WHAT IS YOUR GUESS? 100
YOU ARE HIGH
WHAT IS YOUR GUESS? 75
YOU ARE LOW
WHAT IS YOUR GUESS? 87
YOU ARE LOW
WHAT IS YOUR GUESS? 96
YOU ARE HIGH
WHAT IS YOUR GUESS? 90
YOU GOT IT, RIGHT ON THE NOSE!!!!
YOU ONLY TOOK  6  TRIES

WANT TO TRY AGAIN
TYPE 1=YES OR 2=NO? 2
SCARED HUH!!!!!!


RUN COMPLETE.
```

Program Listing

```
10 REM THIS IS THE GAME OF GUESS
20
30 REM INSTRUCTIONS
40 PRINT"ARE INSTRUCTIONS REQUIRED";
50 PRINT"(1=YES, 2=NO)"
60 INPUT A
70 IF A<>1 THEN 00170
80 PRINT
90 PRINT"AT RANDOM YOUR FRIENDLY COMPUTER WILL"
100 PRINT"CHOOSE A NUMBER BETWEEN 1 AND 100"
110 PRINT"YOU WILL TRY TO GUESS THE RANDOM NUMBER"
120 PRINT"HINT!!THE BINARY SEARCH METHOD!!"
130 PRINT
140 PRINT"               GOOD-LUCK"
150 PRINT"               ---------"
160 PRINT
170 PRINT
180 PRINT"               GUESS"
190 PRINT"               -----"
200 X=0
210 Q=INT(100*RND(0))
220 PRINT
230 PRINT"WHAT IS YOUR GUESS";
240 INPUT Z
250 X=X+1
260 IF Z=Q THEN    300
270 IF Z>Q THEN    330
280 PRINT"YOU ARE LOW"
290 GOTO    230
300 PRINT"YOU GOT IT, RIGHT ON THE NOSE!!!!"
310 PRINT"YOU ONLY TOOK ";X;" TRIES"
320 GOTO    350
330 PRINT"YOU ARE HIGH"
340 GOTO    230
350 PRINT
360 PRINT"WANT TO TRY AGAIN"
370 PRINT"TYPE 1=YES OR 2=NO";
380 INPUT V
390 IF V<>1 THEN    410
400 GOTO    170
410 PRINT"SCARED HUH!!!!!!"
420 END
```

This program also will run on the Radio Shack TRS-80 computer with no modifications needed.

GUESS AGAIN

To win this game you must guess a random fraction, not a decimal number but a common fraction. The fraction, which is picked at random, is less than 1 and is in the following form: x/y where x is an integer from 2 to 9 and x < y.

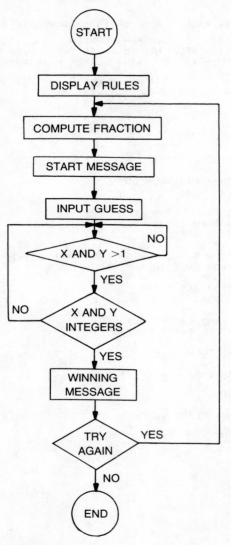

Flowchart for Guess Again

Sample Run

```
RUN
THE COMPUTER IS GOING TO
CHOOSE A FRACTION FROM 0
TO 1
THE FRACTION SO CHOSEN WILL
BE IN THE FOLLOWING FORM
X/Y, WHERE X IS AN INTEGER
FROM 2' TO 9 AND IS ALSO
LESS THAN Y
EXAMPLES:
1/9, 3/8, 4/9, OR 1/4
TO REMIND YOU AGAIN, THE
THE FRACTION COULD DEFINITELY NOT BE
ONE OF THE FOLLOWING OR ANY FRACTION
LIKE THE FOLLOWING
4/10, 3/21, 0/9, OR 2/2
REMEMBER YOUR GUESS FRACTION MUST BE
BETWEEN 0 AND 1
PLEASE ENTER YOUR GUESS AS A
DIGIT THEN A SLASH THEN THE DENOMIN-
ATOR DIGIT
THE COMPUTER HAS PICKED THE FRACTION
GOOD LUCK...
WHAT IS YOUR GUESS
? 2/3
YOU SHOULD TRY A LARGER VALUED
FRACTION
WHAT IS YOUR GUESS
? 5/6
```

THAT'S SUPER, YOU MUST BE A
MATHEMATICIAN
IF YOU WANT TO TRY AGAIN, TYPE 1
OTHERWISE TYPE 2
? 2
GOOD/BYE MATHEMATICIAN
RUN COMPLETE

Program Listing

```
10   REM THE COMPUTER IS TO PICK A
     FRACTION
20   REM AT RANDOM, YOU ARE GOING
30   REM TO HAVE TO GUESS IT
40   PRINT
50   PRINT
60   REM THE RULES OF THE GAME
70   PRINT
80   PRINT ''THE COMPUTER IS GOING TO''
90   PRINT ''CHOOSE A FRACTION FROM 0''
100  PRINT ''TO 1''
110  PRINT ''THE FRACTION SO CHOSEN
     WILL''
120  PRINT ''BE IN THE FOLLOWING FORM''
130  PRINT ''X/Y, WHERE X IS AN INTEG-
     ER''
140  PRINT ''FROM 2 TO 9 AND IS ALSO''
150  PRINT ''LESS THAN Y''
160  PRINT ''EXAMPLES:''
170  PRINT ''1/9, 3/8, 4/9, OR 1/4''
180  PRINT ''TO REMIND YOU AGAIN, THE''
```

```
190   PRINT ''FRACTION COULD DEFINITELY
      NOT BE''
200   PRINT ''ONE OF THE FOLLOWING OR
      ANY FRACTION''
210   PRINT ''LIKE THE FOLLOWING:''
220   PRINT ''4/10, 3/21, 0/9, OR 2/2''
230   PRINT
240   PRINT ''REMEMBER YOUR GUESS FRAC-
      TION MUST BE''
250   PRINT ''BETWEEN 0 AND 1''
260   PRINT ''PLEASE ENTER YOUR GUESS
      AS A''
270   PRINT ''DIGIT THEN A SLASH THEN
      THE DENOMINATOR''
280   PRINT ''DIGIT''
290   REM TIME TO PICK A FRACTION
300   B = INT{RND{0} * 8} + 2
310   A = INT{RND{0} * {B - 1}} + 1
320   PRINT
330   PRINT ''THE COMPUTER HAS PICKED
      THE FRACTION''
340   PRINT ''GOOD LUCK...''
350   PRINT
360   PRINT ''WHAT IS YOUR GUESS''
370   INPUT G$
380   L = LEN{G$}
390   IF L<> 3 THEN 350
400   D$ = SUBSTR{G$,1,1}
410   S$ = SUBSTR{G$,2,1}
420   E$ = SUBSTR{G$,3,1}
```

```
430   D = VAL(D$)
440   E = VAL(E$)
450   IF S$<>''/'' THEN 350
460   IF D < 1 OR E < 1 THEN 350
470   IF D<>INT(D) OR E<>INT(E)
      THEN 350

480   REM NOTICE THAT 470 ALSO CHECKS
      FOR LESS THAN
490   REM 1 LIKE LINE 460, WE HAVE IN-
      CLUDED
500   REM BOTH, BECAUSE OF THE
      DIFFERENCES IN THE
510   REM VERSIONS OF BASIC AVAILABLE
520   IF D > E THEN 350
530   C = A/B
540   F = D/E
550   IF C = F THEN 590
560   IF C > F THEN 710
570   PRINT ''YOU SHOULD TRY A SMALLER
      VALUED NUMBER FRACTION''
580   GOTO 350
590   PRINT
600   PRINT ''THAT'S SUPER, YOU MUST
      BE A
610   PRINT ''MATHEMATICIAN''
630   PRINT ''IF YOU WANT TO TRY AGAIN,
      TYPE 1''
640   PRINT ''OTHERWISE TYPE 2''
650   INPUT C
660   IF C = 1 THEN 690
```

```
670   PRINT ''GOOD-BYE, MATHEMATICIAN''
680   STOP
690   PRINT
700   GOTO 300
710   PRINT ''YOU SHOULD TRY A LARGER
      VALUED FRACTION''
720   GOTO 350
730   END
```

This program will run on the Radio Shack TRS-80 computer with the following modification. Change "SUBSTR" to "MID$" in lines 400, 410, and 420.

PLOT YOUR 4 EQUATIONS

This plotting program allows the user to plot functions by modifying lines 35 to 55. $Q(1)$ to $Q(4)$ are the four equations. If more equations are to be plotted, continue adding $Q(n)$, but be sure to change line 15 to show the change in number of equations.

This program is a sample; the equations already are given. Also, this program consists of an advanced plotting subroutine which may be used by itself in other programs. Note that the characters used for plotting may be changed as well.

We also can change the width of the plot in inches by changing line 20.

A flow chart has been given so the user can, if desired, use this plotting technique with other programs.

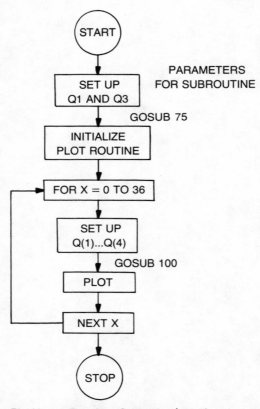

Flowchart for Plot Your 4 Equations Subroutine (1 of 2)

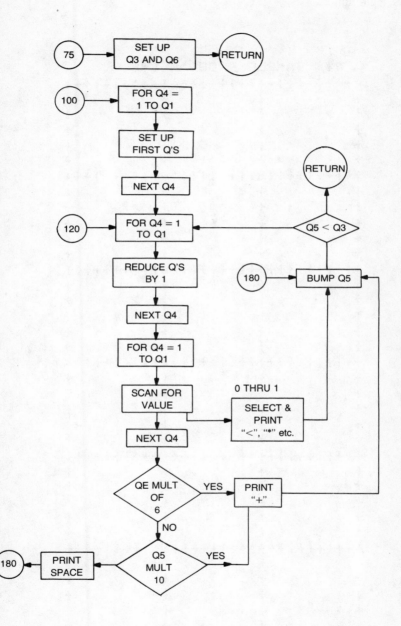

Flowchart for Plot Your 4 Equations Subroutine (2 of 2)

```
  *** SAMPLE PROGRAM ***
*++++++++++++++++++++++++++++++
+ <       +         +         +
+  >      +         +         +
+    *    +         +         +
+      <  +         +         +
+       > +         +         +
++++++++++*++++++++++++++++++++
+         + <       +         +
+         +  >      +         +
+         +    *    +         +
+         +      <  +         +
+         +       > +         +
++++++++++++++++++++*++++++++++
+         +         + <       +
+         +         +  >      +
+         +         +    *    +
+         +         +      <  +
+         +         +       > +
++++++++++++++++++++++++++++++*
+         +         +         +
+         +         +         +
+         +         +         +
+         +         +         +
+         +         +         +
+++++++++++++++++++++++++++++++
+         +         +         +
+         +         +         +
+         +         +         +
+         +         +         +
+         +         +         +
+++++++++++++++++++++++++++++++
+         +         +         +
+         +         +         +
+         +         +         +
+         +         +         +
+         +         +         +
+++++++++++++++++++++++++++++++
```

Sample Program

Program Listing

```
  5 PRINT" *** SAMPLE PROGRAM ***"
 10 REM ASSIGN Q1=NO CURVES,Q3=MAX WIDTH(IN INCHES)
 15 LET Q1 = 4
 20 LET Q3 = 6
 25 GOSUB    75
 30 FOR X = 0 TO 36
 35 LET Q(1) = X/6
 40 LET Q(2) = (36-X)/6
 45 LET Y = SQR(9-((X/6)-3)^2)
 50 LET Q(3) = 3-Y
 55 LET Q(4) = 3+Y
 60 GOSUB   100
 65 NEXT X
 70 STOP
 75 REM  *** ENTRY POINT TO INITIALIZE PLOTTING SUBROUTINE***
 80 LET Q3 = Q3*10 +1
 85 LET Q6 = 0
 90 RETURN
 95 REM *** ENTRY POINT TO PLOT ONE LINE ***
100 FOR Q4 = 1 TO Q1
105 LET Q(Q4) = Q(Q4)*10+1.5
110 NEXT Q4
115 LET Q5 = 0
120 FOR Q4 = 1 TO Q1
125 LET Q(Q4) = Q(Q4)-1
130 NEXT Q4
135 FOR Q4 = 1 TO Q1
140 IF Q(Q4) < 0 THEN    160
145 IF Q(Q4)< .333333334 THEN    205
150 IF Q(Q4) < .666666667 THEN    215
155 IF Q(Q4) <= 1 THEN 00225
160 NEXT Q4
165 IF (Q6/6-INT(Q6/6)) = 0 THEN    235
170 IF (Q5/10-INT(Q5/10))=0 THEN    235
175 PRINT" ";
180 LET Q5 = Q5+1
185 IF Q5<Q3 THEN    120
190 PRINT
195 LET Q6 = Q6+1
200 RETURN
205 PRINT"<";
210 GO TO   180
215 PRINT"*";
220 GO TO  180
225 PRINT">";
230 GO TO  180
235 PRINT"+";
240 GO TO   180
245 REM  *** END OF SUBROUTINE ***
250 END
```

This program is not recommended for use on a TRS-80 computer because of the length of time needed to plot a single line plus the graph does not fit on the video screen.

PLOT YOUR 10 EQUATIONS

This plotting program will plot up to nine curves at once, which are entered at lines 110 to 150 in the form of Q(1) = function to Q(9) = function.

(Q(n) = f(x))

We also can specify, once the functions are entered, which first n (up to nine) will be plotted. We supply the limits of the independent variable x and the limits of the range.

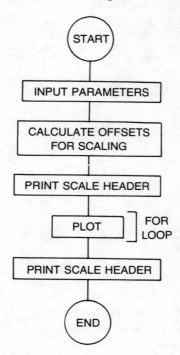

Flowchart for Plot Your 10 Equations

Sample Run

```
ENTER NUMBER OF CURVES TO BE PLOTTED
? 3
ENTER THE LOWER LIMIT OF THE IND VARIABLE
? 10
ENTER THE UPPER LIMIT OF THE IND VARIABLE
? 100
ENTER INCREMENT VALUE OF THE IND VARIABLE
? 5
ENTER THE LOWER LIMIT OF THE RANGE
? 10
ENTER THE UPPER LIMIT OF THE RANGE
? 100
     HORIZONTAL RANGE :  10  TO  100  IN INCREMENTS OF  1.8
     VERTICAL   RANGE :  10  TO  100  IN INCREMENTS OF  5

     0.0          10.0          20.0          30.0          40.0          50.0
     !------------!------------!------------!------------!------------!
   -
   .
   .
   .
   .
   -
   .
   .
   .
   -
   .
   .
   .
   -
   .
   .
   .
   .
     !------------!------------!------------!------------!------------!
     0.0          10.0          20.0          30.0          40.0          50.0
```

```
ENTER NUMBER OF CURVES TO BE PLOTTED
? 8
ENTER THE LOWER LIMIT OF THE IND VARIABLE
? 3.25
ENTER THE UPPER LIMIT OF THE IND VARIABLE
? 7.87
ENTER INCREMENT VALUE OF THE IND VARIABLE
? 4
ENTER THE LOWER LIMIT OF THE RANGE
? 23
ENTER THE UPPER LIMIT OF THE RANGE
? 34
     HORIZONTAL RANGE :  23  TO  34  IN INCREMENTS OF  .22
     VERTICAL   RANGE :  3.25  TO  7.87  IN INCREMENTS OF  4

     0.0          10.0          20.0          30.0          40.0          50.0
     !------------!------------!------------!------------!------------!

     !------------!------------!------------!------------!------------!
     0.0          10.0          20.0          30.0          40.0          50.0
```

Program Listing

```
  5 PRINT"ENTER NUMBER OF CURVES TO BE PLOTTED"
 10 INPUT A
 15 PRINT"ENTER THE LOWER LIMIT OF THE IND VARIABLE"
 20 INPUT B
 25 PRINT"ENTER THE UPPER LIMIT OF THE IND VARIABLE"
 30 INPUT C
 35 PRINT"ENTER INCREMENT VALUE OF THE IND VARIABLE"
 40 INPUT D
 45 PRINT"ENTER THE LOWER LIMIT OF THE RANGE"
 50 INPUT E
 55 PRINT"ENTER THE UPPER LIMIT OF THE RANGE"
 60 INPUT F
 65 LET K=0
 70 LET L=(F-E)/50
 75 PRINT "   HORIZONTAL RANGE : "E;" TO "F;" IN
    INCREMENTS OF "L
 80 PRINT "   VERTICAL   RANGE : "B;" TO "C;" IN
    INCREMENTS OF "D
 85 PRINT
 90 GOSUB   510
 95 GOSUB   520
100 FOR X=B TO C STEP D
105 LET D=0
110
115
120
125
130
135
140
145
150
155 FOR I=1 TO A
160 LET P(I)=INT((Q(I)-E+L/2)/L)+1
165 LET R(I)=I
170 NEXT I
175 FOR I=1 TO A-1
180 FOR J=I+1 TO A
185 IF P(I)<=P(J) THEN    225
190 LET R=P(I)
195 LET P(I)=P(J)
200 LET P(J)=R
205 LET R=R(I)
210 LET R(I)=R(J)
215 LET R(J)=R
220 GOTO    175
225 NEXT J
230 NEXT I
235 LET J=1
240 FOR I=2 TO A
245 IF P(I)<>P(I-J) THEN    270
250 LET P(I)=2E76
255 LET R(I-J)=4E44
260 LET J=J+1
```

```
265 GOTO 00275
270 LET J=1
275 NEXT I
280 LET K=K+1
285 IF 5*INT((K-1)/5)=K-1 THEN   300
290 PRINT " .";
295 GOTO   305
300 PRINT "  -";
305 FOR I=1 TO A
310 IF P(I)=2E76 THEN   480
315 IF (P(I)-1)*(51-P(I))<0 THEN    480
320 LET D=P(I)-D-1
325 IF D=0 THEN   335
330 GOSUB   530
335 IF R(I)=4E44 THEN   470
340 IF R(I)>1 THEN   355
345 PRINT "1";
350 GOTO   475
355 IF R(I)>2 THEN   370
360 PRINT "2";
365 GOTO   475
370 IF R(I)>3 THEN   385
375 PRINT "3";
380 GOTO   475
385 IF R(I)>4 THEN   400
390 PRINT "4";
395 GOTO   475
400 IF R(I)>5 THEN   415
405 PRINT "5";
410 GOTO   475
415 IF R(I)>6 THEN   430
420 PRINT "6";
425 GOTO   475
430 IF R(I)>7 THEN   445
435 PRINT "7";
440 GOTO   475
445 IF R(I)>8 THEN   460
450 PRINT "8";
455 GOTO   475
460 PRINT "9";
465 GOTO   475
470 PRINT "X";
475 LET D=P(I)
480 NEXT I
485 PRINT
490 NEXT X
495 GOSUB   520
500 GOSUB   510
505 STOP
510 PRINT"   0.0        10.0        20.0        30.0        40.0        50.0"
515 RETURN
520 PRINT"   !-----------!-----------!-----------!-----------!-----------!"
525 RETURN
530 LET V=1
535 IF INT(2*D/(2^V))=0 THEN   550
540 LET V=V+1
545 GOTO   535
550 FOR T=1 TO V-1
555 IF D=2*INT(D/2) THEN   640
```

100

```
560 IF T>1 THEN 00575
565 PRINT " ";
570 GOTO   640
575 IF T>2 THEN   590
580 PRINT "  ";
585 GOTO   640
590 IF T>3 THEN   605
595 PRINT "   ";
600 GOTO   640
605 IF T>4 THEN  620
610 PRINT "    ";
615 GOTO   640
620 IF T>5 THEN   635
625 PRINT "       ";
630 GOTO   640
635 PRINT "            ";
640 LET D=INT(D/2)
645 NEXT T
650 RETURN
655 END
```

This program is not recommended for use with the Radio Shack TRS-80 computer because there may be a scrolling problem if the graph is more than 13 lines long.

POLAR GRAPHIC SUBROUTINE

This program allows the user to plot a curve in a polar coordinate plot. The function to be plotted is entered at line 105 in the form of A = F(c). Up to 90 points may be plotted with an increment adjustment to minimize distortion of the generated curve.

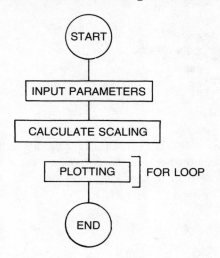

Flowchart for Polar Graphic subroutine

Sample Run

```
00105  A = TAN(23*C)


PROGRAM    POLAR

++++++*******POLAR COORDINATE PLOT*******++++++


ENTER VALUE OF ENDPOINTS (ABS)
? 7

X INCREMENT = .233333

Y INCREMENT = .388889
```

00105 A = TAN(2*C)

RUN

PROGRAM   POLAR

++++++*******POLAR COORDINATE PLOT*******++++++

ENTER VALUE OF ENDPOINTS (ABS)
? 6

X INCREMENT = .2

Y INCREMENT = .333333

```
                                    *
                                    *
                                    *
                                    *
                                    *
                                    *
          +                         *                         +
                                    *
                 +                  *             +
                                    *
                         +          *        +
                 +                  *    +                 +
                              +    *++
                    +        ++  *  ++
                    +          +*+          +
                         +++    +    +++
*****************************************+***********************************X
                         +++    +    +++
                    +          +*+          +
                    +        ++  *  ++        +
                              *
               +        +     *        +                 +
                    +          *             +
                                    *
                         +          *             +
                                    *
          +                         *                         +
                                    *
                                    *
                                    *
                                    *
                                    *
                                    *
                                    Y
```

```
00105 A=SIN(C)
RUN

PROGRAM   POLAR

++++++*******POLAR COORDINATE PLOT*******++++++


ENTER VALUE OF ENDPOINTS (ABS)
? 4

X INCREMENT = .133333

Y INCREMENT = .222222

                              *
                              *
                              *
                              *
                              *
                              *
                              *
                              *
                              *
                              *
                              *
                              *
                              *
                           +++++++
                          ++  *  ++
                          +   *   +
                          ++  *  ++
***************************************+***************************X
                              *
                              *
                              *
                              *
                              *
                              *
                              *
                              *
                              *
                              *
                              *
                              *
                              *
                              Y
```

```
00105  A=TAN(C)
RUN

PROGRAM   POLAR

++++++*******POLAR COORDINATE PLOT******++++++


ENTER VALUE OF ENDPOINTS (ABS)
? 6

X INCREMENT = .2

Y INCREMENT = .333333
                            *
                  +         *         +
                            *
                            *
                            *
                            *
                  +         *         +
                            *
                  +         *         +
                            *
                  +         *         +
                   +        *        +
                   +        *        +
                   +        *        +
                    +       *       +
                    ++      *      ++
                     ++     *     ++
*****************************+*************************************X
                     ++     *     ++
                    ++      *      ++
                    +       *       +
                   +        *        +
                            *        +
                  +         *        +
                  +         *         +
                            *
                  +         *         +
                            *
                            *
                  +         *         +
                            *
                            *
                            *
                            *
                  +         *         +
                            *
                            Y
```

Program Listing

```
    5 REM THIS PROGRAM GENERATES A POLAR PLOT
   10 REM OF THE FUNCTION (EQUATION) PLACED ON LINE 105
   15 REM THE FUNCTION MUST BE WRITTEN AS A=F(C)

   25 PRINT
   30 PRINT"++++++*******POLAR COORDINATE PLOT*******++++++"
   35 PRINT
   40 PRINT
   45 PRINT
   50 DIM X(100),Y(100)
   55 Z=90
   60 PRINT"ENTER VALUE OF ENDPOINTS (ABS)"
   65 INPUT Q
   70 PRINT
   75 PRINT"X INCREMENT =";Q/30
   80 PRINT
   85 PRINT"Y INCREMENT =";Q/18
   90 PRINT
   95 FOR J=1 TO Z
  100 C=.06981317*J
  105
  110 X(J)=INT(((A*COS(C)/Q+1)*30)+.5)
  115 Y(J)=INT(((-A*SIN(C)/Q+1)*18)+.5)
  120 NEXT J
  125 FOR J=1 TO Z
  130 FOR I=1 TO Z-J
  135 D=X(I)
  140 E=Y(I)
  145 IF E<=Y(I+1) THEN     170
  150 X(I)=X(I+1)
  155 Y(I)=Y(I+1)
  160 X(I+1)=D
  165 Y(I+1)=E
  170 NEXT I
  175 NEXT J
  180 R=1
  185 FOR K=0 TO Z-1
  190 IF Y(K+1)>=0 THEN   200
  195 NEXT K
  200 FOR J=0 TO 36
  205 R=R+K
  210 K=0
  215 IF R>Z THEN     225
  220 IF Y(R)=J THEN   250
  225 IF J=18 THEN     240
  230 PRINT TAB(30);"*";
  235 GOTO    470
  240 T=Z+1
  245 GOTO    410
  250 FOR P=R TO Z
  255 IF Y(P)>Y(R) THEN    270
  260 K=K+1
  265 NEXT P
  270 IF K=1 THEN    320
  275 FOR I=1 TO K
  280 FOR P=1 TO K-1
  285 D=X(R+P-1)
  290 E=X(R+P)
  295 IF D<=E THEN    310
  300 X(R+P-1)=E
  305 X(R+P)=D
  310 NEXT P
  315 NEXT I
  320 IF J=18 THEN    405
```

107

```
325 P=-1
330 T=0
335 FOR S=0 TO K-1
340 IF X(R+S)=P THEN    385
345 P=X(R+S)
350 IF P=30 THEN    370
355 IF P<30 THEN    375
360 IF T=1 THEN    375
365 PRINT TAB(30);"*";
370 T=1
375 IF P>60 THEN    470
380 PRINT TAB(P);"+";
385 NEXT S
390 IF T=1 THEN    470
395 PRINT TAB(30);"*";
400 GOTO    470
405 T=R
410 FOR I=0 TO 60
415 IF X(K)<>I THEN    455
420 PRINT"+";
425 FOR S=T TO R+K-1
430 IF X(S)=X(T) THEN    445
435 T=S
440 GOTO    460
445 NEXT S
450 GOTO    460
455 PRINT"*";
460 NEXT I
465 PRINT"X";
470 PRINT
475 NEXT J
480 PRINT TAB(30);"Y"
485 END
```

MATH WHIZ KID QUIZ

The following program is termed a CAI (Computer Assisted Instruction) program. The most famous and possibly the best CAI system is called PLATO. Unfortunately, PLATO requires special equipment such as a full graphics terminal which typically uses a gas plasma display. Quite often the screen also will be touch sensitive. As you can see, the full PLATO set-up can be quite expensive.

This program does not require the features of PLATO, but it does show how such systems respond. Not only does this program instruct with arithmetic problems, but it is also fun to play.

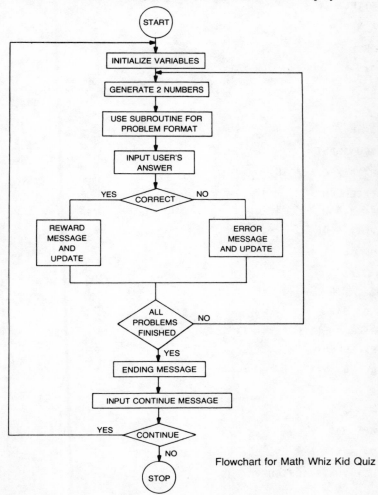

Flowchart for Math Whiz Kid Quiz

109

Sample Run

```
RUN
WE ARE GOING TO PRACTICE MULTIPLICA-
TION
WHAT IS YOUR NAME
? KEN
KEN, THERE ARE 10 PROBLEMS.
THE COMPUTER WILL USE ONE OF TWO FORMS
EITHER
A X B = ?
OR
 A
XB
 ?
1. 6 X 4 = ? 24
YOU DID IT
2. 8 X 2 = ? 16
EXCELLENT
3. 4 X 6 = ? 24
VERY GOOD
4.   8
    X1
    ? 8
NOT BAD
5. 3 X 2 = / ? 6
EXCELLENT
6.   4
    X3
    ? 12
NOT BAD
7. 8 X 8 = ? 64
HEY THATS ALRIGHT
```

8. 9
    X3
     ? 27
EXCELLENT
9. 3
    X4
     ? 12
VERY GOOD
10. 8
     X8
      ? 64
EXCELLENT
WE ARE NOW FINISHED
THE COMPUTER HOPES YOU ENJOYED THIS
WELL, KEN
OF 10 PROBLEMS 100%
WERE CORRECT
AND 0% WERE INCORRECT
TO TRY AGAIN TYPE 1, IF NOT 0
? 0
RUN COMPLETE

Program Listing

```
10   REM THIS PROGRAM DEMONSTRATES THE
20   REM CLASS OF PROGRAMS TERMED CAI
30   REM THIS EXAMPLE GENERATES RANDOM
40   REM PROBLEMS OF MULTIPLICATION AND
50   REM RETURNS REWARD AND PUNISHMENT
60   REM REMARKS AT RANDOM.
70   REM DEFINITION OF VARIABLES
80   REM USERS ANSWER = A
90   REM NUMBER OF PROBLEMS = C
100  REM THE NUMBERS TO BE MULTIPLIED
     = D1, D2
110  REM THE TRUE ANSWER = D3
120  REM POINTER TO MESSAGE = M
130  REM TOTAL NUMBER OF PROBLEMS = N
140  N = 10
150  REM USERS NAME = N$
160  REM PERCENTAGE RIGHT = P1
170  REM PERCENTAGE WRONG = P2
180  REM CORRECT ANSWERS = R
190  REM WRONG ANSWERS = W
200  REM USE RANDOMIZE SO EACH TIME
     THE
210  REM PROGRAM IS USED WE WILL HAVE
     A
220  REM DIFFERENT RANDOM SEQUENCE
     GENERATED
230  RANDOMIZE
240  PRINT
```

```
250   PRINT ''WE ARE GOING TO PRACTICE
      MULTIPLICATION''
260   PRINT
280   PRINT ''WHAT IS YOUR NAME''
285   INPUT N$
290   PRINT
300   PRINT N$; '', THERE ARE ''; N;
      ''PROBLEMS.''
310   PRINT
320   PRINT ''THE COMPUTER WILL USE ONE
      OF TWO FORMS''
330   PRINT
340   PRINT ''EITHER''
350   PRINT '' A X B = ?''
360   PRINT ''OR''
370   PRINT ''A''
380   PRINT ''X B''
390   PRINT ''---''
400   PRINT ''  ?''
410   PRINT
420   PRINT
430   C = 1
440   R = 0
450   W = 0
460   REM GENERATE RANDOM NUMBERS
470   D1 = INT{RND{0} * 10}
480   D2 = INT{RND{0} * 10}
490   D3 = D1 * D2
500   REM BY CHANGING THE STATEMENTS
510   REM 470 AND AND 480 WE CAN
```

```
520   REM CHANGE THE NUMBER OF DIGITS
530   REM OR THE MAGNITUDE OF THE NUM-
      BERS
540   REM TO BE MULTIPLIED.
550   REM BY CHANGING THE STATEMENTS,
560   REM ESPECIALLY THE REMARKS AND THE
570   REM NUMBERS FOR CONSTANTS, WE CAN
      TAILOR
580   REM A GAME OR PROGRAM TO OUR
590   REM TASTES. OF COURSE A PROGRAM
      MAY BE
600   REM RUN EXACTLY AS FOUND, BUT
      THERE IS
610   REM FUN AND INSTRUCTION IN MODI-
      FYING
620   REM PROGRAMS AS WELL.
630   REM THE FOLLOWING SUBROUTINES
      GENERATE
640   REM EITHER ONE OF THE TWO FORMS
      OF PROBLEMS.
650   ON INT(2 * (RND(0))) + 1 GOTO 660, 680
660   GOSUB 1000
670   GOTO 690
680   GOSUB 1050
690   REM WE HAVE RETURNED FROM THE
      SUBROUTINE
700 REM WE NOW NEED AN ANSWER
710   INPUT A
720   REM WE NOW PRINT AT RANDOM
730   REM A MESSAGE ABOUT
```

```
740   REM THE ANSWER. WE ALSO HAVE TO
750   REM INCREMENT THE ANSWER COUNTER.
760   IF A <> D3 THEN 790
770   GOSUB 1130
780   GOTO 800
790   GOSUB 1310
800   REM UPDATE THE VALUE OF C
810   REM THE NUMBER OF PROBLEMS
820   C = C + 1
830   IF C <= N THEN 560
840   REM WE WILL NOW CALCULATE
850   REM THE PERCENTAGE OF RIGHT
860   REM OR WRONG ANSWERS
870   P1 = INT{100 * R/N}
880   P2 = INT{100 * W/N}
890   PRINT
900   PRINT ''WE ARE NOW FINISHED''
910   PRINT ''THE COMPUTER HOPES YOU
      ENJOYED THIS.''
920   PRINT
930   PRINT ''WELL,''; N$
940   PRINT ''OF''; N; ''PROBLEMS,'';
      P1; ''%''
950   PRINT ''WERE CORRECT.''
950   PRINT ''AND''; P2' ''%'' WERE
      INCORRECT.''
960   PRINT ''TO TRY AGAIN, TYPE 1, IF
      NOT, 0''
970   INPUT L
980   IF L = 1 THEN 140
```

```
990   STOP
1000  REM THIS SUBROUTINE PRINTS
1010  REM A HORIZONTAL PROBLEM
1020  PRINT
1030  PRINT C; ''.  ''; D1; '' X'';
      D2; ''='';
1040  RETURN
1050  REM THIS SUBROUTINE PRINTS
1060  REM A VERTICAL PROBLEM
1070  PRINT
1080  PRINT C;''.''; TAB{7}; D1
1090  PRINT TAB{6}; ''X ''; D2
1100  PRINT TAB{7}; ''---''
1110  PRINT TAB{6};
1120  RETURN
1130  REM THIS SUBROUTINE HANDLES
1140  REM RESPONSES TO CORRECT ANSWERS
1150  M = INT{6 * RND{0}} + 1
1160  ON M GOTO 1170, 1190, 1210, 1230,
      1250, 1270
1170  PRINT ''NOT BAD''
1180  GOTO 1280
1190  PRINT ''HEY, THAT'S ALRIGHT.''
1200  GOTO 1280
1210  PRINT ''YOU DID IT''
1220  GOTO 1280
1230  PRINT ''THAT'S CORRECT''
1240  GOTO 1280
1250  PRINT ''EXCELLENT''
1260  GOTO 1280
```

```
1270    PRINT ''VERY GOOD''
1280    PRINT
1290    R = R =+ 1
1300    RETURN
1310    REM THIS SUBROUTINE HANDLES
        INCORRECT
1320    REM ANSWERS AND RESPONDS
1330    M = INT{4 * RND{0}} + 1
1340    ON M GOTO 1350, 1370, 1390,
        1410
1350    PRINT ''SORRY, THAT'S WRONG''
1360    GOTO 1420
1370    PRINT ''HOW COULD YOU?''
1380    GOTO 1420
1390    PRINT ''THAT'S NOT RIGHT''
1400    GOTO 1420
1410    PRINT ''CAN'T YOU MULTIPLY?''
1420    PRINT
1430    PRINT ''THE CORRECT ANSWER IS
        ''; D3
1440    PRINT
1450    W = W =+ 1
1460    RETURN
1470    END
```

This program also will run on the Radio Shack TRS-80 computer with no modifications needed.

SHIP IN THE WATER

This program allows the user to input the parameters of a hull and water conditions. The program returns the ampular and vertical displacements, as well as plotting the displacements separately.

As we are interested in only the horizontal position of the center of gravity, and not the vertical, we can place it as the intersection of water line and lateral division of hull.

The more sections we divide the hull into, the more precise will be the results as numerical integration is used, which depends on the number of entries for precision.

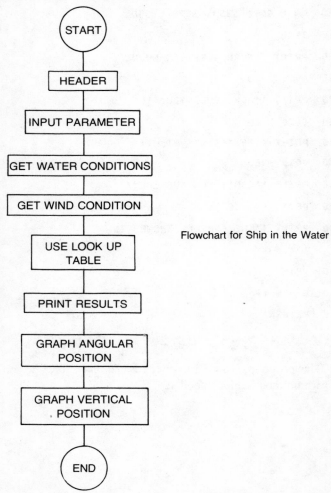

Flowchart for Ship in the Water

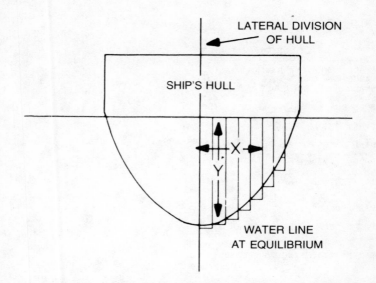

Fig. 1-5—The more sections the hull is divided into, the more precise the result.

Sample Run

```
----------------------------------------
MODELING OF THE MOTION OF A HULL
UNDER DIFFERENT SEA CONDITIONS
----------------------------------------



** HULLS ARE ASSUMED TO BE LATERALLY SYMETRICAL **
** THEREFORE ONLY ENTER THE INFORMATION FOR THE **
** RIGHT SECTIONS, THE LEFT WILL BE MIRRORED **

ENTER # OF SECTIONS ? 5

ENTER BEAM IN METERS? 30

ENTER Y, THE LENGTH OF THE SECTION BELOW
THE WATER LINE AT EQUILIBRIUM
X IS THE DISTANCE FROM THE
CENTER OF GRAVITY OF THE HULL TO
THE CENTER OF EACH SECTION

SECTION # 1    X= 1.5
Y=? 12

SECTION # 2    X= 4.5
Y=? 12

SECTION # 3    X= 7.5
Y=? 11

SECTION # 4    X= 10.5
Y=? 10

SECTION # 5    X= 13.5
Y=? 9.5
```

119

```
ENTER DENSITY OF HULL
? 1.098

TYPE OF WATER BODIES AVAILABLE
-------------------------------
SMALL LAKES AND RIVERS       (1)
LARGE LAKES                  (2)
SMALL BAYS AND COVES         (3)
LARGE BAYS                   (4)
OPEN OCEAN                   (5)

TYPE? 2

WIND SPEEDS AVAILABLE
-------------------------------
2M/SEC (7.2KM/HR)            (1)
5M/SEC (18KM/HR)             (2)
10M/SEC (36KM/HR)            (3)
20M/SEC (72KM/HR)            (4)

WIND SPEED? 3

ENTER TIME INTERVAL (STEP SIZE)
? .5

ENTER TOTAL TIME IN SECONDS ? 10


TIME        VERTICAL POSITION        ANGULAR POSITION
(SEC)          (METERS)                (DEGREES)
----------------------------------------------------------
 .5            -.61229              4.89791E-8
1              -1.73434             359.963
1.5            -2.49834             359.915
2              -2.68613             5.24589E-2
2.5            -2.2433              .250372
3              -1.26507             359.917
3.5            2.48662E-2           359.397
4              1.32621              .132877
4.5            2.33268              1.35089
5              2.80337              359.792
5.5            2.61958              357.06
6              1.81521              .297036
6.5            .571803              6.31512
7              -.823047             359.708
7.5            -2.04294             346.488
8              -2.7983              359.431
8.5            -2.90427             28.8404
9              -2.32651             8.39775
9.5            -1.19069             304.882
10             .257367              296.189
```

ANGULAR POSITION PLOTTED AGAINST TIME

```
FOR X:    TOP =  .5  BOTTOM =  10   INCREMENT =  .5
FOR Y:    LEFT =  0   RIGHT =  360  INCREMENT =  6

   I..........I..........I..........I..........I..........I..........I
 ..'+                                                                +
 .                                                                   +
 . +
 . +
 .                                                                   +
 .                                                                   +
 . +
 . +
 .                                                                   +
 ..                                                                  +
 . +
 .  +
 .                                                                 +
 .                                                             +
 .                                                                 +
 .       +
 . +
 .                                                           +
 .                                                        +
```

VERTICAL POSITION PLOTTED AGAINST TIME

```
FOR X:    TOP =  .5  BOTTOM =  10   INCREMENT =  .5
FOR Y:    LEFT = -25  RIGHT =  25   INCREMENT =  .833333

   I..........I..........I..........I..........I..........I..........I
 .                                 +
 .                                 +
 .                                +
 .                                +
 .                                +
 .                                 +
 .                                  +
 .                                   +
 .                                    +
 .                                    +
 .                                    +
 ..                                  +
 .                                   +
 .                                 +
 .                                +
 .                               +
 .                               +
 .                                +
 .                                 +
```

121

Program Listing

```
100 REM
200 PRINT
300 PRINT
400 PRINT
500 PRINT
600 PRINT
700 PRINT"----------------------------------"
800 PRINT"MODELING OF THE MOTION OF A HULL"
900 PRINT"UNDER DIFFERENT SEA CONDITIONS"
1000 PRINT"----------------------------------"
1100 REM MODEL NEGLECTS VISCOUS DAMPING ACTION
1200 REM OF THE WATER, THUS IF THE RESONANT FREQUENCY AND
1300 REM AND THE PERIOD COINCIDE, THE HULL WILL APPEAR TO
1400 REM JUMP OUT OF THE WATER.
1500 DIM X(50),Y(50)
1600 DIM E4(250)
1700 DIM E3(250)
1800 DIM E1(250)
1900 DIM B(50)
2000 E2=0
2100
2200
2300 REM MODELING OF A SHIP'S HULL
2400 REM INPUT HULL CROSS SECTION
2500 REM INPUT X AND Y
2600 REM X DISTANCE FROM CENTER OF GRAVITY TO
2700 REM CENTER OF SECTION
2800 REM Y LENGTH OF SECTION BELOW WATER AT EQUILIBRIUM
2900 PRINT
3000 PRINT
3100 PRINT
3200 PRINT"** HULLS ARE ASSUMED TO BE LATERALLY SYMETRICAL **"
3300 PRINT"** THEREFORE ONLY ENTER THE INFORMATION FOR THE **"
3400 PRINT"** RIGHT SECTIONS, THE LEFT WILL BE MIRRORED **"
3500 PRINT
3600 PRINT"ENTER # OF SECTIONS";
3700 INPUT S
3800 REM CHECK NOT TO EXCEED X(50)
3900 IF S<1 OR S>50 THEN 4100
4000 GOTO 04300
4100 PRINT"NUMBER OF SECTIONS MUST BE BETWEEN 1 AND 50"
4200 GOTO 03600
4300 PRINT
4400 REM INPUT BEAM AND COMPUTE DISTANCE OF EACH SECTION
4500 PRINT"ENTER BEAM IN METERS";
4600 INPUT B3
4700 IF B3<=0 THEN 4900
4800 GOTO 5100
4900 PRINT"BEAM MUST BE GREATER THAN ZERO"
5000 GOTO 04500
5100 REM FIND HALF BEAM
5200 B3=B3/2
5300 REM FIND WIDTH OF EACH SECTION (COMMON)
5400 B3=B3/S
5500 REM FIND CENTER OF EACH SECTION
5600 REM WITH RESPECT TO CENTER OF GRAVITY
5700 FOR J=1 TO S
5800 X(J)=J*B3-(B3/2)
5900 NEXT J
6000 PRINT
6100 PRINT"ENTER Y, THE LENGTH OF THE SECTION BELOW"
6200 PRINT"THE WATER LINE AT EQUILIBRIUM"
6300 PRINT"X IS THE DISTANCE FROM THE"
6400 PRINT"CENTER OF GRAVITY OF THE HULL TO"
6500 PRINT"THE CENTER OF EACH SECTION"
6600 PRINT
```

```
6700 FOR J=1 TO S
6800 PRINT"SECTION #";J;"  X=";X(J)
6900 PRINT"Y=";
7000 INPUT Y(J)
7100 PRINT
7200 NEXT J
7300 PRINT
7400 PRINT"ENTER DENSITY OF HULL"
7500 INPUT S1
7600 IF S1 <=0 THEN  7800
7700 GOTO  8000
7800 PRINT"DENSITY MUST BE GREATER THAN ZERO"
7900 GOTO  7400
8000 REM APPROXIMATE BOUYANCY FACTOR OF EACH SECTION
8100 B1=S1*9.8
8200 FOR J=1 TO S
8300 B(J)=B3*Y(J)*B1
8400 NEXT J
8500 REM MASS & MOMENT OF INTERIA OF CROSS SECTION
8600 M=0
8700 I=0
8800 FOR J=1 TO S
8900 M1=B(J)/9.8*Y(J)
9000 M=M+M1*2
9100 I=I+M1*X(J)*2
9200 NEXT J
9300 REM INPUT SEA AND WIND CONDITIONS
9400 PRINT
9500 PRINT"TYPE OF WATER BODIES AVAILABLE"
9600 PRINT"-----------------------------"
9700 PRINT"SMALL LAKES AND RIVERS     (1)"
9800 PRINT"LARGE LAKES                (2)"
9900 PRINT"SMALL BAYS AND COVES       (3)"
10000 PRINT"LARGE BAYS                 (4)"
10100 PRINT"OPEN OCEAN                 (5)"
10200 PRINT
10300 PRINT"TYPE";
10400 INPUT S3
10500 S3=INT(S3)
10600 IF S3<1 OR S3>5 THEN 10800
10700 GOTO 11000
10800 PRINT"INPUT MAY RANGE FROM 1 TO 5 ONLY"
10900 GOTO 10300
11000 PRINT
11100 PRINT"WIND SPEEDS AVAILABLE"
11200 PRINT"-----------------------------"
11300 PRINT"2M/SEC (7.2KM/HR)          (1)"
11400 PRINT"5M/SEC (18KM/HR)           (2)"
11500 PRINT"10M/SEC (36KM/HR)          (3)"
11600 PRINT"20M/SEC (72KM/HR)          (4)"
11700 PRINT
11800 PRINT"WIND SPEED";
11900 INPUT S4
12000 S4=INT(S4)
12100 IF S4<1 OR S4>4 THEN 12300
12200 GOTO 12500
12300 PRINT"INPUT MAY RANGE FROM 1 TO 4 ONLY"
12400 GOTO 11800
12500 GOSUB 23600
12600 REM INITIALIZE INTEGRATION VARIABLES
12700 Z=0
12800 Z1=0
12900 V=0
13000 V1=0
13100 A=0
13200 A1=0
13300 R=0
13400 R1=0
13500 Q=0
13600 Q1=0
```

```
13700 C=0
13800 C1=0
13900 T=0
14000 REM INITIALIZE STEP SIZE
14100 REM INITIALIZE PRINT INTERVAL
14200 PRINT
14300 PRINT"ENTER TIME INTERVAL (STEP SIZE)"
14400 INPUT D
14500 IF D<0.1 THEN 14700
14600 GOTO 14900
14700 PRINT"TIME INTERVAL MUST BE GREATER THAN 0.1 SECONDS"
14800 GOTO 14300
14900 K=0
15000 K1=0.1/D
15100 PRINT
15200 REM SET # OF SECONDS OF RUNNING TIME FOR MODEL
15300 PRINT"ENTER TOTAL TIME IN SECONDS";
15400 INPUT S5
15500 S5=INT(S5)
15600 IF S5<1 THEN 15900
15700 IF S5<D THEN 16100
15800 GOTO 16500
15900 PRINT"TOTAL TIME MUST BE GREATER THAN 1 SEC"
16000 GOTO 15300
16100 PRINT"RUNNING TIME MUST BE GREATER THAN TIME INTERVAL"
16200 PRINT"FOR ACCURATE RESULTS RUNNING TIME SHOULD BE AT"
16300 PRINT"LEAST 10 TIMES GREATER THAN THE TIME INTERVAL"
16400 GOTO 15300
16500 PRINT
16600 PRINT
16700 PRINT
16800 PRINT"TIME        VERTICAL POSITION        ANGULAR POSITION"
16900 PRINT"(SEC)           (METERS)                (DEGREES)"
17000 PRINT"---------------------------------------------------------"
17100 REM SUM FORCES AND MOMENTS ON THE SECTIONS
17200 E2=E2+1
17300 REM PREDICT VERTICAL MOTION
17400 REM A V Z ARE ACCELERATION SPEED AND POSITION
17500 A1=F/M-9.8
17600 V=V1+D*A1
17700 Z=Z1+D*V1
17800 REM PREDICT ANGULAR MOTION
17900 REM C Q R ARE ACCELERATION SPEED AND POSITION
18000 C1=G/I
18100 Q=Q1+D*C1
18200 R=R1+D*Q1
18300 REM SUM NEW FORCES AND MOMENTS FOR CORRECTOR FORMULAE
18400 K=K+1
18500 T=T+D
18600 GOSUB 21200
18700 REM CORRECT VERTICAL MOTION
18800 A=F/M-9.8
18900 V=V1+D/2*(A+A1)
19000 Z=Z1+D/2*(V+V1)
19100 REM CORRECT ANGULAR MOTION
19200 C=G/I
19300 Q=Q1+D/2*(C+C1)
19400 R=R1+D/2*(Q+Q1)
19500 REM PREPARE FOR NEXT STEP
19600 V1=V
19700 Z1=Z
19800 Q1=Q
19900 R1=R
20000 IF K<K1 THEN 17200
20100 REM FIND TOTAL DEGREES ROTATION
20200 E=R*57.296
20300 REM FIND POSITION USING MOD 360
20400 E=360*((E/360)-(INT(E/360)))
20500 REM
20600 E4(E2)=Z
```

124

```
20700 E3(E2)=T
20800 E1(E2)=E
20900 PRINT T,Z,E
21000 IF T<S5 THEN 17200
21100 GOTO 36200
21200 REM CAL AND SUM FORCERS AND  MOMENTS ON SECTIONS
21300 F=0
21400 G=0
21500 FOR J=1 TO S
21600 REM POS HALF OF HULL
21700 REM W IS VERTICAL POSITION OF WATER SURFACE AT SECTION J
21800 REM W1 IS LENGTH OF HULL BELOW WATER SURFACE
21900 W=H/2*SIN(6.28318*(T/P+X(J)/L))
22000 W1=Y(J)-Z-SIN(R)*X(J)+W
22100 IF W1>0 THEN 22300
22200 W1=0
22300 F1=B(J)*W1
22400 G1=X(J)*F1
22500 REM MIRROR IMAGE GIVES NEG HALF
22600 W=H/2*SIN(6.28318*(T/P-X(J)/L))
22700 W1=Y(J)-Z+SIN(R)*X(J)+W
22800 IF W1>0 THEN 23000
22900 W1=0
23000 F2=B(J)*W1
23100 G2=-X(J)*F2
23200 F=F+F1+F2
23300 G=G+G1+G2
23400 NEXT J
23500 RETURN
23600 ON S3 GOTO 23700, 26200, 28700, 31200, 33700
23700 ON S4 GOTO 23800, 24400, 25000, 25600
23800 REM 1,1
23900 REM SMALL LAKES AND RIVERS AT 2M/SEC
24000 P=0.6
24100 L=0.56
24200 H=0.02
24300 GOTO 36100
24400 REM 1,2
24500 REM SMALL LAKES AND RIVERS AT 5M/SEC
24600 P=0.8
24700 L=0.1
24800 H=0.05
24900 GOTO 36100
25000 REM 1,3
25100 REM SMALL LAKES AND RIVERS AT 10M/SEC
25200 P=1.25
25300 L=2.4
25400 H=0.08
25500 GOTO 36100
25600 REM 1,4
25700 REM SMALL LAKES AND RIVERS AT 20M/SEC
25800 P=2.5
25900 L=10.0
26000 H=0.25
26100 GOTO 36100
26200 ON S4 GOTO 26300, 26900, 27500, 28100
26300 REM 2,1
26400 REM LARGE LAKES AT 2M/SEC
26500 P=1.0
26600 L=1.5
26700 H=0.06
26800 GOTO 36100
26900 REM 2,2
27000 REM LARGE LAKES AT 5M/SEC
27100 P=1.2
27200 L=2.25
27300 H=0.08
27400 GOTO 36100
27500 REM 2,3
27600 REM LARGE LAKES AT 10M/SEC
```

```
27700 P=2.0
27800 L=6.25
27900 H=0.15
28000 GOTO 36100

28100 REM 2.4
28200 REM LARGE LAKES AT 20M/SEC
28300 P=4.0
28400 L=25.0
28500 H=0.65
28600 GOTO 36100
28700 ON S4 GOTO 28800, 29400, 30000, 30600
28800 REM 3.1
28900 REM SMALL BAYS AND COVES AT 2M/SEC
29000 P=1.5
29100 L=2.3
29200 H=0.12
29300 GOTO 36100
29400 REM 3.2
29500 REM SMALL BAYS AND COVES AT 5M/SEC
29600 P=2.0
29700 L=5.0
29800 H=0.2
29900 GOTO 36100
30000 REM 3.3
30100 REM SMALL BAYS AND COVES AT 10M/SEC
30200 P=3.0
30300 L=14.0
30400 H=0.35
30500 GOTO 36100
30600 REM 3.4
30700 REM SMALL BAYS AND COVES AT 20M/SEC
30800 P=6.0
30900 L=56.0
31000 H=1.4
31100 GOTO 36100
31200 ON S4 GOTO 31300, 31900, 32500, 33100
31300 REM 4.1
31400 REM LARGE BAYS AT 2M/SEC
31500 P=2.0
31600 L=3.1
31700 H=0.15
31800 GOTO 36100
31900 REM 4.2
32000 REM LARGE BAYS AT 5M/SEC
32100 P=2.4
32200 L=9.0
32300 H=0.25
32400 GOTO 36100
32500 REM 4.3
32600 REM LARGE BAYS AT 10M/SEC
32700 P=4.25
32800 L=28.0
32900 H=0.7
33000 GOTO 36100
33100 REM 4.4
33200 REM LARGE BAYS AT 20M/SEC
33300 P=8.5
33400 L=110.0
33500 H=2.8
33600 GOTO 36100
33700 ON S4 GOTO 33800, 34400, 35000, 35600
33800 REM 5.1
33900 REM OPEN OCEAN AT 2M/SEC
34000 P=3.5
34100 L=20.0
34200 H=0.5
34300 GOTO 36100
34400 REM 5.2
34500 REM OPEN OCEAN AT 5M/SEC
34600 P=4.5
```

```
34700  L=30.0
34800  H=0.75
34900  GOTO 36100
35000  REM 5.3
35100  REM OPEN OCEAN AT 10M/SEC
35200  P=7.0
35300  L=80.0
35400  H=2.0
35500  GOTO 36100
35600  REM 5.4
35700  REM OPEN OCEAN AT 20M/SEC
35800  P=14.0
35900  L=300.0
36000  H=7.5
36100  RETURN
36200  REM GRAPHICS ROUTINES
36300  REM FIRST PLOT ANGULAR POSITION
36400  Q0=0
36500  Q1=360
36600  Q2=E3(1)
36700  Q3=E3(E2)
36800  Q4=C
36900  PRINT
37000  PRINT
37100  PRINT"ANGULAR POSITION PLOTTED AGAINST TIME"
37200  PRINT"------------------------------------"
37300  PRINT
37400  GOSUB 39500
37500  REM NOW WE PLOT VERTICAL POSITION
37600  Q0=-25
37700  Q1=25
37800  Q2=E3(1)
37900  Q3=E3(E2)
38000  Q4=C
38100  FOR J=1 TO E2
38200  E1(J)=E4(J)
38300  NEXT J
38400  PRINT
38500  PRINT
38600  PRINT"VERTICAL POSITION PLOTTED AGAINST TIME"
38700  PRINT"------------------------------------"
38800  PRINT
38900  GOSUB 39500
39000  STOP
39100  REM ROUTINE FOR PLOTTING (SUPPLIES THE Y VALUE
39200  Y=E1(N)
39300  RETURN
39400  REM PLOTTING SUBROUTINE
39500  N=0
39600  Q5=(Q1-Q0)/60
39700  Q6=0
39900  FOR X = Q2 TO Q3 STEP Q4
40000  N=N+1
40100  GOSUB 39200
40200  IF Q6 = 0 THEN 42800
40300  IF Q6 = 20 THEN 40600
40400  PRINT " . ";
40500  GOTO 40800
40600  PRINT " - ";
40700  Q6=10
40800  IF Y > Q1 THEN 42500
40900  IF Y < Q0 THEN 42500
41000  Q7=Q0+2*Q5
41100  Z=Q7+0.5*Q5
41200  IF Z<Y THEN 42200
41300  Q6=Q6+1
41400  IF Z-Y>=2*Q5 THEN 42000
41500  IF Z-Y>=Q5 THEN 41800
41600  PRINT " +"
```

127

```
41700 GOTO 43400
41800 PRINT " +"
41900 GOTO 43400
42000 PRINT "+"
42100 GOTO 43400
42200 Q7=Q7+3*Q5
42300 PRINT "   ";
42400 GOTO 41100
42500 PRINT "OFF SCALE    (X,Y) = ";X;",  ";Y
42600 Q6=Q6+1
42700 GOTO 43400
42800 PRINT
42900 PRINT "FOR X      TOP = ";Q2;" BOTTOM = ";Q3;" INCREMENT = ";Q4
43000 PRINT "FOR Y      LEFT = ";Q0;"  RIGHT = ";Q1;" INCREMENT = ";Q5
43100 PRINT
43200 PRINT
"    I..........I..........I..........I..........I..........I..........I"
43300 GOTO 40600
43400 NEXT X
43500 RETURN
43600 END
```

128

LEAP FROG

The game of leap frog is an amusing way to learn the "look ahead logic." You must carefully think of advance moves if you are going to win in a reasonable number of moves.

You indicate the start and end of each leap with a number from 1 to 11. One (1) is the position to the immediate left, while 11 is the last position to the right. Figure 1-6 shows some sample moves.

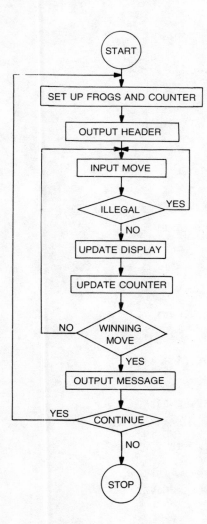

Flowchart for Leap Frog

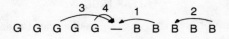

Fig. 1-6—Move 1 is allowed because the frog is landing in an empty space. Move 2 is illegal because there is already a frog in the spot you will land in. Move 3 is also illegal because you may jump only over one frog at a time. Move 4 is permissible. You don't always have to jump over another frog.

Sample Run

```
RUN

THE GAME OF LEAP FROG

OUR GAME STARTS AS:

GGGGGSBBBBB

WE MUST END AS

BBBBBSGGGGG

TO WIN.

NOTE THE S IS THE EMPTY SPACE.

WHAT IS YOUR MOVE {START, END}

? 8,6

CURRENT PATTERN OF FROGS IS

BBBBBGGSGGG

WHAT IS YOUR MOVE {START, END}

? 10,8

CURRENT PATTERN OF FROGS IS

BBBBBGGGGSG

WHAT IS YOUR MOVE {START, END}

?

CURRENT POSITION OF FROGS IS

BBBBBSGGGGG

YOU HAVE DONE IT, IN ONLY X MOVES

DO YOU WANT TO TRY AGAIN?
```

TYPE 1 TO CONTINUE, 2 TO STOP

? 2

RUN COMPLETE

NOTE THE X IN THE LINE

YOU HAVE DONE IT IN ONLY X MOVES

IS THE AMOUNT OF MOVES YOU TOOK TO WIN.

Program Listing

```
10   REM THIS IS THE GAME OF LEAP FROG
20   REM THERE ARE 5 GREEN FROGS LA-
     BELLED
30   REM WITH G'S AND 5 BROWN FROGS
40   REM LABELLED WITH B'S
50   REM THERE IS A SINGLE SPACE LEFT
     OVER
60   REM AND IT IS IN THE MIDDLE BE-
     TWEEN
70   REM THE GREEN AND BROWN FROGS.
80   REM TO WIN WE MUST MOVE ALL THE
90   REM GREEN FROGS TO THE RIGHT AND
     ALL
100  REM THE BROWN FROGS TO THE LEFT
120  REM SET UP DIM FOR FROGS.
130  DIM A$(12)
140  REM SET UP COUNTER
150  C = 0
160  A$(1) = ''G''
170  A$(2) = ''G''
180  A$(3) = ''G''
190  A$(4) = ''G''
```

```
200   A$(5) = ''G''

210   A$(6) = ''S''

220   A$(7) = ''B''

230   A$(8) = ''B''

240   A$(9) = ''B''

250   A$(10) = ''B''

260   A$(11) = ''B''

270   PRINT

280   PRINT ''THE GAME OF LEAP FROG''

290   PRINT ''----------------------''

300   PRINT

310   PRINT

320   PRINT ''OUR GAME STARTS OFF AS:''

330   PRINT

340   PRINT ''GGGGGSBBBBB''

350   PRINT

360   PRINT ''WE MUST END AS''

370   PRINT ''BBBBBSGGGGG''

380   PRINT ''TO WIN.''

385   PRINT ''NOTE THAT S IS THE
      EMPTY SPACE.''

390   PRINT

400   PRINT ''WHAT IS YOUR MOVE (START,
      END)''

410   INPUT S, E

420   IF ABS(S - E)>2 THEN 450

440   GOTO 480

450   PRINT ''SORRY, YOUR LEAP IS TOO
      LARGE''

460   GOTO 390

480   IF A$(S) = ''S'' THEN 510

490   IF A$(E) = ''G'' OR A$(E) = ''B''
      THEN 550
```

132

```
500    GOTO 590
510    PRINT ''HEY, YOU A CANNOT START
       YOUR LEAP''
520    PRINT ''WITHOUT A FROG, YOU HAVE
       GIVEN THE''
530    PRINT ''LOCATION OF THE SPACE.''
540    GOTO 390
550    PRINT ''HEY, YOU CANNOT END YOUR
       LEAP''
560    PRINT ''WITHOUT A SPACE, YOU HAVE
       GIVEN THE''
570    PRINT ''LOCATION OF A FROG''
580    GOTO 390
590    B$ = A$(S)
600    A$(S) = ''S''
610    A$(E) = B$
620    D$ = A$(1)
630    FOR I = 2 TO 11
640    D$ = D$ + A$(I)
650    NEXT I
660    PRINT
670    PRINT ''CURRENT PATTERN OF FROGS
       IS:''
680    PRINT D$
690    C = C + 1
700    IF D$ = ''BBBBBSGGGGG'' THEN 720
710    GOTO 390
720    PRINT
730    PRINT ''YOU HAVE DONE IT, IN ONLY
       ''; C; ''MOVES''
```

```
740  PRINT
750  PRINT ''DO YOU WANT TO TRY
     AGAIN?''
760  PRINT ''TYPE 1 TO CONTINUE, 2 TO
     STOP''
770  INPUT C
780  IF C = 1 THEN 800
790  STOP
800  PRINT
810  GOTO 150
820  END
```

An adaptation of this program designed specifically for the Radio Shack TRS-80 computer using Level II BASIC can be found on page 209 in Section II.

COMPUTERIZED HANGMAN

This amusing algorithm is designed to test your ability to guess words. The computer will choose at random from a list of words. In this program, the DATA statements have been written with one word per line, so that the game player may easily change the words.

You guess at a letter in the word. The computer then responds with the number of times that letter appears in the word, if at all.

After a number of unsuccessful tries, you may be hanged by the computer. Good luck.

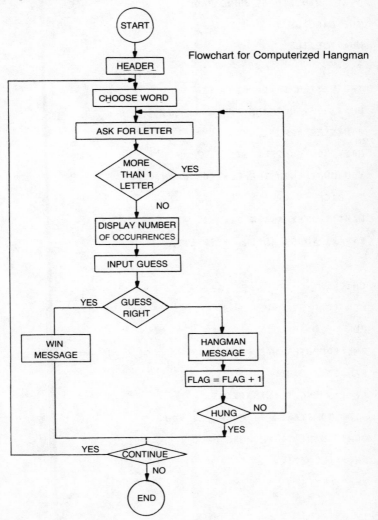

Flowchart for Computerized Hangman

Sample Run

```
RUN
THE COMPUTER HAS PICKED AT
RANDOM A WORD
CONTAINING 11 CHARACTERS
TIME TO START, BE CAREFUL, YOU
DON'T WANT TO BE HUNG FROM
THE GALLOWS
WHAT LETTER
? S
THE LETTER S OCCURS 4 TIMES
WHAT DO YOU THINK THE WORD IS
? MISSISSIPPI
WOW, YOU GUESSED IT
YOU MUST KNOW THE LEXICON FRONT
TO BACK
WANT TO TRY AGAIN
TYPE 1 TO GO AGAIN, 2 TO STOP
? 2
CHICKEN
RUN COMPLETE
RUN
THE COMPUTER HAS PICKED AT
RANDOM A WORD
CONTAINING 5 CHARACTERS
TIME TO START, BE CAREFUL, YOU
DON'T WANT TO BE HUNG FROM
THE GALLOWS...
WHAT LETTER
?X
```

THE LETTER X OCCURS 2 TIMES

WHAT DO YOU THINK THE WORD IS

? XEROX

WOW, YOU GUESSED IT

YOU MUST KNOW THE LEXICON FRONT

TO BACK

WANT TO TRY AGAIN

TYPE 1 TO GO AGAIN, 2 TO STOP

? 2

CHICKEN

RUN COMPLETE

Program Listing

```
10   REM THIS IS THE GAME
20   REM OF HANGMAN
30   REM THE COMPUTER WILL CHOOSE A WORD
40   REM IN ENGLISH AT RANDOM
50   REM EACH TIME IT IS YOUR TURN,
60   REM YOU PICK A LETTER, THE COMPUTER
     WILL
70   REM TELL YOU HOW MANY TIMES IT
     OCCURS IN THE WORD
80   REM YOU THEN TRY TO GUESS THE WORD
90   REM AFTER A CERTAIN NUMBER OF
     GUESSES, IF
100  REM YOU HAVE NOT GUESSED THE
     WORD THE
110  REM COMPUTER WILL HANG YOU.
120  M = 0
130  R = INT(25 * RND(0)) + 1
```

```
140   FOR I = 1 TO R
150   READ W$
160   NEXT I
170   L = LEN(W$)
180   PRINT
190   PRINT ''THE COMPUTER HAS PICKED
      OUT AT''
200   PRINT ''RANDOM A WORD''
210   PRINT ''CONTAINING ''; L; ''
      CHARACTERS''
220   PRINT
230   PRINT ''TIME TO START, BE CAREFUL,
      YOU''
240   PRINT ''DON'T WANT TO BE HUNG
      FROM''
250   PRINT ''THE GALLOWS...''
260   PRINT
270   PRINT ''WHAT LETTER''
280   INPUT L$
290   IF LEN(L$) >1 THEN 310
300   GOTO 325
310   PRINT ''DON'T CHEAT, ONLY 1
      LETTER AT A TIME.''
320   GOTO 260
325   J = 0
330   FOR I = 1 TO L
340   IF SUBSTR(W$,I,1) = L$ THEN 360
350   GOTO 370
360   J = J + 1
370   NEXT I
```

```
380    PRINT
390    PRINT ''THE LETTER''; L$; ''
       OCCURS ''; J$; '' TIMES''
400    PRINT
410    PRINT ''WHAT DO YOU THINK THE
       WORD IS''
420    INPUT B$
425    IF LEN(B$)<>W$ THEN 560
430    IF B$<>W$ THEN 600
440    PRINT
450    PRINT ''WOW, YOU GUESSED IT''
460    PRINT ''YOU MUST KNOW THE LEXICON
       FRONT
470    PRINT ''TO BACK''
480    PRINT
490    PRINT ''WANT TO TRY AGAIN''
500    PRINT ''TYPE 1 TO GO AGAIN, 2 TO
       STOP''
510    INPUT C
520    IF C = 1 THEN 550
530    PRINT ''CHICKEN''
540    STOP
550    GOTO 130
560    PRINT
570    PRINT ''REMEMBER, THERE ARE'';
       L; ''CHARACTERS''
580    PRINT ''IN THE RANDOM WORD''
590    GOTO 400
600  PRINT
610    PRINT ''SORRY, WRONG WORD''
```

```
620   M = M + 1
630   ON M GOTO 640, 660, 680, 710,
      730, 750, 770, 800
640   PRINT ''YOU ARE SENTENCED TO
      HANG''
650   GOTO 260
660   PRINT ''THE GALLOWS ARE NOW
      ERECTED''
670   GOTO 260
680   PRINT ''THE COMPUTER THINKS THIS
      ROPE WILL BE LONG''
690   PRINT ''ENOUGH FOR YOUR HANGING'
700   GOTO 260
710   PRINT ''HOPE THE ROPE IS NOT TOO
      TIGHT AROUND YOUR NECK''
720   GOTO 260
730   PRINT ''THE HANGMAN IS PREPARING
      THE TRAP DOOR''
740   GOTO 260
750   PRINT ''THE SPRING IS SET ON THE
      TRAP DOOR''
760   GOTO 260
770   PRINT ''THIS IS YOUR LAST CHANCE
      YOU STILL MAY''
780   PRINT ''BE SAVED FROM HANGING''
790   GOTO 260
800   PRINT ''THE TRAP DOOR IS OPEN,
      YOU ARE HUNG''
810   PRINT ''GOOD-BYE, CRUEL WORLD''
820   GOTO 480
```

```
830   DATA XEROX

840   DATA MUSHROOM

850   DATA AMERICA

860   DATA COMPUTER

870   DATA TELEVISION

880   DATA ATLANTIC

890   DATA MISSISSIPPI

900   DATA GAMES

910   DATA HOUSE

920   DATA PACIFIC

930   DATA BEAR

940   DATA BLANKET

950   DATA CORVETTE

960   DATA MARBLE

970   DATA ELECTRONICS

980   DATA INTEGRATED

990   DATA CIRCUITS

1000  DATA PRETZEL

1010  DATA VITAMIN

1020  DATA CONTAINER

1030  DATA WHEAT

1040  DATA DEXTROSE

1050  DATA PEOPLE

1060  DATA FAMILY

1070  DATA PROGRAM

1080  END
```

An adaptation of this program designed specifically for the Radio Shack TRS-80 computer using Level II BASIC can be found on page 211 in Section II.

YOUR CHEATING COMPUTER

This game lets you be a private eye. You must find a complete sequence of letters picked at random by the computer. A is lowest and Z is highest; therefore, if you input H and the computer responds too low, the letter must be between I and Z inclusively.

But there is a catch. As you get better, the computer starts cheating. It lies to you about whether the letter is high or low. Of course, if the guess is correct, it will not lie.

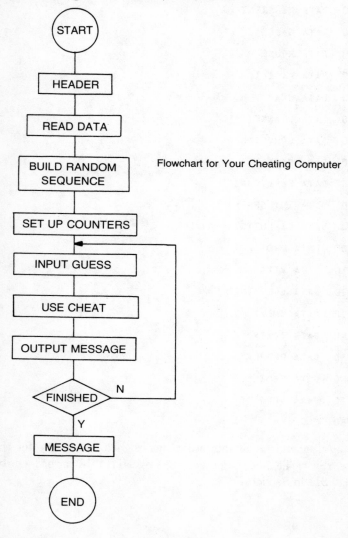

Flowchart for Your Cheating Computer

142

Sample Run

```
THIS PROGRAM LETS YOU BE A DETECTIVE
IT PICKS A LETTER SEQUENCE
 WHICH YOU MUST GUESS
ONE LETTER AT A TIME
TO MAKE THIS GAME VERY DIFFICULT
 THE PROGRAM CHEATS
 ON EACH LETTER
 WITH THE CHEATING A
 FUNCTION OF HOW WELL YOU DID ON THE PREVIOUS TRIES
OBVIOUSLY THE FIRST TRY WILL BE 'HONEST'
THE SEQUENCE IS SET UP FOR YOUR TRIAL
THE CHANCES THAT I WON'T CHEAT ARE   100   %
WHAT IS YOUR GUESS? Q
NOPE YOU ARE TOO LOW
WHAT IS YOUR GUESS? W
NOPE - YOU ARE TOO HIGH
WHAT IS YOUR GUESS? S
NOPE - YOU ARE TOO HIGH
WHAT IS YOUR GUESS? R
OK - YOU GOT THIS LETTER
THE SEQUENCE SO FAR IS R
THE CHANCES THAT I WON'T CHEAT ARE   98.3333   %
WHAT IS YOUR GUESS? M
NOPE YOU ARE TOO LOW
WHAT IS YOUR GUESS? T
NOPE - YOU ARE TOO HIGH
WHAT IS YOUR GUESS? P
NOPE YOU ARE TOO LOW
WHAT IS YOUR GUESS? R
OK - YOU GOT THIS LETTER
THE SEQUENCE SO FAR IS RR
THE CHANCES THAT I WON'T CHEAT ARE   96.6944   %
WHAT IS YOUR GUESS? Q
OK - YOU GOT THIS LETTER
THE SEQUENCE SO FAR IS RRQ
THE CHANCES THAT I WON'T CHEAT ARE   90.2481   %
WHAT IS YOUR GUESS? A
OK - YOU GOT THIS LETTER
THE SEQUENCE SO FAR IS RRQA
THE CHANCES THAT I WON'T CHEAT ARE   84.2316   %
WHAT IS YOUR GUESS? A
NOPE YOU ARE TOO LOW
WHAT IS YOUR GUESS? B
NOPE - YOU ARE TOO HIGH
WHAT IS YOUR GUESS? Z
NOPE - YOU ARE TOO HIGH
WHAT IS YOUR GUESS? M
NOPE YOU ARE TOO LOW
WHAT IS YOUR GUESS? M
NOPE YOU ARE TOO LOW
WHAT IS YOUR GUESS? T
NOPE YOU ARE TOO LOW
WHAT IS YOUR GUESS? V
NOPE YOU ARE TOO LOW
WHAT IS YOUR GUESS? Y
NOPE - YOU ARE TOO HIGH
WHAT IS YOUR GUESS? X
```

143

```
OK - YOU GOT THIS LETTER
THE SEQUENCE SO FAR IS RRQAX
THE CHANCES THAT I WON'T CHEAT ARE  83.6077  %
WHAT IS YOUR GUESS? A
NOPE YOU ARE TOO LOW
WHAT IS YOUR GUESS? B
NOPE - YOU ARE TOO HIGH
WHAT IS YOUR GUESS? C
NOPE - YOU ARE TOO HIGH
WHAT IS YOUR GUESS? L
NOPE YOU ARE TOO LOW
WHAT IS YOUR GUESS? Z
NOPE - YOU ARE TOO HIGH
WHAT IS YOUR GUESS? T
NOPE - YOU ARE TOO HIGH
WHAT IS YOUR GUESS? R
NOPE - YOU ARE TOO HIGH
WHAT IS YOUR GUESS? Q
NOPE YOU ARE TOO LOW
WHAT IS YOUR GUESS? Q
NOPE - YOU ARE TOO HIGH
WHAT IS YOUR GUESS? N
NOPE YOU ARE TOO LOW
WHAT IS YOUR GUESS? O
NOPE - YOU ARE TOO HIGH
WHAT IS YOUR GUESS? M
OK - YOU GOT THIS LETTER
THE SEQUENCE SO FAR IS RRQAXM
THE CHANCES THAT I WON'T CHEAT ARE  83.1432  %
WHAT IS YOUR GUESS? M
NOPE - YOU ARE TOO HIGH
WHAT IS YOUR GUESS? H
NOPE YOU ARE TOO LOW
WHAT IS YOUR GUESS? J
NOPE YOU ARE TOO LOW
WHAT IS YOUR GUESS? M
NOPE YOU ARE TOO LOW
WHAT IS YOUR GUESS? U
NOPE - YOU ARE TOO HIGH
WHAT IS YOUR GUESS? Q
NOPE YOU ARE TOO LOW
WHAT IS YOUR GUESS? T
OK - YOU GOT THIS LETTER
THE SEQUENCE SO FAR IS RRQAXMT
THE CHANCES THAT I WON'T CHEAT ARE  82.3513  %
WHAT IS YOUR GUESS? G
OK - YOU GOT THIS LETTER
THE SEQUENCE SO FAR IS RRQAXMTG
THE CHANCES THAT I WON'T CHEAT ARE  76.8613  %
WHAT IS YOUR GUESS? U
OK - YOU GOT THIS LETTER
THE SEQUENCE SO FAR IS RRQAXMTGU
THE CHANCES THAT I WON'T CHEAT ARE  71.7372  %
WHAT IS YOUR GUESS? M
NOPE - YOU ARE TOO HIGH
WHAT IS YOUR GUESS? A
NOPE YOU ARE TOO LOW
WHAT IS YOUR GUESS? H
NOPE YOU ARE TOO LOW
WHAT IS YOUR GUESS? J
```

```
NOPE - YOU ARE TOO HIGH
WHAT IS YOUR GUESS? I
OK - YOU GOT THIS LETTER
THE SEQUENCE SO FAR IS RRQAXMTGUI
DA CHAMPION HAS STRUK AGIN


NUMBER OF TRIES 45
PROBABILITY OF CHEATING
 ON ALL TRIES   70.7807 %
THE TOTAL SEQUENCE IS RRQAXMTGUI


TRY AGAIN(YES/NO) ? YES
THE SEQUENCE IS SET UP FOR YOUR TRIAL
THE CHANCES THAT I WON'T CHEAT ARE  100  %
WHAT IS YOUR GUESS? M
NOPE YOU ARE TOO LOW
WHAT IS YOUR GUESS? A
NOPE YOU ARE TOO LOW
WHAT IS YOUR GUESS? V
OK - YOU GOT THIS LETTER
THE SEQUENCE SO FAR IS V
THE CHANCES THAT I WON'T CHEAT ARE  97.7778 %
WHAT IS YOUR GUESS? A
NOPE YOU ARE TOO LOW
WHAT IS YOUR GUESS? C
NOPE YOU ARE TOO LOW
WHAT IS YOUR GUESS? E
NOPE YOU ARE TOO LOW
WHAT IS YOUR GUESS? H
NOPE YOU ARE TOO LOW
WHAT IS YOUR GUESS? K
NOPE YOU ARE TOO LOW
WHAT IS YOUR GUESS? L
NOPE YOU ARE TOO LOW
WHAT IS YOUR GUESS? P
NOPE YOU ARE TOO LOW
WHAT IS YOUR GUESS? S
NOPE YOU ARE TOO LOW
WHAT IS YOUR GUESS? U
NOPE YOU ARE TOO LOW
WHAT IS YOUR GUESS? W
NOPE YOU ARE TOO LOW
WHAT IS YOUR GUESS? X
NOPE YOU ARE TOO LOW
WHAT IS YOUR GUESS? Y
NOPE YOU ARE TOO LOW
WHAT IS YOUR GUESS? Z
OK - YOU GOT THIS LETTER
THE SEQUENCE SO FAR IS VZ
THE CHANCES THAT I WON'T CHEAT ARE  97.2764 %
WHAT IS YOUR GUESS? M
OK - YOU GOT THIS LETTER
THE SEQUENCE SO FAR IS VZM
THE CHANCES THAT I WON'T CHEAT ARE  90.7913 %
WHAT IS YOUR GUESS? M
NOPE YOU ARE TOO LOW
WHAT IS YOUR GUESS? V
NOPE - YOU ARE TOO HIGH
```

```
WHAT IS YOUR GUESS? T
NOPE - YOU ARE TOO HIGH
WHAT IS YOUR GUESS? R
NOPE - YOU ARE TOO HIGH
WHAT IS YOUR GUESS? P
NOPE - YOU ARE TOO HIGH
WHAT IS YOUR GUESS? O
NOPE YOU ARE TOO LOW
WHAT IS YOUR GUESS? N
NOPE - YOU ARE TOO HIGH
WHAT IS YOUR GUESS? Q
NOPE - YOU ARE TOO HIGH
WHAT IS YOUR GUESS? P
NOPE - YOU ARE TOO HIGH
WHAT IS YOUR GUESS? N
NOPE - YOU ARE TOO HIGH
WHAT IS YOUR GUESS? H
NOPE YOU ARE TOO LOW
WHAT IS YOUR GUESS? K
NOPE - YOU ARE TOO HIGH
WHAT IS YOUR GUESS? J
NOPE - YOU ARE TOO HIGH
WHAT IS YOUR GUESS? I
NOPE - YOU ARE TOO HIGH
WHAT IS YOUR GUESS? F
NOPE - YOU ARE TOO HIGH
WHAT IS YOUR GUESS? G
NOPE - YOU ARE TOO HIGH
WHAT IS YOUR GUESS? A
NOPE YOU ARE TOO LOW
WHAT IS YOUR GUESS? D
NOPE - YOU ARE TOO HIGH
WHAT IS YOUR GUESS? B
NOPE YOU ARE TOO LOW
WHAT IS YOUR GUESS? C
OK - YOU GOT THIS LETTER
THE SEQUENCE SO FAR IS VZMC
THE CHANCES THAT I WON'T CHEAT ARE  90.4886  %
WHAT IS YOUR GUESS? M
NOPE - YOU ARE TOO HIGH
WHAT IS YOUR GUESS? K
NOPE - YOU ARE TOO HIGH
WHAT IS YOUR GUESS? H
NOPE - YOU ARE TOO HIGH
WHAT IS YOUR GUESS? F
NOPE - YOU ARE TOO HIGH
WHAT IS YOUR GUESS? C
NOPE YOU ARE TOO LOW
WHAT IS YOUR GUESS? E
OK - YOU GOT THIS LETTER
THE SEQUENCE SO FAR IS VZMCE
THE CHANCES THAT I WON'T CHEAT ARE  89.4832  %
WHAT IS YOUR GUESS? M
NOPE YOU ARE TOO LOW
WHAT IS YOUR GUESS? M
NOPE YOU ARE TOO LOW
WHAT IS YOUR GUESS? R
NOPE - YOU ARE TOO HIGH
WHAT IS YOUR GUESS? O
```

```
NOPE - YOU ARE TOO HIGH
WHAT IS YOUR GUESS? N
OK - YOU GOT THIS LETTER
THE SEQUENCE SO FAR IS VZMCEN
THE CHANCES THAT I WON'T CHEAT ARE  88.2901  %
WHAT IS YOUR GUESS? M
NOPE - YOU ARE TOO HIGH
WHAT IS YOUR GUESS? F
NOPE YOU ARE TOO LOW
WHAT IS YOUR GUESS? J
NOPE - YOU ARE TOO HIGH


WHAT IS YOUR GUESS? G
NOPE YOU ARE TOO LOW
WHAT IS YOUR GUESS? I
NOPE YOU ARE TOO LOW
WHAT IS YOUR GUESS? L
NOPE - YOU ARE TOO HIGH
WHAT IS YOUR GUESS? K
NOPE - YOU ARE TOO HIGH
WHAT IS YOUR GUESS? H
OK - YOU GOT THIS LETTER
THE SEQUENCE SO FAR IS VZMCENH
THE CHANCES THAT I WON'T CHEAT ARE  87.5543  %
WHAT IS YOUR GUESS? T
NOPE YOU ARE TOO LOW
WHAT IS YOUR GUESS? X
NOPE - YOU ARE TOO HIGH
WHAT IS YOUR GUESS? U
NOPE YOU ARE TOO LOW
WHAT IS YOUR GUESS? W
OK - YOU GOT THIS LETTER
THE SEQUENCE SO FAR IS VZMCENHW
THE CHANCES THAT I WON'T CHEAT ARE  86.0951  %
WHAT IS YOUR GUESS? M
NOPE YOU ARE TOO LOW
WHAT IS YOUR GUESS? M
NOPE YOU ARE TOO LOW
WHAT IS YOUR GUESS? R
NOPE - YOU ARE TOO HIGH
WHAT IS YOUR GUESS? P
NOPE - YOU ARE TOO HIGH
WHAT IS YOUR GUESS? O
NOPE - YOU ARE TOO HIGH
WHAT IS YOUR GUESS? N
OK - YOU GOT THIS LETTER
THE SEQUENCE SO FAR IS VZMCENHWN
THE CHANCES THAT I WON'T CHEAT ARE  85.1385  %
WHAT IS YOUR GUESS? M
NOPE - YOU ARE TOO HIGH
WHAT IS YOUR GUESS? B
NOPE YOU ARE TOO LOW
WHAT IS YOUR GUESS? K
NOPE - YOU ARE TOO HIGH
WHAT IS YOUR GUESS? F
OK - YOU GOT THIS LETTER
THE SEQUENCE SO FAR IS VZMCENHWNF
HEY BOSS - THIS GUY IS CHAMPIONSHIP MATERIAL
```

```
NUMBER OF TRIES 70
PROBABILITY OF CHEATING
 ON ALL TRIES   83.7195  %
THE TOTAL SEQUENCE IS VZMCENHWNF


TRY AGAIN(YES/NO) ? NO


RUN COMPLETE.
```

Program Listing

```
100  REM THIS PROGRAM "LEARNS" HOW TO CHEAT
200  REM TO USE IT JUST TYPE RUN
300  PRINT "THIS PROGRAM LETS YOU BE A DETECTIVE"
400  PRINT "IT PICKS A LETTER SEQUENCE"
500  PRINT " WHICH YOU MUST GUESS"
600  PRINT "ONE LETTER AT A TIME"
700  PRINT "TO MAKE THIS GAME VERY DIFFICULT"
800  PRINT " THE PROGRAM CHEATS"
900  PRINT " ON EACH LETTER"
1000 PRINT " WITH THE CHEATING A"
1100 PRINT"FUNCTION OF HOW WELL YOU DID ON THE PREVIOUS TRIES"
1200 PRINT "OBVIOUSLY THE FIRST TRY WILL BE 'HONEST'"
1300 READ A$
1400 DATA ABCDEFGHIJKLMNOPQRSTUVWXYZ
1500 DIM G$(10)
1600 REM GET  A SEQUENCE OF TEN RANDOM LETTERS
1700 FOR I=1 TO 10
1800 N=RND(0)*1023
1900 K=N/26
2000 K=K-INT(K)
2100 K=INT(K*26+1)
2200 IF K>26 OR K<1 THEN  1800
2300 G$(I)=SUBSTR(A$,K,1)
2400 NEXT I
2500 REM SET UP COUNTER FOR LETTER IN PROGRESS
2600 C1=0
2700 REM SET UP COUNTER FOR ALL LETTERS
2800 C2=0
2900 REM SET UP POINTER TO LETTER IN QUESTION
3000 L=1
3100 REM SET UP PROBABILITY
3200 P=1
3300 PRINT "THE SEQUENCE IS SET UP FOR YOUR TRIAL"
3400 PRINT "THE CHANCES THAT I WON'T CHEAT ARE ";P*100;" %"
3500 PRINT "WHAT IS YOUR GUESS";
3600 C1=C1+1
3700 C2=C2+1
3800 INPUT T$
3900 IF LEN(T$)>1 THEN  6000
4000 IF T$<>G$(L) THEN  5200
4100 PRINT "OK - YOU GOT THIS LETTER"
4200 PRINT "THE SEQUENCE SO FAR IS ";
4300 FOR I=1 TO L
4400 PRINT G$(I);
```

148

```
4500 NEXT I
4600 PRINT
4700 P=P-P*(1/C1)/15
4800 C1=0
4900 L=L+1
5000 IF L>10 THEN   6700
5100 GOTO   3400
5200 P1=RND(0)
5300 IF P>P1 THEN   5500
5400 GOTO 06500
5500 IF T$ > G$(L) THEN   5800
5600 PRINT "NOPE YOU ARE TOO LOW"
5700 GOTO   3500
5800 PRINT "NOPE - YOU ARE TOO HIGH"
5900 GOTO   3500
6000 PRINT "ONE LETTER AT A TIME - TURKEY"
6100 PRINT " THIS TRY MAKES FURTHER EFFORT WORSE"
6200 IF C1<2 THEN   3500
6300 C1=C1-2
6400 GOTO   3500
6500 IF T$>G$(L) THEN   5600
6600 GOTO 05800
6700 IF C2 > 150 THEN   7900
6800 IF C2> 100 THEN   7700
6900 IF C2 > 80 THEN   7500
7000 IF C2>60 THEN 07300
7100 PRINT "DA CHAMPION HAS STRUK AGIN"
7200 GOTO   8100
7300 PRINT "HEY BOSS - THIS GUY IS CHAMPIONSHIP MATERIAL"
7400 GOTO   8100
7500 PRINT "PRACTICE MAKES PERFECT - KEEP GOING "
7600 GOTO   8100
7700 PRINT "NOT BAD FOR A BEGINNER - BUT LOUSY IF YOU
PLAYED BEFORE"
7800 GOTO   8100
7900 PRINT "HAVE YOU THOUGHT OF PLAYING A SIMPLER GAME
- LIKE";
8000 PRINT " FIND YOUR FINGER?"
8100 PRINT
8200 PRINT "NUMBER OF TRIES",C2
8300 PRINT "PROBABILITY OF CHEATING"
8400 PRINT " ON ALL TRIES",P*100;" %"
8500 PRINT "THE TOTAL SEQUENCE IS ";
8600 FOR I = 1 TO 10
8700 PRINT G$(I);
8800 NEXT I
8900 PRINT
9000 PRINT
9100 PRINT
9200 PRINT "TRY AGAIN(YES/NO)";
9300 INPUT T$
9400 IF T$<>"YES" AND T$<>"NO" THEN   9200
9500 IF T$="YES" THEN  1700
9600 STOP
9700 END
```

An adaptation of this program designed specifically for the Radio Shack TRS-80 computer using Level II BASIC can be found on page 215 in Section II.

COMP-U-STORY

This program demonstrates the use of strings in games. By setting up a possible scenario and then filling in the blanks, we can create a setting as desired.

This type of activity is quite important in interactive games of which *Star Warp* is an example.

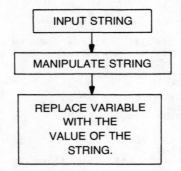

Flowchart for Comp-U-Story

Sample Run

```
RUN
PLEASE ENTER THE FOLLOWING INFORMATION
YOUR NAME
? KEN
NAME A COLOUR
? GREEN
NAME A PIECE OF CLOTHING
? HAT
A PART OF THE BODY
? TOE
ANOTHER PART OF THE BODY
? HAND
ANOTHER COLOUR
```

? ORANGE

WHAT ARE YOU SCARED OF {BEAST}

? MOUSE

A ROOM IN A HOUSE

? BEDROOM

WHO IS YOUR HERO

? HULK

OUR COMPUTER STORY

THIS IS THE STORY OF KEN WHO

ONCE WENT FOR A WALK IN THE WOODS.

WHILE WALKING KEN MET UP WITH A GREEN

MOUSE WHO CHASED THE SCARED KEN.

UNFORTUNATELY KEN FELL ON HIS TOE

AND RIPPED HIS HAT WITH HIS HAND.

KNOWING THAT THE MOUSE WILL EAT HIM,

KEN CALLS ON HIS HERO HULK.

OUR HERO WHICH IS ORANGE DRAGS THE

MOUSE OFF TO THE BEDROOM AND FREES POOR

KEN.

THE COMPUTER SAYS GOOD-BYE

RUN COMPLETE.

Program Listing

```
10   REM THIS PROGRAM ALLOWS YOU TO CON-
     STRUCT A
20   REM STORY USING YOUR NAME
30   REM AND ITEMS ASKED FOR
50   PRINT
60   PRINT
70   PRINT
80   PRINT ''PLEASE ENTER THE FOLLOWING
     INFORMATION''
90   PRINT
100  PRINT ''YOUR NAME''
110  INPUT A$
120  PRINT ''NAME OF A COLOUR''
130  INPUT B$
140  PRINT ''NAME A PIECE OF CLOTHING''
150  INPUT C$
160  PRINT ''A PART OF THE BODY''
170  INPUT D$
180  PRINT ''ANOTHER PART OF THE BODY''
190  INPUT E$
200  PRINT ''ANOTHER COLOUR''
210  INPUT F$
220  PRINT ''WHAT ARE YOU SCARED OF
     {BEAST}''
230  INPUT G$
240  PRINT ''A ROOM IN A HOUSE''
250  INPUT H$
260  PRINT ''WHO IS YOUR HERO''
270  INPUT I$
```

```
280   PRINT
290   PRINT ''OUR COMPUTER STORY''
300   PRINT
310   PRINT
320   PRINT ''THIS IS THE STORY OF '';
      A$; ''WHO''
330   PRINT ''ONCE WENT FOR A WALK IN
      THE WOODS.''
340   PRINT ''WHILE WALKING,'' ''; A$;
      ''MET UP WITH A''
350   PRINT B$; '' ''; G$; '' WHO CHASED
      THE SCARED ''; A$; ''.''
360   PRINT ''UNFORTUNATELY ''; A$;
      ''FELL ON HIS '';D$
370   PRINT ''AND RIPPED HIS ''; C$; ''
      WITH HIS ''; E$; ''.''
380   PRINT ''KNOWING THAT THE ''; G$;
      '' WILL EAT HIM,''
390   PRINT A$; '' CALLS ON HIS HERO '';
      I$; ''.''
400   PRINT '' OUR HERO, WHICH IS '';
      F$; '' DRAGS THE ''; G$
410   PRINT ''OFF TO THE '';H$; '' AND
      FREES POOR ''; A$; ''.''
420   PRINT
430   PRINT
440   PRINT ''THE COMPUTER SAYS GOOD-
      BYE''
450   END
```

This program also will run on the Radio Shack TRS-80 computer with no modifications needed.

AUTO RALLYE

In this auto rallye you can choose both your car and the route. But the better the car, the more gas it eats; and the good routes are more dangerous. It's all lots of fun; but be careful. Don't blow your engine!

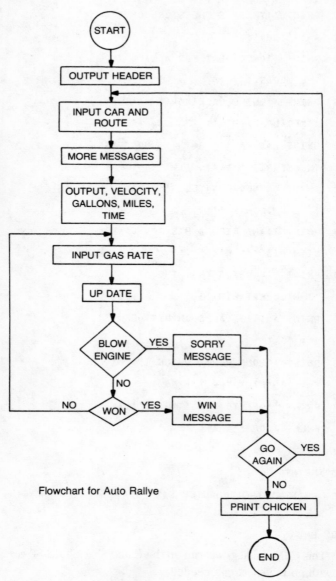

Flowchart for Auto Rallye

Sample Run

```
PROGRAM
                THE CAR RALLY


THIS IS THE SUPER CAR RALLY, THAT ALL
DRIVERS IN THE WORLD WAIT FOR!!!!!!!!!
THE DRIVING IS TOUGH THIS YEAR, AND
WE ALL WISH YOU GOOD-LUCK!!!!!!!!!!!!!


   CHOICE OF CARS
MINI            (1)
LOTUS           (2)
TRANS-AM        (3)
FERRARI         (4)

CHOOSE THE CAR BY THE NUMBER AFTER IT
REMEMBER THE BETTER THE CAR THE MORE GAS IT USES.
WHICH CAR
? 4

YOU NOW CHOOSE WHICH COURSE YOU WANT TO RACE ON.
THE EASIEST COURSE IS NUMBER 1. AND IS THE STRAIGHTEST
ROUTE. NUMBER 5 CONSISTS MOSTLY OF TURNS AND TWISTS
WHICH COURSE DO YOU WANT (1 TO 5) ?
? 1
YOU WILL NEED TO TRAVEL 5 MILES WITH .5 GALLONS OF GAS
YOUR STATUS WILL BE SHOWN EACH 10 SECOND. AFTER EACH STATUS
CHECK YOU WILL BE ASKED FOR A NEW RATE OF GAS. A RATE OF
+10 IS HARD ACCELERATION,AND -10 IS HARD BRAKING. ANY NUMBER
IN BETWEEN IS ALLOWABLE.

PRESENT VELOCITY =  0   NO. OF GALLONS =  .5
NO. OF MILES  =  0   TIME PASSED =  0   SECONDS
WHAT IS YOUR NEW RATE OF GAS  ? 10

ROAD CONDITIONS VEHICLE AHEAD 1000 FEET

PRESENT VELOCITY =  80   NO. OF GALLONS =  .464
NO. OF MILES  =  .173913  TIME PASSED =  10   SECONDS
WHAT IS YOUR NEW RATE OF GAS  ? 10

ROAD CONDITIONS VEHICLE PASSED BY 72   MPH

PRESENT VELOCITY =  128  NO. OF GALLONS =  .428
NO. OF MILES  =  .452174  TIME PASSED =  20   SECONDS
WHAT IS YOUR NEW RATE OF GAS  ? 10

ROAD CONDITIONS VEHICLE AHEAD 1000 FEET

PRESENT VELOCITY =  158  NO. OF GALLONS =  .392
NO. OF MILES  =  .795652  TIME PASSED =  30   SECONDS
WHAT IS YOUR NEW RATE OF GAS  ? 10

ROAD CONDITIONS VEHICLE PASSED BY 121   MPH

PRESENT VELOCITY =  176  NO. OF GALLONS =  .356
NO. OF MILES  =  1.17826  TIME PASSED =  40   SECONDS
WHAT IS YOUR NEW RATE OF GAS  ? 10
DUMMY!! YOU BLEW YOUR ENGINE!!
WHAT TYPE OF FLOWERS DO YOU WISH, AT YOUR FUNERAL??
YOU WANT TO TRY AGAIN, RIGHT !!!!
1-YES, 2-NO ? 2
CHICKEN



RUN COMPLETE.
```

Program Listing

```
10 REM THE CAR RALLY
30 PRINT
40 PRINT
50 PRINT"              THE CAR RALLY"
60 PRINT
70 PRINT
80 PRINT"THIS IS THE SUPER CAR RALLY, THAT ALL"
90 PRINT"DRIVERS IN THE WORLD WAIT FOR!!!!!!!!!"
100 PRINT"THE DRIVING IS TOUGH THIS YEAR, AND"
110 PRINT"WE ALL WISH YOU GOOD-LUCK!!!!!!!!!!!!!!!"
120 PRINT
130 PRINT
140 PRINT"  CHOICE OF CARS"
150 PRINT"MINI              (1)"
160 PRINT"LOTUS             (2)"
170 PRINT"TRANS-AM          (3)"
180 PRINT"FERRARI           (4)"
190 PRINT
200 PRINT"CHOOSE THE CAR BY THE NUMBER AFTER IT"
210 PRINT "REMEMBER THE BETTER THE CAR THE MORE GAS IT USES."
220 PRINT "WHICH CAR"
230 INPUT C1
240 LET C1=INT(C1)
250 IF C1>4 THEN    280
260 IF C1<1 THEN    280
270 GOTO    300
280 PRINT "INVALID CAR NUMBER. NEW CAR ?"
290 GO TO    230
300 PRINT
310 IF N2=1 THEN    350
320 PRINT "YOU NOW CHOOSE WHICH COURSE YOU WANT TO RACE ON."
330 PRINT "THE EASIEST COURSE IS NUMBER 1, AND IS THE STRAIGHTEST"
340 PRINT "ROUTE. NUMBER 5 CONSISTS MOSTLY OF TURNS AND TWISTS"
350 PRINT "WHICH COURSE DO YOU WANT (1 TO 5) ?"
360 INPUT C2
370 LET C2=INT(C2)
380 IF C2<1 THEN    410
390 IF C2>5 THEN    410
400 GOTO    430
410 PRINT "INVALID COURSE NUMBER. NEW CHOICE ?"
420 GOTO    360
430 IF N2=1 THEN    490
440 PRINT "YOU WILL NEED TO TRAVEL 5 MILES WITH .5 GALLONS OF GAS"
450 PRINT "YOUR STATUS WILL BE SHOWN EACH 10 SECOND. AFTER EACH STATUS"
460 PRINT "CHECK YOU WILL BE ASKED FOR A NEW RATE OF GAS. A RATE OF"
470 PRINT "+10 IS HARD ACCELERATION,AND -10 IS HARD BRAKING. ANY NUMBER"
480 PRINT "IN BETWEEN IS ALLOWABLE."
490 FOR I=1 TO C1
500 READ B,M,S
510 LET B=B/10
520 NEXT I
530 LET A1=.5
540 LET M1=0
550 LET C1=C1/2
560 LET V=0
570 PRINT
580 LET R1=0
590 LET T=0
600 LET D=0
610 LET Q1=0
620 PRINT "PRESENT VELOCITY = ";V;" NO. OF GALLONS = ";A1
630 PRINT "NO. OF MILES  = ";M1;" TIME PASSED = ";T;" SECONDS"
640 IF M1 >=5 THEN   1460
650 PRINT "WHAT IS YOUR NEW RATE OF GAS ";
660 INPUT G
670 IF G <=-10 THEN    700
```

156

```
680 IF G>10 THEN      700
690 GOTO      720
700 PRINT "NOT VALID.  NEW RATE";
710 GOTO      660
720 IF G<9 THEN      780
730 LET Z=Z+1
740 IF Z>4 THEN      760
750 GOTO      790
760 PRINT"DUMMY!! YOU BLEW YOUR ENGINE!!"
770 GOTO 1270
780 LET Z=0
790 LET V=INT(B*G-M*V+V)
800 LET I=I+10
810 PRINT
820 PRINT "ROAD CONDITIONS   ";
830 IF V>0 THEN 00850
840 LET V=0
850 LET M1=M1+V/460
860 IF G<0 THEN      890
870 LET A1=A1-(G*S)/5000
875 IF M1 > = 5 THEN 1460
880 IF A1<0 THEN     1380
890 IF R1=1 THEN     1050
900 IF G1=1 THEN     0980
910 LET Q=INT((C2+1)*RND(X))
920 LET R=INT((3.75-C2)*RND(X))
930 IF R>0 THEN 01290
940 IF Q >0 THEN 01340
950 PRINT "CLEAR AND STRAIGHT"
960 PRINT
970 GOTO      620
980 LET H=INT(15+35.*RND(X))
990 LET H=H+5*C1
1000 IF V>H THEN     1500
1010 PRINT "THROUGH CURVE"
1020 PRINT
1030 LET Q1=0
1040 GOTO      620
1050 LET E=E-(V-D)*3.0
1060 IF E<0 THEN     1100
1070 PRINT "VEHICLE ";E;" FEET AHEAD"
1080 PRINT
1090 GOTO      620
1100 IF V-D<5 THEN     1180
1110 PRINT "VEHICLE PASSED BY";
1120 LET D=V-D
1130 PRINT D;
1140 PRINT " MPH"
1150 PRINT
1160 LET R1=0
1170 GOTO      620
1180 PRINT "VEHICLE BEING PASSED "
1190 LET D=INT(25+40*RND(X))
1200 PRINT "GRAYHOUND BUS IN OTHER LANE ";
1210 PRINT"DOING";
1220 PRINT D;
1230 PRINT "MPH";
1240 LET D=V+D
1250 PRINT "CRASH VELOCITY=";
1260 PRINT D
1270 PRINT"WHAT TYPE OF FLOWERS DO YOU WISH, AT YOUR FUNERAL??"
1280 GO TO 01560
1290 PRINT "VEHICLE AHEAD 1000 FEET"
1300 PRINT
1310 LET D=INT(25+35*RND(X))
1320 LET R1=1
1330 GO TO      620
1340 PRINT "WARNING   CURVE AHEAD "
1350 LET Q1=1
1360 PRINT
```

```
1370 GO TO    620
1380 PRINT "EXFLLENT BUT WAIT!"
1390 PRINT
1400 PRINT"TURKEY!! YOU RAN OUT OF GAS!!"
1410 GO TO  1550
1420 PRINT"DON'T KNOW HOW, BUT YOU MADE IT!!"
1430 PRINT
1440 LET R1=0
1450 GO TO    620
1460 PRINT "THE FINISH LINE"
1470 PRINT
1480 PRINT"YOU ARE LUCKY THIS YEAR!!"
1490 GO TO  1560
1500 PRINT "ARE TERRIBLE"
1510 LET H=H-5*C1
1520 PRINT H;"WAS THE SPEED THROUGH THE CURVE"
1530 PRINT V; " WAS YOUR SPEED, BY THE WAY";
1540 GO TO  1270
1550 PRINT "YOU LEAD FOOTED #*$#*$#&"
1560 PRINT "YOU WANT TO TRY AGAIN, RIGHT !!!!"
1570 PRINT "1-YES, 2-NO ";
1580 INPUT V
1590 IF V=2 THEN  1620
1600 N2=1
1610 GO TO  1640
1620 PRINT "CHICKEN"
1630 GO TO  1700
1640 RESTORE
1650 GO TO    220
1660 DATA 45,.53,10
1670 DATA 60,.5,13
1680 DATA 70,.41,15

1690 DATA 80,.39,18
1700 END
```

An adaptation of this program designed specifically for the Radio Shack TRS-80 computer using Level II BASIC can be found on page 217 in Section II.

DECISIONS! DECISIONS!

This program helps you make decisions based on weighing different factors. You input a category, name the items in the category and the factors required. Do not exceed 10 items or 5 factors without changing the DIM statement in lines 30-60. If you modify, make sure you modify all the DIM statements 30-60.

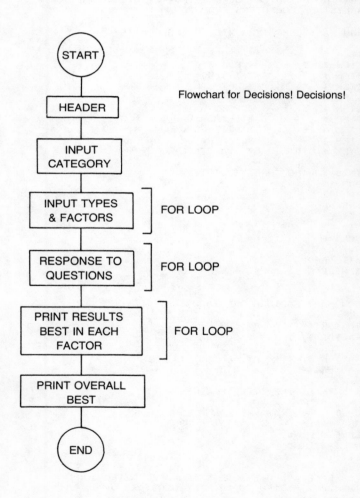

Flowchart for Decisions! Decisions!

Sample Run

```
THE COMPUTER WILL HELP YOU MAKE DECISIONS
      -----
BUT YOU HAVE TO HELP ME AS WELL, OF COURSE

WHAT TYPE OF ITEM,DO YOU NEED HELP WITH
? COMPUTERS

FOR THE COMPUTER TO HELP YOU, IT WILL NEED
A LIST OF COMPUTERS FROM YOU

HOW MANY COMPUTERS WILL WE WORK WITH? 10

ITEM #   1         ? PDP-11
ITEM #   2         ? PDP-8
ITEM #   3         ? TRS-80
ITEM #   4         ? PET
ITEM #   5         ? KIM
ITEM #   6         ? POLY
ITEM #   7         ? SWTPC-6800
ITEM #   8         ? MITS-8800
ITEM #   9         ? SPHERE
ITEM #   10        ? IBM-370

THIS IS THE CORRECT LIST?
PDP-11
PDP-8
TRS-80
PET
KIM
POLY
SWTPC-6800
MITS-8800
SPHERE
IBM-370

HOW MANY FACTORS ARE IMPORTANT TO YOU ? 5

FACTOR #   1       ? COST
FACTOR #   2       ? SOFTWARE
FACTOR #   3       ? EASE OF USE
FACTOR #   4       ? RELIABILITY
FACTOR #   5       ? SIZE

ARE THESE THE RIGHT FACTORS?

COST
SOFTWARE
EASE OF USE
RELIABILITY
SIZE

FOR EACH COMPUTERS WE WILL RATE THE FACTORS
THE BEST RATING IS 10, THE WORST IS 0
PLEASE DO NOT USE THE SAME RATING TWICE
FOR THE SAME FACTOR!!!!!!!!!
```

160

```
PDP-11
COST RATING ? 5
SOFTWARE RATING ? 8
EASE OF USE RATING? 6
RELIABILITY RATING? 8
SIZE RATING ? 9
PDP-8
COST RATING ? 4
SOFTWARE RATING ? 7
EASE OF USE RATING? 5
RELIABILITY RATING? 7
SIZE RATING ? 8
TRS-80
COST RATING ? 4
SOFTWARE RATING ? 1
EASE OF USE RATING? 1C
RELIABILITY RATING? 1C
SIZE RATING ? 10
PET
COST RATING ? 6
SOFTWARE RATING ? 3
EASE OF USE RATING? 8
RELIABILITY RATING? 9
SIZE RATING ? 3
KIM
COST RATING ? 10
SOFTWARE RATING ? 5
EASE OF USE RATING? 1
RELIABILITY RATING? 1
SIZE RATING ? 10
POLY
COST RATING ? 9
SOFTWARE RATING ? 4
EASE OF USE RATING? 2
RELIABILITY RATING? 1
SIZE RATING ? 5
SWTPC-6800
COST RATING ? 7
SOFTWARE RATING ? 3
EASE OF USE RATING? 4
RELIABILITY RATING? 2
SIZE RATING ? 5
MITS-8800
COST RATING ? 1
SOFTWARE RATING ? 7
EASE OF USE RATING? 2
RELIABILITY RATING? 2
SIZE RATING ? 7
SPHERE
COST RATING ? 3
SOFTWARE RATING ? 9
EASE OF USE RATING? 3
RELIABILITY RATING? 6
SIZE RATING ? 2
IBM-370
COST RATING ? 1
SOFTWARE RATING ? 10
EASE OF USE RATING? 1
RELIABILITY RATING? 10
SIZE RATING ? 1
```

```
                    RATINGS
                    ----------


COST
BEST RATING IS THE KIM
ITS RATING WAS   10

SOFTWARE
BEST RATING IS THE IBM-370
ITS RATING WAS   10

EASE OF USE
BEST RATING IS THE TRS-80
ITS RATING WAS   10

RELIABILITY
BEST RATING IS THE IBM-370
ITS RATING WAS   10

SIZE
BEST RATING IS THE KIM
ITS RATING WAS   10
          OVERALL BEST RATING
          -----------------------------
THE PDP-11 HAS THE BEST RATING
ITS AVERAGE RATING WAS   7.2

THE COMPUTER HOPES HE HELPED YOU!!!



RUN COMPLETE.
```

Program Listing

```
 10 REM THIS PROGRAM HELPS TO MAKE DECISIONS
 30 DIM A$(10)
 40 DIM B$(5)
 50 DIM Q(10,5)
 60 DIM C(10)
 70 PRINT
 80 PRINT
 90 PRINT"THE COMPUTER WILL HELP YOU MAKE DECISIONS"
100 PRINT"                     ----"
110 PRINT"BUT YOU HAVE TO HELP ME AS WELL, OF COURSE"
120 PRINT
130 PRINT"WHAT TYPE OF ITEM,DO YOU NEED HELP WITH"
140 INPUT I$
150 PRINT
160 PRINT"FOR THE COMPUTER TO HELP YOU, IT WILL NEED"
170 PRINT"A LIST OF ";I$;" FROM YOU"
180 PRINT
190 PRINT"HOW MANY ";I$;" WILL WE WORK WITH";
200 INPUT X
210 IF X<2 OR X>10 THEN    190
220 PRINT
```

```
230 FOR J=1 TO X
240 PRINT"ITEM # ";J,
250 INPUT A$(J)
260 NEXT J
270 PRINT
280 PRINT"THIS IS THE CORRECT LIST?"
290 FOR J=1 TO X
300 PRINT A$(J)
310 NEXT J
320 PRINT
330 PRINT"HOW MANY FACTORS ARE IMPORTANT TO YOU";
340 INPUT F
350 IF F<1 OR F>5 THEN    330
360 PRINT
370 FOR J=1 TO F
380 PRINT"FACTOR # ";J,
390 INPUT B$(J)
400 NEXT J
410 PRINT
420 PRINT"ARE THESE THE RIGHT FACTORS?"
430 PRINT
440 FOR J=1 TO F
450 PRINT B$(J)
460 NEXT J
470 PRINT
480 PRINT"FOR EACH ";I$;" WE WILL RATE THE FACTORS"
490 PRINT"THE BEST RATING IS 10, THE WORST IS 0"
500 PRINT"PLEASE DO NOT USE THE SAME RATING TWICE"
510 PRINT"FOR THE SAME FACTOR!!!!!!!!!"
520 PRINT
530 FOR K=1 TO X
540 PRINT A$(K)
550 FOR L=1 TO F
560 PRINT B$(L);" RATING";
570 INPUT R
580 Q(K,L)=R
590 NEXT L
600 NEXT K
610 PRINT
620 PRINT"            RATINGS"
630 PRINT"            -------"
640 PRINT
650 FOR T=1 TO F
660 PRINT B$(T)
670 Y=1
680 FOR N=2 TO X
690 IF Q(Y,T)>Q(N,T) THEN    710
700 Y=N
710 NEXT N
720 PRINT"BEST RATING IS THE ";A$(Y)
730 PRINT"ITS RATING WAS ";Q(Y,T)
740 PRINT
750 NEXT T
760 PRINT
770 FOR Y=1 TO X
780 FOR T=1 TO F
790 C(Y)=C(Y)+Q(Y,T)
800 NEXT T
810 NEXT Y
```

163

```
820 J=1
830 FOR I=2 TO X
840 IF C(J)>C(I) THEN 00860
850 J=1
860 NEXT I
870 PRINT"        OVERALL BEST RATING"
880 PRINT"        --------------------"
890 PRINT"THE ";A$(J);" HAS THE BEST RATING"
900 PRINT"ITS AVERAGE RATING WAS ";C(J)/F
910 PRINT
920 PRINT"THE COMPUTER HOPES HE HELPED YOU!!!"
930 END
```

COMPUTER CRAPS

This program lets the user input a BASIC program and then search for all variables found within it. Variables must be single character. When using the assignment statement, the LET keyword must be used. When printing, do not type commas (,) between variables, therefore; 10 PRINT A,B,C

must be entered as 10 PRINT A B C

This program is useful in analyzing variables to see whether they have been printed, if they are assigned before being used, etc.

Of course, the clever user can use this program as a text editor. Remember to indent the END four spaces, pretending that a line number was present. Line numbers are not required with the rest of the lines, and the other commands will still function except the TEST function.

We can modify a line or add lines whether using it with variables or as a text editor.

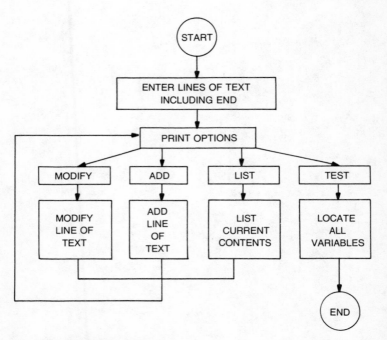

Flowchart for Computer Craps

Sample Run

```
+++++++++++++++++++++++++++++++
-------------------------------
**********VARIABLES**********
-------------------------------
+++++++++++++++++++++++++++++++


ENTER PROGRAM, REMEMBER TO USE LINE NUMBERS FROM
01 TO A MAXIMUM OF 25 (00<LN<26)
ENTER NO MORE THAN 5 VARIABLES PER LINE
USE AS THE LINE NUMBER THE SAME NUMBER AS THE
ENTRY NUMBER SUPPLIED BY THE PROGRAM TO INSURE
PROPER OPERATION OF THE PROGRAM


ENTRY # 1
? 01.LET A=B*C
ENTRY # 2
? 02 INPUT A
ENTRY # 3
? 03 INPUT B
ENTRY # 4
? 04 INPUT C
ENTRY # 5
? 05 INPUT D
ENTRY # 6
? 06 IF A>B THEN 08
ENTRY # 7
? 07 LET C+D
ENTRY # 8
? 08 LET C+A/D
ENTRY # 9
? PRINT A
ENTRY # 10
? END
ENTRY # 11
? 11 END


THE FOLLOWING OPTIONS ARE AVAILABLE
                LIST
                MODIFY
                ADD
                TEST

OPTION? LIST

ENTRY #   1     01 LET A=B*C
ENTRY #   2     02 INPUT A
ENTRY #   3     03 INPUT B
ENTRY #   4     04 INPUT C
ENTRY #   5     05 INPUT D
ENTRY #   6     06 IF A>B THEN 08
ENTRY #   7     07 LET C+D
ENTRY #   8     08 LET C+A/D
ENTRY #   9     PRINT A
ENTRY #  10     END
ENTRY #  11     11 END

OPTION? M

WHICH ENTRY NUMBER
? 1
01 LET A=B*C
```

166

```
ENTER REPLACEMENT LINE
? 01 REM TEST PROGRAM
01 REM TEST PROGRAM

OPTION? M

WHICH ENTRY NUMBER
?.9
PRINT A
ENTER REPLACEMENT LINE
?.09 PRINT
09 PRINT

OPTION? M

WHICH ENTRY NUMBER
?.9
09 .PRINT
ENTER REPLACEMENT LINE
?.09 PRINT A
09 PRINT A

OPTION? M

WHICH ENTRY NUMBER
?.10
END
ENTER REPLACEMENT LINE
? 10 PRINT A+B*C
10 PRINT A+B*C

OPTION? L

ENTRY #   1     01 REM TEST PROGRAM
ENTRY #   2     02 INPUT A
ENTRY #   3     03 INPUT B
ENTRY #   4     04 INPUT C
ENTRY #   5     05 INPUT D
ENTRY #   6     06 IF A>B THEN 08
ENTRY #   7     07 LET C+D
ENTRY #   8     08 LET C+A/D
ENTRY #   9     09 PRINT A
ENTRY #   10    10 PRINT A+B*C
ENTRY #   11    11 END


OPTION? TEST
```

VARIABLES FOUND IN THE GIVEN PROGRAM

VARIABLES FOUND IN INPUT STATEMENTS

```
A                 LINE # 02
B                 LINE # 03
C                 LINE # 04
D                 LINE # 05
```

VARIABLES FOUND IN PRINT STATEMENTS

```
A                 LINE # 09
A                 LINE # 10
B                 LINE # 10
C                 LINE # 10
```

VARIABLES FOUND IN IF STATEMENTS

```
A                 LINE # 06
B                 LINE # 06
```

VARIABLES FOUND IN LET STATEMENTS

```
C              LINE # 07
D              LINE # 07
C              LINE # 08
A              LINE # 08
B              LINE # 08
```

******RUN COMPLETE*******

RUN COMPLETE,

Program Listing


```
 10 REM VARIABLE PATH-FLOW ANALYSIS
 30 REM THIS PROGRAM ASSUMES THAT THE LINE NUMBERS
 40 REM ENTERED BY THE USER ARE CONSISTENT WITH THAT OF
 50 REM THE ENTRY NUMBERS
 50 REM DIMENSION ALL VARIABLES USED AS MATRICES AND VECTORS
 70 DIM P$(25), Q$(25,5), R$(25,5), T$(25,5)
 80 DIM U$(25,5)
 90 REM CLEAR ALL MATRICES AND VECTORS
100 REM BY SETTING THEM EQUAL TO A BLANK SPACE
110 REM CLEAR VECTOR P$
120 FOR I=1 TO 25
130 P$(I)=" "
140 NEXT I
150 REM CLEAR MATRIX Q$
160 FOR I=1 TO 25
170 FOR J=1 TO 5
180 Q$(I,J)=" "
190 NEXT J
200 NEXT I
210 REM CLEAR MATRIX R$
220 FOR I=1 TO 25
230 FOR J=1 TO 5
240 R$(I,J)=" "
250 NEXT J
260 NEXT I
270 REM CLEAR MATRIX T$
280 FOR I=1 TO 25
290 FOR J=1 TO 5
300 T$(I,J)=" "
310 NEXT J
320 NEXT I
330 REM CLEAR MATRIX U$
340 FOR I=1 TO 25
350 FOR J=1 TO 5
360 U$(I,J)=" "
370 NEXT J
380 NEXT I
390 REM OUTPUT STARTING LABEL
400 PRINT
410 PRINT
420 PRINT
430 PRINT"+++++++++++++++++++++++++++++++"
440 PRINT"-------------------------------"
450 PRINT"***********VARIABLES***********"
460 PRINT"-------------------------------"
470 PRINT"+++++++++++++++++++++++++++++++"
480 PRINT
490 PRINT
500 PRINT"ENTER PROGRAM, REMEMBER TO USE LINE NUMBERS FROM"
```

```
510 PRINT"01 TO A MAXIMUM OF 25 (00<LN<26)"
520 PRINT"ENTER NO MORE THAN 5 VARIABLES PER LINE"
530 PRINT"USE AS THE LINE NUMBER THE SAME NUMBER AS THE"
540 PRINT"ENTRY NUMBER SUPPLIED BY THE PROGRAM TO INSURE"
550 PRINT"PROPER OPERATION OF THE PROGRAM"
560 PRINT
570 REM ENTRY OF USER'S PROGRAM TO BE ANALYZED
580 N=1
590 PRINT "ENTRY #";N
600 INPUT L$
610 P$(N)=L$
620 REM IF THE LAST ENTRY WAS AN END STATEMENT
630 REM TERMINATE ENTRY MODE
640 IF SUBSTR(L$,4,3)="END" THEN   670
650 N=N+1
660 GOTO   590
670 PRINT
680 REM DISPLAY AVAILABLE OPTIONS TO THE USER
690 PRINT"THE FOLLOWING OPTIONS ARE AVAILABLE"
700 PRINT"            LIST"
710 PRINT"            MODIFY"
720 PRINT"            ADD"
730 PRINT"            TEST"
740 PRINT
750 PRINT"OPTION";
760 INPUT L$
770 IF L$="L" OR L$="LIST" THEN   840
780 IF L$="M" OR L$="MODIFY" THEN   900
790 IF L$="T" OR L$="TEST" THEN   1140
800 IF L$="A" OR L$="ADD" THEN   1030
810 PRINT"COMMAND IS NOT RECOGNIZED"
820 GOTO   740
830 REM PROCESS LIST OPTION
840 PRINT
850 FOR I=1 TO N
860 PRINT"ENTRY # ";I;"   ";P$(I)
870 NEXT I
880 PRINT
890 GOTO   740
900 PRINT
910 REM PROCESS MODIFY OPTION
920 PRINT"WHICH ENTRY NUMBER"
930 INPUT L
940 IF L<01 OR L>N THEN   960
950 GOTO   980
960 PRINT"LINE NUMBER";L;"HAS NOT BEEN ENTERED"
970 GOTO   920
980 PRINT P$(L)
990 PRINT"ENTER REPLACEMENT LINE"
1000 INPUT P$(L)
1010 PRINT P$(L)
1020 GOTO   740
1030 PRINT
1040 REM PROCESS ADD OPTION
1050 PRINT"LAST LINE ENTERED IS"
1060 PRINT P$(N)
1070 PRINT"ENTER NEW LINES"
1080 PRINT"ENTRY";N;
1090 INPUT L$
1100 P$(N)=L$
1110 IF SUBSTR(L$,4,3)="END" THEN   740
1120 N=N+1
1130 GOTO   1080
1140 PRINT
1150 REM ANALSIS
1160 REM FIND OUT WHAT THE STATEMENT IS ON LINE K
1170 K=1
1180 IF SUBSTR(P$(K),4,3)="END" THEN   1690
1190 IF SUBSTR(P$(K),4,5)="INPUT" THEN   1280
1200 IF SUBSTR(P$(K),4,3)="LET" THEN   1380
```

```
1210 IF SUBSTR(P$(K),4,5)="PRINT" THEN  1480
1220 IF SUBSTR(P$(K),4,2)="IF" THEN  1580
1230 IF K>25 THEN  1260
1240 K=K+1
1250 GOTO  1180
1260 PRINT"PROGRAM ERROR, NO END STATEMENT"
1270 REM PROCESS INPUT STATEMENTS
1280 J=1
1290 FOR I=10 TO LEN(P$(K))
1300 Z$=SUBSTR(P$(K),I,1)
1310 CHANGE Z$ TO A
1320 IF A(2)<0 OR A(2)>26 THEN  1350
1330 U$(K,J)=SUBSTR(P$(K),I,1)
1340 J=J+1
1350 NEXT I
1360 GOTO  1240
1370 REM LET STATEMENT SUBROUTINE (Q$)
1380 J=1
1390 FOR I=8 TO LEN(P$(K))
1400 Z$=SUBSTR(P$(K),I,1)
1410 CHANGE Z$ TO A
1420 IF A(2)<0 OR A(2)>26 THEN  1450
1430 Q$(K,J)=SUBSTR(P$(K),I,1)
1440 J=J+1
1450 NEXT I
1460 GOTO  1240
1470 REM PRINT STATEMENT SUBROUTINE (R$)
1480 J=1
1490 FOR I=10 TO LEN(P$(K))
1500 Z$=SUBSTR(P$(K),I,1)
1510 CHANGE Z$ TO A
1520 IF A(2)<0 OR A(2)>26 THEN  1550
1530 R$(K,J)=SUBSTR(P$(K),I,1)
1540 J=J+1
1550 NEXT I
1560 GOTO 01240
1570 REM IF STATEMENT SUBROUTINE (T$)
1580 J=1
1590 FOR I=7 TO LEN(P$(K))
1600 IF SUBSTR(P$(K),I,4)="THEN" THEN  1670
1610 Z$=SUBSTR(P$(K),I,1)
1620 CHANGE Z$ TO A
1630 IF A(2)<0 OR A(2)>26 THEN  1660
1640 T$(K,J)=SUBSTR(P$(K),I,1)
1650 J=J+1
1660 NEXT I
1670 GOTO  1240
1680 REM *****ANALYSIS*****

1690 PRINT
1700 PRINT"_____"
1710 PRINT"VARIABLES FOUND IN THE GIVEN PROGRAM"
1720 PRINT"----------------------------------------"
1730 PRINT
1740 REM PRINT ALL VARIABLES FOUND
1750 PRINT"VARIABLES FOUND IN INPUT STATEMENTS"
1760 PRINT
1770 FOR K=1 TO 25
1780 FOR J=1 TO 5
1790 A(2)=27
1800 Z$=U$(K,J)
1810 CHANGE Z$ TO A
1820 IF A(2)<1 OR A(2)>26 THEN  1840
1830 PRINT U$(K,J),"LINE # ";SUBSTR(P$(K),1,2)
1840 NEXT J
1850 NEXT K
1860 PRINT
1870 PRINT"VARIABLES FOUND IN PRINT STATEMENTS"
1880 PRINT
1890 FOR K=1 TO 25
```

170

```
1900 FOR J=1 TO 5
1910 A(2)=27
1920 Z$=R$(K,J)
1930 CHANGE Z$ TO A
1940 IF A(2)<1 OR A(2)>26 THEN  1960
1950 PRINT R$(K,J),"LINE # ";SUBSTR(P$(K),1,2)
1960 NEXT J
1970 NEXT K
1980 PRINT
1990 PRINT"VARIABLES FOUND IN IF STATEMENTS"
2000 PRINT
2010 FOR K=1 TO 25
2020 FOR J=1 TO 5
2030 A(2)=27
2040 Z$=T$(K,J)
2050 CHANGE Z$ TO A
2060 IF A(2)<1 OR A(2)>26 THEN  2080
2070 PRINT T$(K,J),"LINE # ";SUBSTR(P$(K),1,2)
2080 NEXT J
2090 NEXT K
2100 PRINT
2110 PRINT"VARIABLES FOUND IN LET STATEMENTS"
2120 PRINT
2130 FOR K=1 TO 25
2140 FOR J=1 TO 5
2150 A(2)=27
2160 Z$=Q$(K,J)
2170 CHANGE Z$ TO A
2180 IF A(2)<1 OR A(2)>26 THEN  2200
2190 PRINT Q$(K,J),"LINE # ";SUBSTR(P$(K),1,2)
2200 NEXT J
2210 NEXT K
2220 PRINT
2230 PRINT"******RUN COMPLETE******"
2240 END
```

ART GRAPHICS

Art Graphics lets you draw semi-random pictures based on the binomial theorem. You may specify the array size and which elements to blank, such as every multiple of N except where N = 1, in which case everything will be blanked and nothing will be printed. Give it a try.

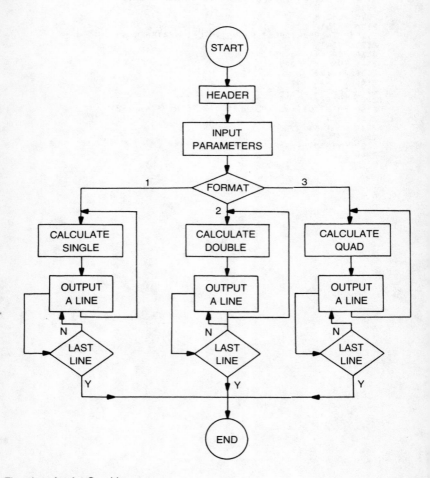

Flowchart for Art Graphics

Sample Run

```
                RANDOM ART
                ----------------

AVAILABLE PATTERNS
----------------------

1          SINGLE
2          DOUBLE
3          QUAD
OKAY ART FELLOWS, WHAT TYPE ? 1
WHICH MULTIPLES SHOULD BE BLANKS? 3
HOW MANY ROWS AND COLUMNS
DO NOT EXCEED 36....PLEASE? 12
 *  *  *  *  *  *  *  *  *  *
 *  *  *  *  *  *  *  *  *  *  *
 *  *  *  *  *  *  *  *  *  *  *
 *  *  *  *  *  *  *  *  *  *  *
 *  *  *  *  *  *  *  *  *  *  *
 *  *  *  *  *  *  *  *  *  *  *
 *  *  *  *  *  *  *  *  *  *  *
 *  *  *  *  *  *  *  *  *  *  *
 *  *  *  *  *  *  *  *  *  *  *
 *  *  *  *  *  *  *  *  *  *  *
 *  *  *  *  *  *  *  *  *  *  *
 *  *  *  *  *  *  *  *  *  *  *


RUN COMPLETE.
RUN



                RANDOM ART
                ----------------

AVAILABLE PATTERNS
----------------------

1          SINGLE
2          DOUBLE
3          QUAD
OKAY ART FELLOWS, WHAT TYPE ? 1
WHICH MULTIPLES SHOULD BE BLANKS? 2
HOW MANY ROWS AND COLUMNS
DO NOT EXCEED 36....PLEASE? 17
 *  *  *  *  *  *  *  *  *  *  *  *  *  *
 *  *   *  *  *   *  *  *   *  *  *   *  *
 *  *  *   *  *  *  *   *  *  *  *  *  *  *
 *  *  *  *   *  *  *  *   *  *  *  *
 *  *  *  *   *  *  *  *  *  *  *  *  *
 *  *  *  *  *   *  *  *  *  *  *  *  *  *
 *  *  *  *  *  *   *  *  *  *  *  *  *  *
 *  *  *  *  *  *  *   *  *  *  *  *  *
 *  *  *  *  *  *  *  *   *  *  *  *  *  *
```

```
* * * * * * * * *   * * * * * *
* * * * * * * * * *   * * * * *
* * * * * * * * * * *   * * * *
* * * * * * * * * * * *   * * *
* * * * * * * * * * * * *   * *
* X * * * * * * * * * * * *   *
* * * * * * * * * * * * * * *
* * * * * * * * * * * * * * * *
```

RUN COMPLETE.
RUN

                    RANDOM ART

AVAILABLE PATTERNS
----
1   SINGLE
2   DOUBLE
3   QUAD
OKAY ART FELLOWS, WHAT TYPE ? 2
WHICH MULTIPLES SHOULD BE BLANKS? 3
HOW MANY ROWS AND COLUMNS
DO NOT EXCEED 36....PLEASE? 17

```
* * * * * * * * * * * * * * * *
* *   * *   * *   * *   * *     *
*   *     *     *     *     *
* * * * *       * * *       * *
* *   * *       * *     * * * *
*   *         *       *     *
* * *           *     * * * *
* *             * * * * * *
*                       *
* * * * * * *             * *
* *   * *       * *       * * *
*   *     *         *       *
* * *   * *         * *   * *
* *   * * * *         * * * * * *
*     *     *     *       *
*     * *   * *   * *   * *   * *
  * * * * * * * * * * * * * * *
```


RUN COMPLETE.
RUN
```
```

```
            RANDOM ART
            ----------
```

AVAILABLE PATTERNS

```
1          SINGLE
2          DOUBLE
3          QUAD
OKAY ART FELLOWS, WHAT TYPE ? 3
WHICH MULTIPLES SHOULD BE BLANKS? 3
HOW MANY ROWS AND COLUMNS
DO NOT EXCEED 36....PLEASE? 18
* * * * * * * * * * * * * * *
* *   * *   * *   * * * * * * *
*   *   *     * * * * * * *
* * * * *       * * * * * *
* * * *         * * * * *
*   *           * * * *
* * *           * * *
* *             * *
*               *
*               *
* *             * *
* * *           * * *
* * * *         * *
* * * * *       * * * *
* * * * * *     * * * * *
* * * * * * *   * *   * *
* * * * * * * * * * * * * * *
* * * * * * * * * * * * * * * * *
```

RUN COMPLETE.
RUN
```
            RANDOM ART
            ----------
```

AVAILABLE PATTERNS

```
1          SINGLE
2          DOUBLE
3          QUAD
OKAY ART FELLOWS, WHAT TYPE ? 3
WHICH MULTIPLES SHOULD BE BLANKS? 5
HOW MANY ROWS AND COLUMNS
DO NOT EXCEED 36....PLEASE? 36
```

RUN COMPLETE.

Program Listing

```
10 REM PRINT TITLE
20 PRINT
30 PRINT"          RANDOM ART"
40 PRINT"          ----------"
50 PRINT
60 REM ART USING BINOMIAL THEOREM
80 DIM P(36,36)
90 MAT P=ZER
100 PRINT"AVAILABLE PATTERNS"
110 PRINT"-----------------"
120 PRINT"1          SINGLE"
130 PRINT"2          DOUBLE"
140 PRINT"3          QUAD"
150 PRINT"OKAY ART FELLOWS, WHAT TYPE";
160 INPUT O
170 IF O<>1 AND O<>2 AND O<>3 THEN 00150
180 PRINT"WHICH MULTIPLES SHOULD BE BLANKS";
190 INPUT Q
200 PRINT"HOW MANY ROWS AND COLUMNS"
210 PRINT"DO NOT EXCEED 36....PLEASE";
220 INPUT T
230 IF T*(36-T)<0 THEN   200
240 IF O=1 THEN      270
250 IF O=2 THEN      460
260 IF O=3 THEN      690
270 FOR R=1 TO T
280 FOR C=1 TO T
290 IF (R-1)*(C-1)=0 THEN   320
300 P(R,C)=P(R,C-1)+(P(R-1,C)/Q)
310 GOTO   330
320 P(R,C)=1
330 NEXT C
340 NEXT R
350 FOR R=1 TO T
360 FOR C=1 TO T
370 IF P(R,C)=0 THEN    410
380 IF (P(R,C)/Q)=INT(P(R,C)/Q) THEN    410
390 PRINT"* ";
400 GOTO    420
410 PRINT"  ";
420 NEXT C
430 PRINT
440 NEXT R
450 STOP
460 Z=T
470 N=Z
480 FOR R=1 TO N
490 FOR C=1 TO Z-1
500 IF (R-1)*(C-1)=0 THEN    530
510 P(R,C)=P(R,C-1)+P(R-1,C)
520 GOTO    540
530 P(R,C)=1
540 NEXT C
550 Z=Z-1
560 NEXT R
570 Z=N
580 N=2
590 FOR R=Z TO 1 STEP -1
600 FOR C=Z TO N STEP -1
```

176

```
610 IF (R-Z)*(C-Z)=0 THEN      640
620 P(R,C)=P(R,C+1)+P(R+1,C)
630 GOTO    650
640 P(R,C)=1
650 NEXT C
660 N=N+1
670 NEXT R
680 GOTO    350
690 M=Q
700 Y=T
710 Z=INT(Y/2)
720 A5=Z*2
730 Z1=Z
740 Z2=Z1
750 Z3=Z2
760 X4=Z3
770 X5=X4
780 FOR I=1 TO Z1
790 FOR J=1 TO Z
800 IF (J-1)*(I-1)=0 THEN      830
810 P(I,J)=P(I,J-1)+P(I-1,J)
820 GOTO    840
830 P(I,J)=1
840 NEXT J
850 Z=Z-1
860 NEXT I
870 N=Z1
880 FOR I=1 TO Z1
890 FOR J=Y TO X5+1 STEP -1
900 IF I=1 THEN    940
910 IF J=Y THEN    940
920 P(I,J)=P(I,J+1)+P(I+1,J)
930 GOTO    950
940 P(I,J)=1
950 NEXT J
960 X5=X5+1
970 NEXT I
980 N=Z2
990 FOR I=Y TO X4+1 STEP -1
1000 FOR J=1 TO Z2
1010 IF J=1 THEN    1050
1020 IF I=Y THEN    1050
1030 P(I,J)=P(I,J-1)+P(I-1,J)
1040 GOTO    1060
1050 P(I,J)=1
1060 NEXT J
1070 Z2=Z2-1
1080 NEXT I
1090 N=Z3
1100 FOR I=Y TO N+1 STEP -1
1110 FOR J=Y TO Z3+1 STEP -1
1120 IF J=Y THEN    1160
1130 IF I=Y THEN    1160
1140 P(I,J)=P(I+1,J)+P(I,J+1)
1150 GOTO    1170
1160 P(I,J)=1
1170 NEXT J
1180 Z3=Z3+1
1190 NEXT I
1200 GOTO    350
1210 END
```

LOVE THAT PRINTER GRAPHICS

You may input any message. The program will spell out "love" using your message as the background. For best results your message should be less than 60 characters.

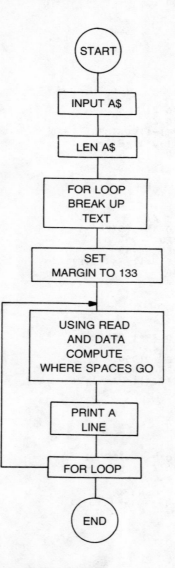

Flowchart for Love that Printer Graphics

Sample Run

Program Listing

```
10 REM LOVE
20 REM KT APRIL 1978
30 DIM I$(240)
40 INPUT A$
50 L=LEN(A$)
60 FOR J=0 TO INT(120/L)
70 FOR I=1 TO L
80 I$(J*L+I)=SUBSTR(A$,I,1)
90 NEXT I
100 NEXT J
110 MARGIN 133
120 C=0
130 A1=F=1
140 C=C+1
150 IF C=37 THEN 00430
160 PRINT
170 READ A
180 A=2*A
190 A1=A1+A
200 IF F=1 THEN 00260
210 FOR I=1 TO A
220 PRINT" ";
230 NEXT I
240 F=1
250 GO TO 00300
260 FOR I=A1-A TO A1-1
270 PRINT I$(I);
280 NEXT I
290 F=0
300 IF A1>120 THEN 00130
310 GO TO 00170
320 DATA 60,1,12,26,9,12,3,8,24,17,8,4,6,23,21,6,4,6,22,12,5,6,5
330 DATA 4,6,21,11,8,6,4,4,6,21,10,10,5,4,4,6,21,9,11,5,4,4,6,21,8
340 DATA 11,6,4,4,6,21,7,11,7,4,4,6,21,6,11,8,4,4,6,19,1,1,5,11,9
350 DATA 4,4,6,19,1,1,5,10,10,4,4,6,18,2,1,6,8,11,4,4,6,17,3,1,7,5
360 DATA 13,4,4,6,15,5,2,23,5,1,29,5,17,8,1,29,9,9,12,1,13,5,40,1
370 DATA 1,13,5,40,1,4,6,13,3,10,6,12,5,1,5,6,11,3,11,6,14,3,1,5
380 DATA 6,11,3,11,6,15,2,1,6,6,9,3,12,6,16,1,1,6,6,9,3,12,6,7,1
390 DATA 10,7,6,7,3,13,6,6,2,10,7,6,7,3,13,14,10,8,6,5,3,14,6,6,2
400 DATA 10,8,6,5,3,14,6,7,1,10,9,6,3,3,15,6,16,1,1,9,6,3,3,15,6,15
410 DATA 2,1,10,6,1,3,16,6,14,3,1,10,10,16,6,12,5,1,11,8,13,27,1,11,8
420 DATA 13,27,1,60
430 FOR J=1 TO 25
440 PRINT
450 NEXT J
460 STOP
470 END
```

180

Section II
Programs For
TRS-80 and PET® Computers

This section contains programs written specifically for the Radio Shack TRS-80 computer using Level II BASIC. Program listings are included for 12 of the games found in Section I. Some programs were completely rewritten. For instance, *Computerized Hangman* now includes a graphic display as well as twice as many vocabulary words.

Some of the other programs will run with no modifications. In general, none of the three plotting routines, *Plot Your 4 Equaitons, Plot Your 10 Equations,* or *Polar Graphic Subroutine* should be used on a TRS-80. This is because of problems with screen size, scrolling, and execution time.

You will need Level II BASIC and 8K of memory. The program *Star Warp* needs 16K of memory.

Most of the programs in this book will run on the Commodore PET®, however, some conversion may be required. Before keying in one of the programs, examine the listings carefully. If two listings are shown for the same program, determine which listing more closely resembles the PET®BASIC. In most cases, this will be the listing in Section I of this book. Section II contains listings in TRS-80 BASIC. If you desire to convert the TRS-80 version to your PET®, there are several important differences you should be aware of.

- Video screen size for the TRS-80 is 64 characters by 16 lines.
- TRS-80 Level II BASIC allows up to 256 characters in a single instruction.
- Several TRS-80 instructions do not have an equivalent in PET®BASIC (such as DEFINT, DEFDBL, DEFSTR, and PRINT@).
- Video display graphics are handled completely differently.

The following is a list of TRS-80 instructions along with their PET®equivalents. This should give you an idea of some of the subtle differences between the two.

TRS-80	PET
CLS	PRINT"♥"
RND(X)	INT(X*RND(0) + .1)
A$ = INKEY$	GET A$
PRINT TAP (5) A	PRINT TAB(5); A
FOR I = 1 TO 5: NEXT	FOR I = 1 TO 5: NEXT I
NEXT K,L	NEXT K: NEXT L

Cursor movement is also handled differently on the two machines. On the TRS-80 the PRINT @ command is used to position the cursor at an absolute location on the screen. Position 0 is in the upper left-hand corner and position 1023 is the lower left. For example, PRINT @ 64, "HI THERE" would cause HI THERE to appear, starting in the first character position of the second line of the display. Other cursor movement is done using the PRINT command with a CHR$ operand. For example, PRINT CHR$(28) causes the cursor to return to position 0. Other values which may be used, along with their functions, are in the following table:

PRINT	(8)	Backspace and erase current character
CHR$	(13)	Carriage return
	(14)	Turn on cursor (The cursor on the TRS-80 is the underscore (--).)
	(15)	Turn off cursor
	(23)	Convert to 32 character mode (all characters become twice their normal size)
PRINT	(24)	Move cursor one position left
CHR$	(25)	Move cursor one position right
	(26)	Move cursor one line down
	(27)	Move cursor one line up
	(28)	Return cursor to position 0
	(29)	Move cursor to beginning of line
	(30)	Erase to end of line
	(31)	Erase to end of screen

WUMPUS

Program Listing

```
10 REM HUNT THE WUMPUS
20 RANDOM
30 DIM P(5)
40 PRINT"INSTRUCTIONS? (Y-N)";
50 INPUT I$
60 IF I$="N" THEN 80
70 GOSUB 640
80 CLS:DIM S(20,3)
90 FOR J=1TO20
100 FOR K=1TO3
110 READ S(J,K)
120 NEXT K,J
130 DATA 2,5,8,1,3,10,2,4,12,3,5,14,1,4,6
140 DATA 5,7,15,6,8,17,1,7,9,8,10,18,2,9,11
150 DATA 10,12,19,3,11,13,12,14,20,4,13,15,6,14,16
160 DATA 15,17,20,7,16,18,9,17,19,11,18,20,13,16,19
170 REM LOCATE L ARRAY ITEMS
180 REM 1=YOU, 2=WUMPUS, 3&4=PITS, 5&6=BATS
190 DIM L(6)
200 DIM M(6)
210 FOR J=1TO6
220 L(J)=RND(20)
230 M(J)=L(J)
240 NEXT J
250 REM CHECK FOR CROSSOVERS
260 FOR J=1TO6
270 FOR K=JTO6
280 IF J=K THEN 300
290 IF L(J)=L(K) THEN 210
300 NEXT K
310 NEXT J
320 REM SET ARROWS
330 A=5
340 LL=L(1)
350 REM RUN THE GAME
360 PRINTTAB(20)"HUNT THE WUMPUS"
370 PRINTTAB(20)"----------------"
380 REM HAZARD WARNINGS AND LOCATIONS
390 GOSUB 1100
400 REM MOVE OR SHOOT
410 GOSUB 1280
420 IF O=2 THEN 470
```

183

```
430 GOSUB 1340
440 IF F=0 THEN 390
450 GOTO 490
460 REM MOVE
470 GOSUB 1840
480 IF F=0 THEN 390
490 IF F>0 THEN 540
500 REM LOSE
510 PRINT"DUMMY, YOU LOSE.   WUMPII JUST LOVE YOU ! ! !"
520 GOTO 560
530 REM WIN
540 PRINT"OKAY, HOT-SHOT.   THE WUMPII WILL GET THEIR REVENGE."
550 PRINT"WUMPII SPIRITS WILL HAUNT YOU 'TIL THEN."
560 FOR J=1TO6
570 L(J)=M(J)
580 NEXT J
590 PRINT"SAME SET UP? (Y-N)";
600 INPUT I$
610 CLS
620 IF I$<>"Y" THEN 210
630 GOTO 330
640 REM INSTRUCTIONS
650 PRINT"WELCOME TO 'HUNT THE WUMPUS.'"
660 PRINT:PRINT"   THE WUMPUS LIVES IN A CAVE OF 20 ROOMS.   EACH ROOM"
670 PRINT"HAS 3 TUNNELS LEADING INTO OTHER ROOMS.   (LOOK AT A"
680 PRINT"DUODECAHEDRON TO SEE HOW THIS WORKS -- IF YOU DON'T KNOW"
690 PRINT"WHAT A DUODECAHEDRON IS, ASK SOMEONE.)"
700 PRINT:PRINT"HAZARDS"
710 PRINT"* BOTTOMLESS PITS
720 PRINT"     THERE ARE TWO OF THESE.   FALL INTO ONE OF THEM"
730 PRINT"     AND YOU WILL LAND IN CHINA."
740 PRINT"* SUPER-BATS
750 PRINT"     TWO OTHER ROOMS HAVE SUPER-BATS.   IF YOU GO THERE,"
760 PRINT"     A BAT GRABS YOU AND TAKES YOU TO SOME OTHER ROOM AT"
770 PRINT"     RANDOM (WHICH MIGHT BE TROUBLESOME)."
780 INPUT"PRESS ENTER TO CONTINUE"; I$
790 CLS:PRINT:PRINT"THE WUMPUS -"
800 PRINT:PRINT"   THE WUMPUS IS NOT BOTHERED BY THE HAZARDS (HE HAS"
810 PRINT"SUCKER FEET AND IS TOO BIG FOR A BAT TO LIFT).   USUALLY"
820 PRINT"HE IS ASLEEP.   TWO THINGS WAKE HIM UP:   YOUR ENTERING"
830 PRINT"HIS ROOM OR YOUR SHOOTING AN ARROW."
840 PRINT:PRINT"   IF THE WUMPUS WAKES, HE MOVES (75% CHANCE) ONE ROOM"
850 PRINT"OR STAYS STILL (25% CHANCE).   AFTER THAT, IF HE IS WHERE"
860 PRINT"YOU ARE, HE EATS YOU UP (AND, BOY, DO YOU LOSE!).
870 PRINT:INPUT"PRESS ENTER TO CONTINUE"; I$
880 CLS:PRINT:PRINT"YOU -"
```

```
890 PRINT:PRINT"   EACH TURN, YOU MAY MOVE OR SHOOT A CROOKED ARROW. "
900 PRINT:PRINT"* MOVING"
910 PRINT"    YOU CAN GO ONE ROOM (THROUGH ONE TUNNEL). "
920 PRINT:PRINT"* ARROWS"
930 PRINT"    YOU HAVE 5 ARROWS.   YOU LOSE WHEN YOU RUN OUT. "
940 PRINT"    EACH ARROW CAN GO FROM 1 TO 5 ROOMS.   YOU AIM BY"
950 PRINT"    TELLING THE COMPUTER THE ROOM(S) YOU WANT THE ARROW"
960 PRINT"    TO GO.   IF THE ARROW CAN'T GO THAT WAY (I.E. NO "
970 PRINT"    TUNNEL) IT MOVES AT RANDOM TO THE NEXT ROOM. "
980 PRINT"    IF THE ARROW HITS THE WUMPUS, YOU WIN. "
990 PRINT"    IF THE ARROW HITS YOU, YOU LOSE. "
1000 INPUT"PRESS ENTER TO CONTINUE"; I$
1010 CLS:PRINT:PRINT"WARNINGS -"
1020 PRINT:PRINT"   WHEN YOU ARE ONE ROOM AWAY FROM THE WUMPUS OR HAZARD, "
1030 PRINT"THE COMPUTER SAYS:"
1040 PRINT:PRINT"   WUMPUS - 'I SMELL A WUMPUS'"
1050 PRINT"    BAT   - 'BATS NEARBY'"
1060 PRINT"    PIT   - 'I FEEL A DRAFT'"
1070 PRINT:PRINT:INPUT"PRESS ENTER TO BEGIN THE GAME"; I$
1080 CLS:PRINT
1090 RETURN
1100 REM PRINT LOCATION AND HAZARD WARNINGS
1110 PRINT
1120 FOR J=2TO6
1130 FOR K=1TO3
1140 IF S(L(1),K)<>L(J) THEN 1220
1150 IF J=3 OR J=4 THEN 1190
1160 IF J=5 OR J=6 THEN 1210
1170 PRINT"I SMELL A WUMPUS!"
1180 GOTO 1220
1190 PRINT"I FEEL A DRAFT!"
1200 GOTO 1220
1210 PRINT"BATS NEARBY!"
1220 NEXT K
1230 NEXT J
1240 PRINT"YOU ARE IN ROOM ";L(1)
1250 PRINT"TUNNELS LEAD TO ";S(LL,1),S(LL,2),S(LL,3)
1260 PRINT
1270 RETURN
1280 REM CHOOSE OPTION
1290 PRINT"SHOOT OR MOVE? (S-M)";
1300 INPUT I$
1310 IF I$="S" THEN O=1:RETURN
1320 IF I$="M" THEN O=2:RETURN
1330 GOTO 1290
1340 REM ARROW ROUTINE
1350 F=0
```

```
1360 REM PATH OF ARROW
1370 PRINT"NUMBER OF ROOMS? (1-5)";
1380 INPUT J9
1390 IF J9<1 OR J9>5 THEN 1370
1400 FOR K=1TOJ9
1410 PRINT"ROOM NUMBER";
1420 INPUT P(K)
1430 IF K<=2 THEN 1470
1440 IF P(K) <> P(K-2) THEN 1470
1450 PRINT":?"ARROWS ARE NOT SUPER MAGIC!--BE REALISTIC (RE-ENTER)";
1460 PRINT:GOTO 1410
1470 NEXT K
1480 REM SHOOT ARROW
1490 LL=L(1)
1500 FOR K=1TOJ9
1510 FOR K1=1TO3
1520 IF S(LL,K1)=P(K) THEN 1680
1530 NEXT K1
1540 REM NO TUNNEL FOR ARROW
1550 LL=S(L,RND(3))
1560 GOTO 1690
1570 NEXT K
1580 PRINT"MISSED"
1590 LL=L(1)
1600 REM MOVE WUMPUS
1610 GOSUB 1760
1620 REM AMMO CHECK
1630 A=A-1
1640 IF A>0 THEN 1660
1650 F=-1
1660 RETURN
1670 REM SEE IF ARROW IS AT L(1) OR L(2)
1680 LL=P(K)
1690 IF LL <> L(2) THEN 1730
1700 PRINT"AHA!  YOU GOT THE WUMPUS!"
1710 F=1
1720 RETURN
1730 IF LL <> L(1) THEN 1570
1740 PRINT"OUCH ! ! !  THE ARROW GOT YOU !"
1750 GOTO 1650
1760 REM MOVE WUMPUS ROUTINE
1770 K=RND(4)
1780 IF K=4 THEN 1800
1790 L(2)=S(L(2),K)
1800 IF L(2)<>LL THEN 1830
1810 PRINT"WUMPUS GOT YA ! ! !  TURKEY ! ! !"
```

```
1820 F=-1
1830 RETURN
1840 REM MOVE ROUTINE
1850 F=0
1860 PRINT"OKAY, WHERE TO NOW";
1870 INPUT LL
1880 IF LL<1 OR LL>20 THEN 1860
1890 FOR K=1TO3
1900 REM CHECK IF LEGAL MOVE
1910 IF S(L(1),K)=LL THEN 1970
1920 NEXT K
1930 IF LL=L(1) THEN 1970
1940 PRINT"ARE YOU FOR REAL, THAT'S NOT POSSIBLE":PRINT
1950 GOTO 1860
1960 REM CHECK FOR HAZARDS
1970 L(1)=LL
1980 REM WUMPUS
1990 IF LL<>L(2) THEN 2060
2000 PRINT"TURKEY!  YOU BUMPED INTO A WUMPUS ! !"
2010 REM MOVE WUMPUS
2020 GOSUB 1770
2030 IF F=0 THEN 2060
2040 RETURN
2050 REM PIT
2060 IF LL<>L(3) AND LL<>L(4) THEN 2110
2070 PRINT"A PIT ! ! ! CHINA, HERE YOU COME ! ! ! ! "
2080 F=-1
2090 RETURN
2100 REM BATS
2110 IF LL<>L(5) AND LL<>L(6) THEN 2150
2120 PRINT"SUPER-BATS ! ! !  GOOD LUCK ! !"
2130 LL=RND(20)
2140 GOTO 1970
2150 RETURN
2160 END
```

SUB HUNT

Program Listing

```
10 REM THE GAME OF SUB HUNT
20 REM THE SUB HUNT IS PLAYED
30 REM ON A 10 X 10 GRID WITH
40 REM THE ORIGIN ON THE LEFT
50 REM TOP CORNER.
60 REM THE X AXIS READS FROM
70 REM 1 TO 10 GOING LEFT TO
80 REM RIGHT, THE Y AXIS READS
90 REM FROM 1 TO 10 GOING
100 REM FROM TOP TO BOTTOM, THEREFORE
110 REM COORDINATE 10,10 IS THE RIGHT,
120 REM LOWER CORNER OF THE GRID
130 REM SUBS ARE CRAFTY, WATCH THEM
140 REM CAREFULLY
150 CLS:PRINT
160 PRINTTAB(20)"S U B   H U N T"
170 PRINT:PRINT" WELCOME TO THE GAME OF SUB HUNT.  THE ENEMY MAY BE"
180 PRINT"LURKING ANYWHERE WITHIN THE GRID.  TO COMPLICATE FINDING"
190 PRINT"IT AND DESTROYING IT WITH DEPTH CHARGES, THE SUB CAN ALSO"
200 PRINT"DIVE.  DEPTH CHARGES MAY BE DROPPED ANYWHERE ON THE GRID,"
210 PRINT"BUT THEY ARE NOT EFFECTIVE UNLESS THEY HAVE BEEN SET"
220 PRINT"FOR THE RIGHT DEPTH.
230 PRINT" SINCE THE SUB CAN DIVE TO THE SEA BOTTOM, DEPTH CHARGES"
240 PRINT"MAY ALSO BE SET FOR THIS DEPTH.  10 IS THE SEA BOTTOM,"
250 PRINT"WHILE 1 IS THE SURFACE OF THE SEA.  THE SUB'S POSITION"
260 PRINT"WILL BE UPDATED AFTER EACH MOVE, AS IT WAITS TO SEE WHAT"
270 PRINT"YOUR MOVE IS.  THE SUB, BEING NUCLEAR POWERED, CAN STAY"
280 PRINT"AT ANY DEPTH FOR ANY PERIOD OF TIME."
290 PRINT:PRINT"PRESS ENTER TO CONTINUE";:INPUT A$
300 CLS:PRINT:PRINT"  TO DESTROY THE SUB, YOU MUST DROP THE DEPTH CHARGE"
310 PRINT"NOT ONLY AT THE RIGHT COORDINATES, BUT IT MUST BE FUSED"
320 PRINT"FOR THE RIGHT DEPTH.  IF NOT YOU HAVE WASTED A DEPTH CHARGE."
330 PRINT"  YOU HAVE A DISADVANTAGE AND AN ADVANTAGE OVER THE SUB."
340 PRINT"THE DISADVANTAGE IS YOU'RE LIMITED TO THE NUMBER OF DEPTH"
350 PRINT"CHARGES YOU HAVE (AT LEAST 16).  THE ADVANTAGE IS THAT THE"
360 PRINT"SUB CAN ONLY MOVE ONE SQUARE AT A TIME, AND ALSO IT CAN"
370 PRINT"MOVE UP OR DOWN ONE COORDINATE AT A TIME."
380 PRINT:PRINT"GOOD LUCK, COMMANDER - PRESS ENTER TO BEGIN";:INPUT A$
390 RANDOM
400 REM
410 REM AMOUNT OF DEPTH CHARGES
420 C1=RND(11)+15
```

188

```
430 CLS:PRINT:PRINT"YOU, COMMANDER ARE AT COORDINATES 1,1"
440 PRINT
450 REM SET UP POSITION FOR SUB
460 A=RND(10):B=RND(10):D=RND(10)
470 REM A IS THE X AXIS
480 REM B IS THE Y AXIS
490 REM D IS THE DEPTH
500 REM SHIP'S STARTING COORDINATES
510 X1=1
520 Y1=1
530 REM GET SHIP'S MOVE
540 PRINT
550 PRINT"COMMANDER, WHERE DO WE SAIL FOR";
560 INPUT X,Y
570 REM TEST THAT X,Y ARE NOT OUT OF BOUNDS
580 IF X>0 AND X<11 AND Y>0 AND Y<11 THEN 600
590 PRINT:PRINT"COMMANDER, STAY WITHIN THE GRID":GOTO 550
600 X1=X
610 Y1=Y
620 PRINT
630 PRINT"COMMANDER, WHAT SETTING FOR DEPTH CHARGES"
640 PRINT"A SETTING OF 0 RELEASES NO CHARGES";
650 INPUT C
660 IF C=0 THEN 710
670 IF C>0 AND C<11 THEN 830
680 PRINT"COMMANDER, THE SUB IS IN THE WATER."
690 PRINT"NEITHER ABOVE THE SURFACE, NOR BELOW THE BOTTOM."
700 GOTO 620
710 PRINT
720 PRINT"THE SUB IS AT COORDINATES:"
730 PRINT"X =";A,"Y =";B,"DEPTH =";D
740 REM NEW SUB POSITION
750 A1=RND(3)-2:B1=RND(3)-2:D1=RND(3)-2
760 A=A+A1:IF A < 1 THEN A=2
770 IF A>10 THEN A=9
780 B=B+B1:IF B < 1 THEN B=2
790 IF B>10 THEN B=9
800 D=D+D1:IF D<1 THEN D=2
810 IF D>10 THEN D=9
820 GOTO 540
830 IF X=A AND Y=B AND C=D THEN 920
840 PRINT:PRINT"SORRY, COMMANDER, YOU MISSED"
850 C1=C1-1:IF C1>0 THEN 710
860 PRINT"SORRY, COMMANDER, NO MORE DEPTH CHARGES."
870 PRINT"BETTER LUCK NEXT TIME.":PRINT
880 PRINT"WOULD YOU LIKE TO PLAY AGAIN (YES - NO)";:INPUT A$
```

```
890 IF A$="YES" THEN 400
900 PRINT:PRINT"THE COMPUTER KNEW YOU WERE A LANDLUBBER !!!"
910 END
920 PRINT
930 PRINT"NELSON WOULD BE PROUD OF YOU"
940 PRINT"YOU GOT THE SUB !!"
950 PRINT"YOU STILL HAVE ";C1;" DEPTH CHARGES":PRINT
960 GOTO 880
```

SINK THE BISMARK

Program Listing

```
10 RANDOM
20 REM ESTABLISH DISTANCE AT START OF GAME
30 D=1000+RND(2000)
40 REM NUMBER OF SHOTS FOR ENEMY
50 S=RND(25)+20
60 REM YOUR SHOTS
70 S1=RND(25)+20
80 V=0
90 E=0
100 CLS:PRINT:PRINTTAB(20)"DESTROYER"
110 PRINTTAB(20)"---------":PRINT:PRINT
120 PRINT"THIS IS THE GAME OF DESTROYER.  BOTH YOUR VESSEL AND THAT"
130 PRINT"OF THE ENEMY HAVE HIGH EXPLOSIVE SHELLS.  YOUR MISSION"
140 PRINT"IS TO SINK THE ENEMY VESSEL BEFORE IT CAN SINK YOU.":PRINT
150 PRINT"THE NUMBER OF SHELLS FOR BOTH YOU AND THE ENEMY ARE"
160 PRINT"RANDOM, BUT BOTH SHIPS HAVE AT LEAST 21.":PRINT
170 PRINT"WITH EACH TURN, YOU MAY MOVE OR SHOOT.  NOTE THAT SHELLS"
180 PRINT"ARE LESS EFFECTIVE THE FURTHER APART YOU ARE.":PRINT
190 INPUT"PRESS ENTER TO BEGIN";A$
200 CLS
210 PRINT:PRINT"THE PRESENT DISTANCE IS NOW";D
220 PRINT:PRINT"WHAT IS YOUR COMMAND - MOVE OR SHOOT ('M' OR 'S')";
230 INPUT C$:IF C$="M" THEN 260
240 IF C$="S" THEN 920
250 PRINT:PRINT"YOU MUST ENTER 'M' OR 'S'";:GOTO230
260 PRINT:PRINT"HOW FAR ('-' = TOWARD, '+' = AWAY)";
270 INPUTD1
280 IF SGN(D1)=1 OR ABS(D1)<D THEN 340
290 FOR I=1 TO 5:CLS:FOR I1=1 TO 100:NEXT I1::PRINTCHR$(23)::PRINT:PRINTTAB
    (10)"COLLISION !"
300 FOR J=1 TO 100:NEXT J
310 NEXT I
320 CLS:PRINT:PRINT:PRINT"BOTH SHIPS ARE GOING DOWN ! ! !"
330 FOR I=1 TO 500:NEXT I:GOTO 830
340 D=D+D1
350 REM GET ENEMY SHOT
360 FOR I=1 TO 1000:NEXT I
370 S=S-1
380 IF S<0 THEN 700
390 REM Q IS TEMPORARY VARIABLE
400 Q=ABS(RND(10)-INT(D/400))
410 V=V+Q
420 Q=INT(V/10)
```

191

```
430 ON Q GOTO 490,520,540,570,590,610,630,660,680,800
440 GOTO 460
450 FOR I=1 TO 500:NEXT I
460 PRINT:PRINT"THE ENEMY HAS NOW ONLY";S;"SHELLS LEFT"
470 PRINT"YOUR SHIP HAS";S1;"SHELLS LEFT"
480 GOTO 210
490 PRINT:PRINT"CAUTION, YOU'RE TAKING ON WATER"
500 PRINT"NO SERIOUS DAMAGE YET"
510 GOTO 450
520 PRINT:PRINT"THERE ARE A FEW SMALL FIRES,"
530 PRINT"BUT THEY ARE UNDER CONTROL":GOTO 450
540 PRINT:PRINT"YOU ARE LISTING TO PORT 5 DEGREES."
550 PRINT"WATER LEVEL IS STILL NOT DANGEROUS."
560 PRINT"CAUTION -- FIRES ARE SPREADING!":GOTO 450
570 PRINT:PRINT"ENGINES ARE OVERHEATING AND THE BILGE PUMPS"
580 PRINT"ARE ACTING UP -- TAKING ON A LOT OF WATER NOW":GOTO 450
590 PRINT:PRINT"MOST OF YOUR CREW IS SERIOUSLY HURT."
600 PRINT"THE FIRES ARE APPROACHING THE AMMO MAGAZINES.":GOTO 450
610 PRINT:PRINT"THE LIFE BOATS ARE BEING READIED. SMOKE FILLS MOST"
620 PRINT"OF THE CORRIDORS.  BILGE PUMPS ARE NEAR FAILURE.":GOTO 450
630 PRINT:PRINT"YOUR CREW IS ABANDONING SHIP.  BILGE PUMPS ARE"
640 PRINT"COMPLETELY GONE.  ONE ENGINE HAS BURNED OUT."
650 GOTO 450
660 PRINT:PRINT"THE ENTIRE SHIP IS BURNING AND IS"
670 PRINT"LISTING BADLY TO PORT.":GOTO 450
680 PRINT:PRINT"SHE'S GOING UNDER, CAPTAIN.  YOU MAY GET"
690 PRINT"IN ONE OR TWO LAST SHOTS.":GOTO 450
700 CLS:FOR I=1 TO 500:NEXT I:PRINT:PRINT"THE ENEMY IS RETREATING !!"
710 PRINT"YOU HAVE WON THE BATTLE !!"
720 PRINT:PRINT"YOU STILL HAD";S1;"SHELLS LEFT, CAPTAIN"
730 PRINT:PRINT"SINCE YOU ARE SUCH A GREAT CAPTAIN, THE COMPUTER"
740 PRINT"WANTS TO KNOW IF YOU WANT TO FIGHT AGAIN (YES OR NO)";
750 INPUT L$:IF L$="YES" THEN 30
760 PRINT:PRINT"OKAY, QUIT WHILE YOU'RE AHEAD"
770 PRINT:PRINT"THE COMPUTER SAYS, ";CHR$(34);"GOOD-BYE";CHR$(34)
780 PRINT:PRINT"THE ENEMY SAYS, ";CHR$(34);"THANK GOODNESS!!";CHR$(34)
790 END
800 PRINT:PRINT"YOU'D BETTER GET INTO THE LIFEBOAT !"
810 PRINT"HURRY, CAPTAIN! IF YOU'RE GOING TO MAKE IT!!"
820 FOR I=1 TO 1000:NEXT I
830 PRINT:PRINT"YOU LOST THIS TIME--DO YOU WANT"
840 PRINT"TO TRY AGAIN, CAPTAIN (YES OR NO)";
850 INPUT L$:IF L$="YES" THEN 880
860 PRINT:PRINT"HAD ENOUGH, HUH?"
870 END
880 PRINT:PRINT"GOOD!  THE COMPUTER IS HAPPY TO SEE YOU HAVE"
```

```
890 PRINT"FIGHTING SPIRIT"
900 FOR I=1 TO 1500:NEXT I
910 GOTO 30
920 IF S1>0 THEN S1=S1-1:GOTO 960
930 CLS:PRINT:PRINT"SORRY, CAPTAIN, YOU HAVE NO MORE SHELLS. "
940 PRINT"BETTER RETREAT TO PORT.   BETTER LUCK NEXT TIME. "
950 GOTO 830
960 REM Q IS A TEMPORARY VARIABLE
970 Q=ABS(RND(10)-INT(D/400))
980 E=E+Q
990 Q=INT(E/10)
1000 ON Q GOTO 1070,1090,1110,1140,1160,1180,1200,1230,1250,1040
1010 CLS:PRINT:PRINT"THE ENEMY IS TAKING ON WATER. "
1020 PRINT"THERE SEEMS TO BE SOME SMOKE. "
1030 GOTO 350
1040 CLS:PRINT:PRINT"CONGRADULATIONS, CAPTAIN, YOU HAVE SUNK THE"
1050 PRINT"ENEMY SHIP ! !"
1060 GOTO 720
1070 CLS:PRINT"THE ENEMY SHIP IS LOSING GROUND. "
1080 PRINT"ALREADY THERE ARE SMALL FIRES. ":GOTO 350
1090 CLS:PRINT:PRINT"LOOKS LIKE SOME OF THE ENEMY'S CREW"
1100 PRINT"IS TAKING TO THE LIFE BOATS, CAPTAIN. ":GOTO 350
1110 CLS:PRINT:PRINT"CAPTAIN, THE RADIO ROOM HAS PICKED UP A TRANSMISSION"
1120 PRINT"FROM THE ENEMY--THEY ARE TAKING ON WATER. "
1130 GOTO 350
1140 CLS:PRINT:PRINT"THE FIRES ON THE ENEMY SHIP SEEM TO BE"
1150 PRINT"SPREADING, CAPTAIN. ":GOTO 350
1160 CLS:PRINT:PRINT"THE ENEMY SHIP IS STARTING TO LIST, CAPTAIN. "
1170 PRINT"HER BILGES MUST BE OUT!":GOTO 350
1180 CLS:PRINT:PRINT"THE ENEMY SHIP IS LISTING BADLY--SHE CAN'T"
1190 PRINT"LAST MUCH LONGER.   KEEP IT UP, CAPTAIN. ":GOTO 350
1200 CLS:PRINT:PRINT"THE ENEMY'S ENGINES MUST BE OUT, CAPTAIN. "
1210 PRINT"SHE'S NOT MANUEVERING, BUT SHE'S STILL FIRING AT US. "
1220 GOTO 350
1230 CLS:PRINT:PRINT"IT LOOKS LIKE THE ENEMY IS ABANDONING SHIP. "
1240 PRINT"POUR IT ON, CAPTAIN. ":GOTO 350
1250 CLS:PRINT:PRINT"SHE'S GOING DOWN, CAPTAIN.   I THINK THE"
1260 PRINT"ENEMY HAS HAD IT THIS TIME. ":GOTO 350
```

MOUSE HUNT
Program Listing

```
100 REM CHANGE A MOUSE
150 CLS:PRINT:PRINT
200 PRINT"THIS PROGRAM ALLOWS YOU TO GO ON A MOUSE HUNT"
300 PRINT"FOR A VERY OBNOXIOUS MOUSE. "
400 PRINT"THE MOUSE TRIES TO DODGE YOU BY HOPPING"
500 PRINT"RANDOMLY. "
600 PRINT"YOU CAN CATCH IT BY BEING WHERE THE MOUSE LANDS. "
700 PRINT"YOU CAN CHANGE DIRECTION, TOO. "
800 PRINT:RANDOM
900 T=RND(100)+100
1100 PRINT"YOU HAVE TO GET WITHIN";T;"FEET OF THE MOUSE TO 'KETCH' IT. "
1200 T=T*T
1300 REM SET UP THE LOCATIONS AND SPEEDS
1400 REM TO "KETCH" THE MOUSE
1500 REM YOU ARE THE FOX
1600 R1=RND(10)*10+50
1700 R2=(INT(RND(0)*2+.5)+1)*R1
1800 K1=RND(0)
1900 K2=RND(0)
2000 IF K1>.5 THEN 2300
2100 K1=-1
2200 GOTO 2400
2300 K1=1
2400 IF K2>.5 THEN 2700
2500 K2=1
2600 GOTO 2800
2700 K2=-1
2800 Q1=RND(400)+100
2900 Q1=Q1*K1
3000 Q2=RND(400)+100
3100 Q2=Q2*K2
3200 IF Q2=0 OR Q1=0 THEN 1800
3300 Q3=0:Q4=0
3400 PRINT:INPUT"PRESS ENTER TO BEGIN";A$
3500 CLS:PRINT:PRINT"HOP SIZES","DA MOUSE";R1,"YOUSE";R2
3600 PRINT
3700 PRINT"THE COMPUTER SAYS: I WISH YOU GREAT FORTUNE IN YOUR ENDEAVOR"
3800 PRINT"FROM THE MOUSE:  DROP DEAD - TURKEY"
3900 PRINT"FROM THE COMPUTER:  KEEP IT CLEAN, BOYS"
4000 PRINT
4100 P1=3.14159254/130
4200 K3=1
4300 Z1=(Q3-Q1)*(Q3-Q1)+(Q4-Q2)*(Q4-Q2)
4400 REM
4500 REM PRINT A CYCLE
```

194

```
4600 REM
4700 PRINT
4800 PRINT"TRY #",K3
4900 PRINT"THE MOUSE IS";SQR(Z1);"FEET AWAY"
5000 PRINT"AT LOCATION  ";Q1;"  BY  ";Q2
5100 D1=RND(359)
5200 IF Z1<=T THEN 5400
5300 PRINT"AND TOOK OFF AT AN ANGLE OF ";D1;"DEGREES"
5400 PRINT"YOU ARE AT LOCATION ";Q3;"  BY  ";Q4
5600 IF Z1>2*T THEN 6200
5700 IF Z1>T THEN 6400
5750 CLS:PRINT:PRINT
5800 PRINT"SPLAT ! ! !"
5900 PRINT"YOU GOT IT ! ! !"
6000 PRINT"BOY, WHAT A MESS - SQUASHED MOUSE EVERYWHERE"
6100 GOTO 8800
6200 PRINT"OWWW THAT HURTS - YOU'RE NOT EVEN CLOSE"
6300 GOTO 6500
6400 PRINT"MISSED AGAIN - BUT PRETTY CLOSE"
6500 PRINT"WHAT DIRECTION DO YOU WISH TO JUMP";
6600 INPUT D2
6700 IF D2>=0 AND D2<=360 THEN 7000
6800 PRINT"BETWEEN 0 AND 360 DEGREES ONLY"
6900 GOTO 6500
7000 Q5=R1*COS(D1*P1)/100
7100 Q6=R1*SIN(D1*P1)/100
7200 Q7=R2*COS(D2*P1)/100
7300 Q8=R2*SIN(D2*P1)/100
7400 C1=Z1
7500 C2=Z1
7600 FOR I=1 TO 100
7700 Q1=Q1+Q5
7800 Q2=Q2+Q6
7900 Q3=Q3+Q7
8000 Q4=Q4+Q8
8100 C2=(Q3-Q1)*(Q3-Q1)+(Q4-Q2)*(Q4-Q2)
8200 IF C2>C1 THEN 8400
8300 C1=C2
8400 NEXT
8500 IF C1<=T THEN 5750
8600 K3=K3+1
8700 GOTO 4800
8800 PRINT"YOU TOOK",K3;"TRIES TO 'KETCH(UP)' THE MOUSE"
8900 PRINT"WANT TO TRY AGAIN? (YES/NO)";
9000 INPUT A$
9100 IF A$="YES" THEN 900
9200 IF A$<>"NO" THEN 8900
9300 END
```

CAPTURE THE ALIEN

Program Listing

```
10 REM LETS CAPTURE AN ENEMY VESSEL
20 REM INSTEAD OF DESTROYING HIM
30 RANDOM:CLS
40 DIM Q(10,10)
50 PRINT:PRINT"ENTER YOUR NAME FOR THE LOG, SIR";:INPUTA$
60 S=25
70 PRINT:PRINT"DO YOU WANT INSTRUCTIONS, COMMANDER ";A$;:INPUTC$
80 IF C$<>"YES" THEN 200
90 CLS:PRINT:PRINT"YOU MISSION, COMMANDER ";A$;", IS TO CAPTURE AN"
100 PRINT"ENEMY BATTLE CRUISER.  YOU MUST NOT DESTROY THE ENEMY --"
110 PRINT"YOU MUST TAKE HIM ALIVE.  TO EFFECT CAPTURE, YOU MUST"
120 PRINT"DESTROY ALL OF THE REGIONS SURROUNDING THE ENEMY VESSEL."
130 PRINT"THE ONBOARD COMPUTER WILL KEEP YOU UP-TO-DATE ON THE"
140 PRINT"ENEMY'S LAST POSITION."
150 PRINT:PRINT"THESE IS ALSO A PROTECTED AREA USING THE AREAS WHERE"
160 PRINT"X = 0 OR Y = 0, SO THAT THE ALIEN HAS A CHANCE.  IF YOU"
170 PRINT"FIRE INTO THIS REGION, IT IS THE SAME AS FIRING INTO A"
180 PRINT"PREVIOUSLY DESTROYED AREA.":PRINT:PRINT"GOOD LUCK, COMMANDER."
190 PRINT:INPUT"PRESS ENTER TO BEGIN";B$
200 CLS:PRINT:PRINT"COMMANDER ";A$;", YOU HAVE 25 SHOTS."
210 FOR X=0TO10
220 FOR Y=0TO10
230 Q(Y,X)=0:Q(0,X)=-1:Q(Y,0)=-1
240 Q(10,X)=-1:Q(Y,10)=-1
250 NEXT Y,X
260 X=RND(10)-1:Y=RND(10)-1
270 PRINT:PRINT"ENEMY'S LAST KNOWN POSITION -- SECTOR";X;",";Y
280 IF S<=0THEN740
290 C=X
300 A=RND(3)-2:X=X+A:IF X<0 OR X>9 THEN X=C:GOTO 290
310 D=Y
320 A=RND(3)-2:Y=Y+A:IF Y<0 OR Y>9 THEN Y=D:GOTO 310
330 IF Q(Y,X)=-1 THEN X=C:Y=D:GOTO290
340 IF X=C AND D=Y THEN 290
350 PRINT:PRINT"    0 1 2 3 4 5 6 7 8 9"
360 FOR A=0TO9
370 PRINTA;
380 FOR B=0TO9
390 IF Q(A,B)=0 THEN PRINT" *"; ELSE PRINT"  ";
400 NEXT B
410 IF A=4 THEN PRINTTAB(40)"LAST KNOWN POSITION";
420 IF A=5 THEN PRINTTAB(42)"SECTOR";C;",";D;
430 PRINT
```

```
440 NEXT A
450 A=RND(10):IF A>4 THEN 520
460 PRINT"COMMANDER ";A$;", YOU HAVE BEEN ATTACKED"
470 PRINT"ENERGY USED TO REPLENISH SHIELDS. "
480 S=S-1
490 IF S<=0 THEN 740
500 PRINT"ONLY";S;"SHOTS REMAINING"
510 GOTO 580
520 A=RND(10):IF A<9 THEN 580
530 A=RND(10)-1:B=RND(10)-1
540 IF A=X AND B=Y THEN 530
550 IF Q(B,A)=-1 THEN 530
560 Q(B,A)=-1
570 PRINT"NOVA IS SECTOR";A;",";B
580 PRINT:PRINT"ENTER YOU PHASER SHOT (X,Y)";
590 INPUT A,B
600 IF A>9 OR B>9 THEN 580
610 S=S-1
620 IF A=X AND B=Y THEN 770
630 IF Q(B,A)=-1 THEN 820
640 Q(B,A)=-1
650 FOR A=X-1 TO X+1
660 FOR B=Y-1 TO Y+1
670 IF A=X AND B=Y THEN 690
680 IF Q(B,A)<>-1 THEN 270
690 NEXT B,A
700 PRINT"GOOD SHOW, COMMANDER ";A$;" --
710 PRINT"YOU HAVE CAPTURED THE ALIEN ENEMY AND YOU STILL"
720 PRINT"HAVE";S;"SHOTS REMAINING. "
730 END
740 PRINT"COMMANDER ";A$
750 PRINT"YOU HAVE NO MORE ENERGY FOR PHASERS. "
760 GOTO 800
770 PRINT"COMMANDER ";A$
780 PRINT"DID YOU EVER BLOW IT THIS TIME"
790 PRINT"YOU ZAPPED THE ALIEN ! ! ! ! ! ! "
800 PRINT"WELL, BETTER LUCK NEXT TIME. "
810 END
820 PRINT"COMMANDER ";A$
830 PRINT"GOOD SHOT! YOU FIRED AT A PREVIOUSLY DESTROYED AREA!"
840 PRINT"TURKEY!"
850 GOTO 270
```

STAR WARP

Program Listing

```
10 REM SPACE
20 RANDOM
30 CLS
40 DIM N$(5),O$(21),Z$(21),L$(8),R$(4),K$(3),T$(5)
50 FOR I=1TO8:READL$(I):NEXT
60 DATA GAMMA 7,ALPHA CENTAURI,SIRIUS 12,BETEGEUSE 7,SOL 3,ANTARES 9,ALDERBARAN,ANDROMEDA
70 FORI=1TO5:READN$(I):NEXT
80 DATA ENTERPRISE,EXCALIBER,DEFIANT,EXETER,ENTERPRISE
90 FORI=1TO3:READK$(I):NEXT
100 DATA KLINGON,ROMULAN,ALIEN
110 FORI=1TO4:READR$(I):NEXT
120 DATA CTHULU,QUARK,CLIXNIP,XOTOP
130 FORI=1TO5:READT$(I):NEXT
140 DATA KLEEK,RYJKA,DYSNIP,JOJLM,TWEEL
150 FORI=1TO21:READO$(I):NEXT
160 DATA RANGE AND BEARING OF THE ENEMY
170 DATA FIRE FORWARD PHASER BANK
180 DATA FIRE REAR PHASER BANK
190 DATA FIRE FORWARD PHOTON TORPEDOES
200 DATA FIRE REAR PHOTON TORPEDOES
210 DATA LAUNCH ANTI-MATTER PROBE
220 DATA COME UP ON THE ENEMY VESSEL
230 DATA RETREAT FROM THE ENEMY
240 DATA APPROACH ENEMY AT WARP SPEED
250 DATA RETREAT AT TOP WARP SPEED
260 DATA "USE OPTIMUM SHIELD DEPLOYMENT, MR. SULU"
270 DATA "TURN US ABOUT 180 DEGREES, MR. SULU"
280 DATA "MR. SPOCK, WHAT ARE OUR CHANCES OF A HIT?"
290 DATA "MR. SPOCK, WHAT OPTIONS ARE AVAILABLE?"
300 DATA "MR. SPOCK, FULL DAMAGE REPORT"
310 DATA "LIEUTENANT, OPEN A VOICE CHANNEL TO STAR FLEET"
320 DATA "LET'S WAIT, WHAT WILL THE ENEMY DO NEXT?"
330 DATA ACTIVATE COMPUTER DESTRUCT SEQUENCE
340 DATA "LIEUTENANT, OPEN A VOICE CHANNEL TO THE ENEMY."
350 DATA "TURN 90 DEGREES TO PORT, MR. CHEKOV"
360 DATA "TURN 90 DEGREES TO STARBOARD, MR. CHEKOV"
370 FORI=1TO21:READZ$(I):NEXT
380 DATA RANGE,PHASEF,PHASER,TORPF,TORPR,PROBE,CLOSE,AWAY
390 DATA PURSE,ESCAPE,SHIELDS,ROTATE,CHANCES,COMMANDS
400 DATA DAMAGE,BLUFF,WAIT,SUICIDE,SURRENDER,LVEER,RVEER
410 PRINT:S$=N$(RND(5))
420 PRINT"SPACE. THE FINAL FRONTIER...."
430 PRINT"THIS IS THE VOYAGE OF THE STARSHIP ";S$;". IT'S FIVE"
440 PRINT"YEAR MISSION. TO EXPLORE STRANGE NEW WORLDS, TO SEEK"
450 PRINT"OUT NEW LIFE AND NEW CIVILIZATIONS, TO BOLDLY GO WHERE"
460 PRINT"NO MAN HAS GONE BEFORE."
470 PRINT:PRINT:PRINT:FORI=1TO1000:NEXT
480 PRINT"YEOMAN ";TAB(10)"SIR, ENTER YOUR NAME FOR THE LOG";:INPUT C$
490 PRINT
500 PRINT"SPOCK. ";TAB(10)"YOU ARE IN COMMAND OF THE ";S$;", CAPTAIN ";C$;". "
510 PRINTTAB(10)"DO YOU WISH A LIST OF POSSIBLE COMMANDS, SIR";:INPUT A$
520 IF A$="YES"THEN GOSUB 3070:GOSUB3250
530 PRINT:E$=K$(RND(3)):F=R$(RND(4)):U$=T$(RND(5)):D$=L$(RND(8)):Y=50*(RND(0)-.5)
540 REM
550 PRINTC$;". ";TAB(10)"CAPTAIN'S LOG, STARDATE";INT(RND(10000))/10+2000
560 PRINTTAB(10)"WE ARE PRESENTLY ON COURSE FOR ";D$
570 ON RND(5):GOTO580,600,620,630,640
580 PRINTTAB(10)"TO RESCUE MINERS UNDER ATTACK BY ";E$
590 PRINTTAB(10)"BATTLE CRUISERS.":GOTO650
600 PRINTTAB(10)"WITH A CARGO OF DILITHIUM CRYSTALS TO POWER"
610 PRINTTAB(10)"THE COLONISTS STATION.".GOTO650
620 PRINTTAB(10)"TO SEARCH FOR NEW MINERALS FOR THE FEDERATION.".GOTO650
630 PRINTTAB(10)"WITH THE CURE FOR MARTIAN FLU.".GOTO650
```

198

```
640 PRINTTAB(10)"FOR OBSERVATION OF A BLACK HOLE. "
650 GOSUB3490:PRINT"SULU:";TAB(10)"SIR, I'M PICKING UP A VESSEL ON AN ATTACK"
660 PRINTTAB(10)"VECTOR WITH THE ";S$;". "
670 GOSUB3490:PRINT"SPOCK:";TAB(10)"SHIP'S COMPUTER INDICATES THAT IT IS THE"
680 PRINTTAB(10)E$;" VESSEL, ";F$;", CAPTAIN. "
690 PRINTTAB(10)"UNDER COMMAND OF CAPTAIN ";U$;". "
700 PRINTC$;".";TAB(10)"SOUND RED ALERT, LIEUTENANT UHURA. "
710 GOSUB3490:PRINT"UHURA:      AYE, SIR. "
720 IFRND(2)=1THENX$="SULU"ELSEX$="CHEKOV"
730 H1=0:H2=0:G=0:X=0:S=0
740 P=0
750 FORI=1TO4:Z(I)=100:S(I)=100:NEXT
760 R=1000-RND(100)
770 B=RND(360)-180
780 B1=RND(360)-180
790 GOTO820
800 IF I<7THEN840
810 IF I>12THEN840
820 GOSUB3200
830 GOSUB3490
840 PRINT:PRINTX$;":";TAB(10)"WHAT ARE YOUR ORDERS, SIR";:INPUTM$
850 PRINT:I=0
860 FORJ=1TO21:IFZ$(J)=M$THENI=J
870 NEXT
880 IF I<1ORI>21THENPRINTX$";";TAB(10)"TROUBLE HEARING YOU, SIR":GOTO840
890 PRINTC$;":";TAB(10)O$(I)
900 ONIGOTO820,910,920,930,940,950,960,960,970,970,1500,960,1550,1600,1610,980,2090,2090,1990,2040,3430,3450
910 IFH1<7THEN1060ELSEPRINT"CHEKOV:    FORWARD PHASERS ARE DEAD, SIR. ":GOTO2090
920 IFH1<6THEN1360ELSEPRINT"CHEKOV:    REAR PHASERS ARE DEAD, SIR. ":GOTO2090
930 IFH1<9THEN1370ELSEPRINT"CHEKOV:    FORWARD PHOTON TORPEDOES ARE DEAD, SIR. ":GOTO2090
940 IFH1<8THEN1410ELSEPRINT"CHEKOV:    REAR PHOTON TORPEDOES ARE DEAD, SIR. ":GOTO2090
950 IFH1<11THEN1420ELSEPRINT"CHEKOV:    PROBE LAUNCHER IS DEAD, SIR. ":GOTO2090
960 IFH1<14THEN1450ELSEPRINT"SULU:      IMPULSE ENGINES ARE DEAD, SIR. ":GOTO2090
970 IFH1<11THEN1450ELSEPRINT"SULU:      WARP DRIVE IS OUT, SIR. ":GOTO2090
980 IFH2<11THEN990ELSEPRINT"SPOCK:     THE ";E$;" HAS NO ENGINES, SIR. ":GOTO2090
990 IFG=0THEN1790
1000 PRINT"SPOCK:     I DO NOT THINK THAT THE ";E$;"S WILL BE"
1010 PRINTTAB(10)"FOOLED BY THAT MANEUVER AGAIN, SIR. "
1020 GOTO2090
1030 IFABS(B)<90THEN1050
1040 PRINT"CHEKOV:    WRONG PHASER BANK, CAPTAIN. ":GOTO2090
1050 PRINT"CHEKOV:    PHASERS FIRING, SIR. "
1060 R9=R:B9=B:GOSUB3390
1070 IFRND(0)<F8THEN1090
1080 PRINT"CHEKOV:    MISSED HIM, SIR. ":GOTO2090
1090 IFRND(0)<.2THEN1220
1100 V=.5
1110 K=1
1120 FORK1=2TO4:IFS(K)>=S(K1)THEN1140
1130 K=K1
1140 NEXT
1150 IFS(K)>50THEN1170
1160 K=RND(4)
1170 H2=H2+V
1180 PRINT"SPOCK:     A HIT ON SHIELD #";K;". "
1190 IFS(K)=0THEN1230
1200 S(K)=S(K)-30*V+(RND(0)+.1)
1210 IFS(K)<0THEN2090ELSEPRINTTAB(10)"WHICH IS NOW GONE, SIR. ":S(K)=0:GOTO2090
1220 V=1:PRINT"CHEKOV:    DIRECT HIT, SIR. ":GOTO1110
1230 PRINT:PRINT"CHEKOV:    GOT HIM, SIR. "
1240 IFRND(0)>.5THEN820
1250 GOSUB3490:PRINT"SPOCK:     THE ";E$;" VESSEL REMAINS INTACT, CAPTAIN. "
1260 GOSUB3490:PRINTC$;":";TAB(10)"OPEN A HAILING FREQUENCY, LIEUTENANT. "
1270 GOSUB3490:PRINT"UHURA:     HAILING FREQUENCY OPEN, SIR. "
1280 GOSUB3490:PRINTC$;":";TAB(10)"THIS IS CAPTAIN ";C$;" OF THE STARSHIP"
1290 PRINTTAB(10)S$;". PREPARE TO BEAM OVER SURVIVORS. "
1300 IF RND(0)>.5THEN1350
1310 GOSUB3490:PRINTU$;":";TAB(10)"I AM AFRAID THAT WILL BE IMPOSSIBLE,"
1320 PRINTTAB(10)"CAPTAIN, SINCE I JUST ACTIVATED OUR AUTO-DESTRUCT. "
```

199

```
1330 FORI=10TO1STEP-1:GOSUB3500:PRINTTAB(10),I:NEXT
1340 PRINT:GOTO3020
1350 GOSUB3490:PRINTU$;":";TAB(10)"VERY WELL, CAPTAIN, OUR SHIELDS HAVE BEEN LOWERED.":GOTO3220
1360 IFABS(B)<90THEN1040ELSEGOTO01050
1370 IF ABS(B)>=90THEN1040
1380 R9=R:B9=B:GOSUB3350
1390 IF RND(0)>F9THEN1080
1400 IF RND(0)<.25THEN1100ELSEGOTO01220
1410 IFABS(B)<90THEN1040ELSEGOTO01380
1420 IFX<10THEN1430ELSEPRINT"CHEKOV:    WE HAVE NO MORE PROBES, SIR.":GOTO2100
1430 X=X+1:IFRND(0)<.07135THEN1440ELSEGOSUB3490:PRINT"SPOCK:    PROBE LOST, CAPTAIN ":GOTO2090
1440 GOSUB3490:PRINT"SPOCK:    THE PROBE IS HOMING IN ON THE ";F$;", SIR.":GOTO3020
1450 ONI-6GOTO01460,1470,1480,1490,1500,1530
1460 GOSUB2790:R=ABS(R-Y):GOTO2090
1470 GOSUB2820:R=ABS(R+Y):IFR>5000THEN2700ELSEGOTO02090
1480 GOSUB2830:R=ABS(R-2*Y):GOTO2090
1490 GOSUB2840:R=ABS(R+2*Y):IFR>5000THEN2700ELSEGOTO02090
1500 S=1:FORJ=2TO4:IFZ(J)<=Z(S)THEN1510ELSES=J
1510 NEXT
1520 GOSUB3500:PRINT:PRINT"SULU:";TAB(10)"SHIELD #";S;"IS IN POSITION, SIR.":GOTO840
1530 B=B+180
1540 IFB<=180THEN2090ELSEB=B-360:GOTO2090
1550 GOSUB3490:PRINT"SPOCK:    AT RANGE",R;"I WOULD ESTIMATE THE PROBABILITY"
1560 R9=R:B9=B:GOSUB3390:F8=F8*100
1570 PRINTTAB(10)"OF A PHASER HIT AT";F8;"AND THE PROBABILITY"
1580 R9=R:B9=B:GOSUB3350:F9=F9*100
1590 PRINTTAB(10)"OF A PHOTON TORPEDO HIT AT";F9;".".GOTO840
1600 GOSUB2070:GOTO0840
1610 GOSUB3500:PRINT:PRINT"SPOCK:    DAMAGES ARE AS FOLLOWS:":PRINT
1620 PRINTTAB(12)"SHIELD #";TAB(22)S$;TAB(35)F$
1630 FORJ=1TO4:PRINT:PRINTTAB(15)J;TAB(25)Z(J);TAB(38)S(J):NEXT
1640 PRINT:PRINTTAB(10)S$;" DAMAGE ",
1650 IFH1>5.5THEN1660ELSEPRINT"NONE":GOTO1730
1660 PRINT:PRINTTAB(20)"REAR PHASERS OUT"
1670 IFH1<7THEN1730ELSEPRINTTAB(20)"FORWARD PHASERS OUT"
1680 IFH1<8THEN1730ELSEPRINTTAB(20)"REAR PHOTON TORPEDOES DEAD"
1690 IFH1<9THEN1730ELSEPRINTTAB(20)"FORWARD PHOTON TORPEDOES DEAD"
1700 IFH1<11THEN1730ELSEPRINTTAB(20)"PROBE LAUNCHER DESTROYED"
1710 PRINTTAB(20)"WARP DRIVE LOST"
1720 IFH1<14THEN1730ELSEPRINTTAB(20)"IMPULSE POWER LOST"
1730 PRINT:PRINTTAB(10)F$;" DAMAGE ",
1740 IFH2>5.5THEN1750ELSEPRINT"NONE":PRINT:GOTO840
1750 PRINT:PRINTTAB(20)"ALL PHASERS DEAD"
1760 IF H2<9THENPRINT:GOTO840ELSEPRINTTAB(20)"ALL TORPEDOES DEAD"
1770 IFH2<11THENPRINT:GOTO840ELSEPRINTTAB(20)"WARP DRIVE LOST"
1780 IFH2<14THENPRINT:GOTO840ELSEPRINTTAB(20)"IMPULSE ENGINES OUT":PRINT:GOTO840
1790 PRINTTAB(10)"USE CODE 2."
1800 GOSUB3490:PRINT"UHURA:    BUT, SIR, THE ";E$;"S BROKE CODE 2 YESTERDAY, SIR."
1810 GOSUB3490:PRINTC$;":";TAB(10)"CODE 2, LIEUTENANT, IMMEDIATELY!"
1820 GOSUB3490:PRINT"UHURA:    AYE, AYE, SIR.  GO AHEAD, SIR."
1830 GOSUB3490:PRINTC$;":";TAB(10)"THIS IS CAPTAIN ";C$;" OF THE STARSHIP ";S$;"."
1840 GOSUB3500:PRINTTAB(10)"WE ARE UNDER ATTACK BY THE ";E$;" SHIP ";F$
1850 GOSUB3500:PRINTTAB(10)"AND, IN ORDER TO PREVENT THIS SHIP FROM FALLING"
1860 GOSUB3500:PRINTTAB(10)"INTO ENEMY HANDS, WE ARE ACTIVATING THE CORBOMITE"
1870 GOSUB3500:PRINTTAB(10)"DEVICE.  SINCE THIS WILL RESULT IN THE COMPLETE"
1880 GOSUB3500:PRINTTAB(10)"ANNIHILATION OF ALL MATTER WITHIN A RANGE OF 5000"
1890 GOSUB3500:PRINTTAB(10)"MEGAMETERS, ALL VESSALS SHOULD BE WARNED TO STAY"
1900 GOSUB3500:PRINTTAB(10)"CLEAR OF THIS AREA FOR THE NEXT";RND(4);
1910 PRINTTAB(10)"SOLAR YEARS."
1920 G=1:IFRND(0)>.2THEN1360
1930 GOSUB3490:PRINT"SULU:    THE ";E$;" IS MOVING AWAY AT WARP 10, SIR."
1940 GOSUB3490:PRINT"SPOCK:    THE TACTIC APPEARS TO HAVE BEEN EFFECTIVE, SIR."
1950 PRINTTAB(10)"THE ";E$;"S HAVE BEEN REPULSED.":GOTO3220
1960 GOSUB3490:PRINT"SULU:    NO IMMEDIATE CHANGE IN ";E$;"'S COURSE OR SPEED, SIR."
1970 GOSUB3490:PRINT"SPOCK:    IT WOULD SEEM THAT THEY HAVE, AS YOU HUMANS"
1980 PRINTTAB(13)"PUT IT, 'CALLED OUR BLUFF,' CAPTAIN.":GOTO2090
1990 GOSUB3490:PRINT"COMPUTER:";FORJ=12TO1STEP-1:PRINTTAB(9)JJ:GOSUB3500:NEXT
2000 PRINTTAB(13)"THE ";S$;"HAS BEEN DESTROYED."
2010 Q=RND(200):GOSUB3500:PRINTTAB(10)"RADIUS OF EXPLOSION" Q;"MEGAMETERS."
2020 IFQ>RTHENPRINTTAB(10)E$;" VESSEL DESTROYED."ELSEPRINTTAB(10)E$;" VESSEL REMAINS INTACT."
```

200

```
2030 GOTO3220
2040 IFE$="ROMULAN"THENPRINT"UHURA:    NO ANSWER FROM THE ";F$;", SIR.":GOTO2090
2050 GOSUB3490:PRINTC$;":";TAB(10)"THIS IS CAPTAIN ";C$;" OF THE STARSHIP ";S$;"."
2060 PRINTTAB(10)"WILL YOU ACCEPT OUR UNCONDITIONAL SURRENDER?"
2070 GOSUB3490:PRINTU$;":";TAB(10)"ON BEHALF OF THE ";E$;" EMPIRE, I ACCEPT YOUR"
2080 PRINTTAB(10)"SURRENDER, PREPARE FOR IMMEDIATE BOARDING.":GOTO3220
2090 REM ENEMY MOVE
2100 IFH2<9THEN2290
2110 IFH2<11THEN2190
2120 IFH2>12.9THEN2650
2130 IFH1>10.9THEN2700
2140 IFH1>8.9THEN2170
2150 IFR<RND(200)THEN2740
2160 GOSUB2790:R=ABS(R+V):IFR>5000THEN2700ELSEGOTO820
2170 IFRND(0)<.5THEN2160
2180 GOSUB2820:R=ABS(R-V):IFR>5000THEN2700ELSEGOTO820
2190 IFH1<7THEN2250
2200 IFH1<9THEN2150
2210 IFH1>10.9THEN2700
2220 IFRND(0)<.5THEN2170
2230 IFRND(0)<.5THEN2250
2240 GOSUB2830:R=ABS(R+2*V):IFR>5000THEN2700ELSEGOTO820
2250 GOSUB2840:R=ABS(R-2*V):GOTO820
2260 IFR>700THEN2250
2270 IFR>200THEN2240
2280 GOTO2150
2290 IFH2<6THEN2390
2300 IFH1<7THEN2370
2310 IFR<200THEN2250
2320 IFR>700THEN2240
2330 IFH1>7.3THEN2250
2340 IFINT(ABS(B1/90))>INT(ABS(B/90))THEN2250
2350 IFABS(B1-90)=ABS(B-90)-20THEN2850
2360 IFRND(0)<.5THEN2250ELSEGOTO2240
2370 R9=R:B9=B1:GOSUB3390 R9=R:B9=B1:GOSUB3350
2380 IFF8>F9THEN2250ELSEGOTO2310
2390 IFH1<7THEN2450
2400 IFR>150THEN2420
2410 IFRND(0)<.5THEN2180ELSEGOTO2250
2420 IFR>=400THEN2440
2430 IFABS(B1-90)<20THEN2880ELSEGOTO2180
2440 IFR>700THEN2240ELSEGOTO2340
2450 IFR>700THEN2240
2460 R9=R:B9=B1:GOSUB3350:R9=R:B9=B1:GOSUB3390
2470 IFF9>F3THEN2340
2480 IFH1>6.9THEN2500
2490 IFINT(ABS(B1/90))>INT(ABS(B/90))THEN2250
2500 IFABS(B1-90)=ABS(B-90)-20THEN2880ELSEGOTO2250
2510 IFH1<6THEN2640
2520 T=H1-V:IFABS(T-6)<.1THEN2540
2530 IFABS(H1-6.26)>.3THEN2540ELSEPRINT"CHEKOV:    REAR PHASERS DEAD, SIR.":GOTO2640
2540 IFABS(T-7)<.1THEN2560
2550 IFABS(H1-7.25)>.3THEN2560ELSEPRINT"CHEKOV:    FORWARD PHASERS DEAD, SIR.":GOTO2640
2560 IFABS(T-8)<.1THEN2580
2570 IFABS(H1-8.25)>.3THEN2580ELSEPRINT"CHEKOV:    REAR PHOTON TORPEDOES DEAD, SIR.":GOTO2640
2580 IFABS(T-9)<.1THEN2600
2590 IFABS(H1-9.25)>.3THEN2600ELSEPRINT"CHEKOV:    FORWARD PHOTON TORPEDOES DEAD, SIR.":GOTO2640
2600 IFABS(T-11)<.1THEN2620
2610 IFABS(H1-11.25)>.3THEN2620ELSEPRINT"CHEKOV:    PROBE LAUNCHER AND WARP DRIVE GONE, SIR.":GOTO2640
2620 IFABS(T-14)<.1THEN2640
2630 IFABS(H1-14.25)>.3THEN2640ELSEPRINT"CHEKOV:    IMPULSE ENGINES DEAD, SIR."
2640 RETURN
2650 IFP>0THEN800
2660 P=1:GOSUB3490:PRINT"SPOCK:    THE ";E$;" SHIP IS COMPLETELY CRIPPLED, SIR."
2670 PRINTTAB(10)"WILL YOU ALLOW THEM TO SURRENDER";:INPUTA$:IFA$="YES"THEN1260
2680 PRINT"SPOCK:    DO YOU WANT TO DESTROY THE ";F$;", CAPTAIN";:INPUTA$:IFA$="YES"THEN840ELSEGOTO2710
2690 REM LOSS OF CONTACT
2700 GOSUB3490:PRINT"SULU:    CONTACT WITH THE ";E$;" VESSEL HAS BEEN LOST, SIR."
2710 GOSUB3490:PRINTC$;":";TAB(10)"RESUME COURSE FOR ";D$;", MR. SULU."
2720 GOSUB3490:PRINT"SULU:    AYE, AYE, SIR.":GOTO3220
```

```
2730 REM
2740 GOSUB3490:PRINT"SPOCK:    SENSORS INDICATE THAT THE ";F$;" IS OVERLOADING"
2750 PRINTTAB(10)"WHAT REMAINS OF ITS ANTI-MATTER PODS.  UNDOUBTEDLY"
2760 PRINTTAB(10)"A SUICIDAL MOVE, CAPTAIN.  PODS WILL DETONATE"
2770 PRINTTAB(10)"IN 12 SECONDS...."
2780 GOSUB3490:FORJJ=10TO1STEP-1:PRINTTAB(10)JJ:GOSUB3500:NEXTJJ:GOTO3020
2790 R=R-RND(200)
2800 B=RND(360)-180:B1=RND(360)-180:IFR<0THENR=-R


2810 RETURN
2820 R=R+RND(200):GOTO2800
2830 R=R-RND(400):GOTO2800
2840 R=R-RND(400):GOTO2800
2850 GOSUB3490:PRINT"SPOCK:    THE ";E$;" IS FIRING PHOTON TORPEDOES AT US."
2860 R9=R:B9=B1:GOSUB3350:IFRND(0))F9THEN3010
2870 IFRND(0)< 4THEN2980ELSEGOTO2910
2880 GOSUB3490:PRINT"SPOCK:    THE ";E$;" IS FIRING PHASERS AT US, SIR."
2890 R9=R:B9=B1:GOSUB3390:IFRND(0))F8THEN3010
2900 IFRND(0)< 2THEN2980
2910 V=.5:K=RND(4):IFS=0THEN2930
2920 K=S
2930 PRINTTAB(10)"A HIT ON SHIELD #";K
2940 IFZ(K)<=0THEN2970ELSEZ(K)=Z(K)-30*V*(RND(0)+.1)
2950 H1=H1+V:GOSUB2510:IFZ(K))0THEN800
2960 Z(K)=0:PRINTTAB(10)"THAT'S IT FOR SHIELD #";K;", SIR.":GOTO800
2970 GOSUB3490:PRINT"COMPUTER: THE ";S$;" HAS BEEN DESTROYED.":GOTO3220
2980 V=1:K=RND(4):IFS=0THEN3000
2990 K=S
3000 PRINTTAB(10)"A DIRECT HIT ON SHIELD #";K;", SIR.":GOTO2940
3010 PRINTTAB(10)"EVASIVE MANEUVERS WERE EFFECTED, NO DAMAGE.":GOTO800
3020 PRINT:Q=RND(200):IFQ<RTHEN3050
3030 GOSUB3490:PRINT"COMPUTER: RADIUS OF EXPLOSION";Q;"MGM."
3040 PRINTTAB(10)S$;" HAS BEEN DESTROYED.":GOTO3220
3050 GOSUB3490:PRINT"SPOCK:";TAB(10)E$;" VESSEL DESTROYED, SIR."
3060 PRINTTAB(10)"RADIUS OF EXPLOSION WAS";Q;"MGM.:GOTO3220
3070 PRINT:PRINT"SPOCK:    THE POSSIBLE COMMANDS ARE AS FOLLOWS:"
3080 PRINT:PRINT"CODE    COMMAND           CODE    COMMAND"
3090 PRINT"RANGE    RANGE/BEARING     PHASEF  FORWARD PHASERS"
3100 PRINT"PHASER   REAR PHASERS      TORPF   FORWARD TORPEDO"
3110 PRINT"TORPR    REAR TORPEDO      PROBE   ANTI-MATTER PROBE"
3120 PRINT"CLOSE    APPROACH (IMPULSE) AWAY   RETREAT (IMPULSE)"
3130 PRINT"PURSE    APPROACH (WARP)   ESCAPE  RETREAT (WARP)"
3140 PRINT"SHIELDS  OPTIMUM SHIELDS   ROTATE  180 TURN"
3150 PRINT"CHANCES  FIRING CHANCES    COMMANDS REPEAT COMMANDS"
3160 PRINT"DAMAGE   FULL REPORT       BLUFF   TRY BLUFF"
3170 PRINT"WAIT     ENEMY'S TURN      SUICIDE SELF-DESTRUCT"
3180 PRINT"LVEER    TURN LEFT         RVEER   TURN RIGHT"
3190 PRINT"SURRENDER":PRINT:PRINT"PRESS ENTER TO CONTINUE";:INPUTA$:CLS:RETURN
3200 PRINT:PRINT"SPOCK:";TAB(10)F$;" IS AT RANGE";R;"MGM. BEARING";B;
3210 PRINTTAB(10)"DEGREES.":RETURN
3220 PRINT:PRINT"COMPUTER: DO YOU WISH TO ATTEMPT ANOTHER BATTLE"
3230 PRINTTAB(10)"IN COMMAND OF THE ";S$;:INPUTA$:IFA$="YES"THEN540
3240 PRINT:PRINT"COMPUTER: DO YOU WISH TO CHANGE SHIPS";:INPUTA$
3250 IFA$="YES":THENS=N$(RND(5)):GOTO500ELSEGOTO3480
3260 PRINT:PRINT"NOTE WEAPON RANGES ARE:"
3270 PRINT:PRINT"     PHASERS      0-400 MGM (OPTIMUM 200 MGM)"
3280 PRINT"     TORPEDOES    300-700 MGM (OPTIMUM 500 MGM)"
3290 PRINT"     PROBES       ALL RANGES":PRINT
3300 PRINT"PHASERS ARE MORE DEADLY THAN TORPEDOES.  PROBES CAUSE"
3310 PRINT"TOTAL DESTRUCTION, BUT ARE EFFECTIVE ONLY 7 PERCENT"
3320 PRINT"OF THE TIME.  TORPEDOES AND PHASERS ARE MORE DEADLY"
3330 PRINT"WHEN THE BEARING OF THE ENEMY IS CLOSE TO 0 OR 180"
3340 PRINT"DEGREES.":PRINT:PRINT"PRESS ENTER TO CONTINUE";:INPUTA$:CLS:RETURN
3350 F9=0:IFABS(R9-500))200THEN3380
3360 F9=1-(R9-500)[2/40000:GOSUB3510
3370 F9=F9*SIN(B7)*(3-INT(ABS(B9/90)))/3
3380 RETURN
```

```
3390 F8=0:IFR9>400THENRETURN
3400 F8=1-(R9-200)[2/40000:GOSUB3510
3410 F8=F8*SIN(B7)*(5-INT(ABS(B9/90)))/5
3420 RETURN
3430 IFH1>=14THEN960
3440 B=B+90:GOTO1540
3450 IFH1>=14THEN960
3460 B=B-90.IFB>=0THENB=360-B
3470 GOTO1540
3480 END
3490 PRINT.FORII=1TO1000:NEXTII.RETURN
3500 FORII=1TO500:NEXTII:RETURN
3510 B7=3.1415926*ABS(90-ABS(B9))/180.RETURN
```

BOMB DISPOSAL SQUAD

This is a spiced up version of the original program. There is a flashing "TICK" while the computer waits for your input. The setup procedure also is reduced.

Program Listing

```
10 REM THIS IS THE PROGRAM OF TIME BOMB
20 REM THE BOMB CONSISTS OF 4 STICKS OF
30 REM DYNAMITE AND IS CONNECTED TO A
40 REM DIGITAL CLOCK AND OTHER SENSORS.
50 REM UNFORTUNATELY, YOU CANNOT JUST
60 REM CUT THE WIRES FROM THE CLOCK.
70 REM IF THE WIRES ARE NOT CUT ACCORDING
80 REM TO SEQUENCE, BANG! YOU BLOW UP.
90 RANDOM:CLS:PRINTTAB(20)"TIME BOMB"
100 PRINTTAB(20)"---------"
110 PRINT:PRINT"THE TIME BOMB IS SET TO EXPLODE AFTER 6 MOVES.  YOU"
120 PRINT"MUST DEFUSE THE BOMB BEFORE THEN, OR ELSE THE RESULTING"
130 PRINT"EXPLOSION WILL GET YOU !!!":PRINT
140 PRINT"THERE ARE 10 WIRES LABELED 1 TO 10, 2 OF THESE WIRES WILL"
150 PRINT"CAUSE IMMEDIATE EXPLOSION IF CUT !!":PRINT
160 PRINT"OF THE REMAINING 8 WIRES, 4 ARE NOT CONNECTED TO ANY"
170 PRINT"SENSOR, INCLUDING THE CLOCK.  THE BOMB MAKER PLANTS"
180 PRINT"THESE FALSE WIRES, JUST TO GIVE YOU A HARD TIME IN"
190 PRINT"DEFUSING THE BOMB.":PRINT
200 INPUT"PRESS ENTER WHEN READY TO BEGIN";A$
210 CLS
220 REM THE WIRES ARE
230 F=4
240 FOR I=1TO10:W(I)=2:NEXT
250 REM SET TWO WIRES TO CAUSE EXPLOSION
260 FOR I=1 TO 2
270 J=RND(10):IF W(J)<>2 THEN 270
280 W(J)=3:NEXT
290 REM SET UP HARMLESS WIRES
300 FOR I=1 TO 4
310 J=RND(10):IF W(J)<>2 THEN 310
320 W(J)=1:NEXT
330 REM THE REST ARE LIVE
340 M=0
350 M=M+1:IF M>6 THEN 680
360 CLS:PRINT:PRINT"THE BOMB IS ";
370 IF M=1 THEN PRINT"TICKING AWAY" ELSE PRINT"STILL TICKING"
380 PRINT:PRINT"WHICH WIRE TO CUT?";:P=POS(0)
```

```
390 L=0:A$=" ":J=1
400 IF A$=" " THEN A$="TICK !" ELSE A$="    "
410 PRINT@91,A$;CHR$(30);:I=0
420 I=I+1:IF I>50 THEN 400
430 L$(J)=INKEY$:IF L$(J) = "" THEN 420
440 IF L$(J)=CHR$(8) THEN J=J-1:PRINT@193+P,CHR$(8);:P=P-1:GOTO 420
450 IF L$(J)=CHR$(13) THEN PRINT@193+P,CHR$(13):GOTO 470
460 PRINT@193+P,L$(J);:J=J+1:P=P+1:GOTO 420
470 P$="":FOR I=1 TO J:P$=P$+L$(I):NEXT I
480 L=VAL(P$):IF L<1 OR L>10 THEN 510
490 IF W(L)<>0 THEN 530
500 PRINT:PRINT"SORRY THAT'S BEEN USED":FOR I=1 TO 1000:NEXT I:GOTO 360
510 PRINT:PRINT"TRY PICKING A NUMBER FROM 1 TO 10 THIS TIME"
520 FOR I=1 TO 1000:NEXT I:GOTO 360
530 IF W(L)=3 THEN 680
540 IF W(L)=1 THEN 600
550 W(L)=0:F=F-1
560 IF F=0 THEN 640
570 IF M=6 THEN 680
580 PRINT:PRINT"GOOD SHOW ! NOW ONLY";F;"MORE TO GO."
590 FOR I=1 TO 1500:NEXT:GOTO 350
600 IF M=6 THEN 680
610 W(L)=0:PRINT:PRINT"OH! OH! THAT WAS A HARMLESS ONE"
620 PRINT"STILL";F;"MORE LIVE ONES TO GO !"
630 GOTO 590
640 CLS:PRINT:PRINT"WOW ! WHAT A GREAT JOB !"
650 PRINT:PRINT"YOU SHOULD HAVE BEEN WITH THE BOMB"
660 PRINT"DISPOSAL SQUAD. AND YOU DID IT IN";M;"MOVES."
670 GOTO 720
680 CLS:PRINTCHR$(23);
690 PRINT@520,"BAAA";
700 FOR I=1TO150:NEXT
710 PRINT"RRROOOOOOMMMMM !!"
720 FOR I=1 TO 2000:NEXT
730 CLS:PRINT:PRINT:PRINT"WANT TO TRY ANOTHER BOMB (YES OR NO)";
740 INPUT A$:IF A$="YES" THEN 210
750 PRINT:PRINT"NEVER DID LIKE EXPLOSIONS. DID YA?":PRINT
760 END
```

BIORHYTHM

This program is changed from the original. It will display 13 days starting with the date you specify. Press ENTER to scroll one day at a time. Press the "up-arrow" to scroll the next 13 days. Press "X" to terminate the program.

Program Listing

```
10 CLS
20 QQ=2*3.14159
30 DIM A(12)
40 DIM M$(12)
50 DIM X$(51)
60 INPUT"ENTER YOUR BIRTHDAY (MM,DD,YY)";M,D,Y
70 INPUT"ENTER TODAY'S DATE (MM,DD,YY)";M1,D1,Y1
80 IF M > 12 OR M1 > 12 THEN 190
90 Y1 = 1900 + Y1
100 Y = 1900 + Y
110 P=0:Q=0
120 R = Y1 - Y
130 S = R * 365
140 FOR I = 1 TO 12
150 READ A(I),M$(I)
160 NEXT I
170 IF D1 > A(M1) THEN 190
180 IF D <= A(M) THEN 200
190 PRINT"WOULD YOU LIKE TO TRY THAT AGAIN?":RESTORE:GOTO 60
200 IF INT(Y / 4) <> Y / 4 THEN 220
210 A(2) = 29
220 FOR J = M TO 12
230 P = P + A(J)
240 NEXT J
250 P = P - D
260 A(2) = 28
270 IF INT(Y1/4) <> Y1/4 THEN 290
280 A(2) = 29
290 FOR J = M1 TO 12
300 Q = Q + A(J)
310 NEXT J
320 Q = Q - D1
330 S = S + INT(R / 4) + P - Q
340 PRINT
```

```
350 PRINT "YOU ARE ";S;" DAYS OLD"
360 PRINT
370 PRINT"YOUR BIORHYTHM PROFILE IS:"
380 P=INT(23*(S/23-INT(S/23))+.5)
390 PRINT TAB(5),"PHYSICAL = ";P
400 T = INT(28*(S/28-INT(S/28))+.5)
410 PRINT TAB(5),"EMOTIONAL = ";T
420 E = INT(33*(S/33-INT(S/33))+.5)
430 PRINT TAB(5),"INTELLECTUAL = ";E
440 PRINT
450 PRINT"THE FOLLOWING IS A GRAPH OF YOUR BIORHYTHM. "
460 PRINT"PRESS ENTER TO SCROLL ONE DAY AT A TIME.   PRESS"
470 PRINTCHR$(34);"[";CHR$(34);" TO SEE THE NEXT 12 DAYS. "
480 PRINT"TYPE ";CHR$(34);"X";CHR$(34);" TO STOP. "
490 FOR N = 1 TO 3
500 NEXT N
510 GOSUB 640
520 A$=INKEY$:IF A$="" THEN 520
530 IF A$=CHR$(13) THEN 560
540 IF A$="[" THEN GOSUB 670:GOTO 520
550 IF A$="X" THEN 1070 ELSE GOTO 520
560 REM PRINT 13 LINES
570 GOSUB 600
580 PRINT@960,;
590 GOTO 520
600 REM PRINT A LINE
610 GOSUB 710
620 PRINT@0,"P = PHYSICAL   I = INTELLECTUAL     E = EMOTIONAL"
630 RETURN
640 CLS
650 GOSUB 620
660 PRINT
670 FOR II=1 TO 13
680 GOSUB 710
690 NEXT II
700 RETURN
710 PRINT M$(M1);D1;TAB(9);
720 D1=D1+1
730 IF D1 > A(M1) THEN D1 = 1:M1=M1+1
740 IF M1 > 12 THEN M1=1
750 FOR I=1 TO 51
760 X$(I)=" "
```

207

```
770 NEXT I
780 X$(26)="!"
790 I1=INT(SIN(P/23*QQ)*25)+26
800 I2=INT(SIN(T/28*QQ)*25)+26
810 I3=INT(SIN(E/33*QQ)*25)+26
820 X$(I1)="P"
830 X$(I2)="E"
840 X$(I3)="I"
850 IF I1=I2 OR I1=I3 THEN X$(I1)="*"
860 IF I2=I3 THEN X$(I2)="*"
870 FOR I=1 TO 51
880 PRINT X$(I);
890 NEXT I
900 P=P+1:IF P = 23 THEN P=0
910 E=E+1:IF E = 33 THEN E=0
920 T=T+1:IF T = 28 THEN T=0
930 PRINT
940 RETURN
950 DATA 31,JAN
960 DATA 28,FEB
970 DATA 31,MAR
980 DATA 30,APR
990 DATA 31,MAY
1000 DATA 30,JUN
1010 DATA 31,JUL
1020 DATA 31,AUG
1030 DATA 30,SEP
1040 DATA 31,OCT
1050 DATA 30,NOV
1060 DATA 31,DEC
1070 END
```

LEAP FROG

Program Listing

```
10 REM THIS IS THE GAME OF LEAP FROG
20 REM THERE ARE 5 GREEN FROGS LABELLED
30 REM WITH G'S AND 5 BROWN FROGS
40 REM LABELLED WITH B'S
50 REM THERE IS A SINGLE SPACE LEFT OVER
60 REM AND IT IS IN THE MIDDLE BETWEEN
70 REM THE GREEN AND BROWN FROGS
80 REM TO WIN YOU MUST MOVE ALL THE
90 REM GREEN FROGS TO THE RIGHT SIDE AND ALL
100 REM THE BROWN FROGS TO THE LEFT
110 REM SET UP DIM FOR FROGS
120 DIM A$(12)
130 REM SET UP COUNTER
140 C=0
150 FOR I=1TO5:A$(I)="G":NEXT
160 FOR I=7TO11:A$(I)="B":NEXT
170 A$(6)=" "
180 CLS:PRINT:PRINT
190 PRINT"THE GAME OF LEAP FROG"
200 PRINT"---------------------"
210 PRINT:PRINT
220 PRINT"OUR GAME STARTS OFF AS:"
230 PRINT:PRINT"GGGGG";CHR$(95);"BBBBB"
240 PRINT:PRINT"TO WIN, YOU MUST END WITH:"
250 PRINT:PRINT"BBBBB";CHR$(95);"GGGGG"
260 PRINT:PRINT"NOTE THAT THE '";CHR$(95);"' IS THE EMPTY SPACE."
270 PRINT:PRINT"WHAT IS YOUR MOVE (START,END)";
280 INPUT S,E
290 IF ABS(S-E)>2 THEN PRINT"SORRY, YOUR LEAP IS TOO SMALL":GOTO270
300 IF A$(S)=" "THEN 320
310 IF A$(E) <> " " THEN 350 ELSE GOTO 370
320 PRINT:PRINT"HEY, YOU CANNOT START YOUR LEAP WITHOUT"
330 PRINT"A FROG, YOU HAVE GIVEN THE LOCATION OF THE"
340 PRINT"SPACE":GOTO 270
350 PRINT:PRINT"HEY, YOU MUST END YOUR LEAP ON A SPACE. "
360 PRINT"YOU HAVE GIVEN ME THE LOCATION OF A FROG. ":GOTO270
370 A$(E)=A$(S):A$(S)=" "
380 D$=""
```

```
390 FOR I=1 TO 11
400 B$=A$(I)
410 IF B$=" " THEN B$=CHR$(95)
420 D$=D$+B$
430 NEXT
440 PRINT:PRINT"THE CURRENT PATTERN OF FROGS IS:"
450 PRINTD$
460 C=C+1
470 IF LEFT$(D$,5)="BBBBB" AND RIGHT$(D$,5)="GGGGG" THEN 490
480 GOTO 270
490 PRINT:PRINT"YOU HAVE DONE IT, IN ONLY";C;"MOVES"
500 PRINT:PRINT"DO YOU WANT TO TRY AGAIN";:INPUT I$
510 IF LEFT$(I$,1)="Y" THEN 140
520 END
```

COMPUTERIZED HANGMAN

This program was rewritten from the original program to include a graphics display of the gallows and a piece by piece assembly of a body as shown in Fig. 2-1. Also, 50 vocabulary words are included.

Pressing ENTER in response to "PICK A LETTER" will allow you to guess at the whole word. No penalty for a wrong guess. When you pick a wrong letter, it's recorded at the bottom of the display.

PICK A LETTER?

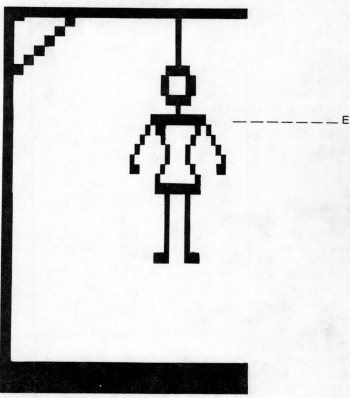

– – – – – – – E

LETTERS GUESSED—X, Y, Z

Fig. 2-1—As the Hangman game progresses, the body is assembled on the TRS-80 video display.

Program Listing

```
10 RANDOM
20 DIM W$(50),W(50)
30 DIM G$(20)
40 REM GET WORDS
50 FOR I=1 TO 50:READ W$(I):W(I)=0:NEXT
60 REM DRAW GALLOWS
70 CLS
80 FOR X=6 TO 53
90 SET(X,6):SET(X,42):SET(X,43):SET(X,44)
100 NEXT
110 FOR Y=7 TO 41
120 SET(6,Y):SET(7,Y)
130 NEXT
140 Y=12:FOR X=8 TO 18 STEP 2
150 SET(X,Y):SET(X+1,Y):Y=Y-1
160 NEXT
170 FOR Y=7 TO 11:SET(40,Y):NEXT
180 REM OK NOW PICK A WORD AT RANDOM
190 I=RND(50):IF W(I)<>0 THEN 190
200 W(I)=1:P$=W$(I):P=LEN(P$):P1=0:Q=0
210 REM CLEAR OUT ALREADY GUESSED LETTERS
220 FOR J=1 TO 20:G$(J)="":NEXT:G1=0
230 REM DRAW CHARACTER POSITIONS
240 FOR X=418 TO 418+2*(LEN(P$)-1) STEP 2
250 PRINT@X,CHR$(14);
260 NEXT
270 PRINT@980,"LETTERS GUESSED -";CHR$(15);:L=998
280 A$=" ":PRINT@30,"PICK A LETTER";:INPUT A$
290 IF LEN(A$)>1 THEN PRINT@30,"ONE LETTER AT A TIME, PLEASE";:GOTO 340
300 IF A$<>" " THEN 360
310 PRINT@30,"WHAT IS YOUR GUESS";:INPUT B$
320 IF B$=P$ THEN 890
330 PRINT@94,"SORRY ! WRONG WORD";
340 FOR J=1 TO 1500:NEXT
350 PRINT@30,CHR$(30);:PRINT@94,CHR$(30);:PRINT@158,CHR$(30);:GOTO 280
360 G2=0
370 G2=G2+1:IF G2>G1 THEN 400
380 IF A$=G$(G2) THEN PRINT@94,"ALREADY USED";:GOTO 340
390 GOTO 370
400 G$(G1)=A$:G1=G1+1
410 J=0
420 FOR I=1 TO P
430 IF A$ = MID$(P$,I,1) THEN PRINT@418+2*(I-1),A$;:J=J+1
440 NEXT
450 Q=Q+J:IF Q = P THEN 880
```

212

```
460 IF J<>0 THEN 350
470 P1=P1+1
480 IF L=998 THEN PRINT@L,A$; :L=999 ELSE PRINT@L,", ";A$; :L=L+3
490 ON P1 GOTO 500,550,670,710,750,790
500 PRINT@94,"OH! OH! THERE'S YOUR HEAD";
510 FOR X=38 TO 42:SET(X,12):SET(X,15):NEXT
520 SET(37,13):SET(38,13):SET(42,13):SET(43,13)
530 SET(37,14):SET(38,14):SET(42,14):SET(43,14)
540 GOTO 340
550 PRINT@94,"THERE'S YOUR BODY (HUMMM, ";
560 PRINT@158,"PUTTING ON WEIGHT?";
570 SET(40,16)
580 FOR X=36 TO 44:SET(X,17):NEXT
590 SET(36,18):SET(44,18)
600 SET(37,19):SET(43,19)
610 SET(38,20):SET(42,20)
620 SET(38,21):SET(42,21)
630 SET(37,22):SET(43,22)
640 SET(36,23):SET(44,23)
650 FOR X=36 TO 44:SET(X,24):NEXT
660 GOTO 340
670 PRINT@94,"OOPS, THERE GOES THE RIGHT ARM";
680 X=35:FOR Y=17 TO 21:SET(X,Y):X=X-1:NEXT
690 SET(31,22):SET(32,22)
700 GOTO 340
710 PRINT@94,"NOW THE LEFT !!!";
720 X=45:FOR Y=17 TO 21:SET(X,Y):X=X+1:NEXT
730 SET(48,22):SET(49,22)
740 GOTO 340
750 PRINT@94,"YOU'RE IN TROUBLE NOW!";
760 FOR Y=25 TO 31:SET(38,Y):NEXT
770 SET(36,31):SET(37,31)
780 GOTO 340
790 PRINT@94,"GOOD-BYE, CRUEL WORLD!!!";
800 FOR Y=25 TO 31:SET(42,Y):NEXT
810 SET(43,31):SET(44,31)
820 PRINT@158,"THE WORD WAS ";P$:
830 FOR I=1 TO 2000 NEXT
840 CLS:PRINT:PRINT:PRINT"WANT TO TRY AGAIN (YES OR NO)";
850 INPUT C$:IF C$="YES" THEN 60
860 PRINT:PRINT"CHICKEN!":PRINT
870 END
880 FOR I=1 TO 1000:NEXT
890 CLS:PRINT:PRINT:IF P1<2 THEN PRINT"WAY TO GO! THAT WAS EXCELLENT:GOTO 920
900 IF P1<4 THEN PRINT"PRETTY GOOD! YOU'RE DOING WELL":GOTO 920
910 PRINT"THAT WAS CLOSE, BUT YOU GOT IT!"
920 PRINT:PRINT"WOULD YOU LIKE TO TRY YOUR LUCK AGAIN";
```

```
930 GOTO 850                    1180 DATA PURPLE
940 DATA THUMB                  1190 DATA SANITY
950 DATA MUSHROOM               1200 DATA WIDOW
960 DATA AMERICA                1210 DATA TREMENDOUS
970 DATA COMPUTER               1220 DATA FANTASTIC
980 DATA TELEVISION             1230 DATA THOUSAND
990 DATA ATLANTIC               1240 DATA WHEAT
1000 DATA GAMES                 1250 DATA GREASE
1010 DATA HOUSE                 1260 DATA MEADOW
1020 DATA PACIFIC               1270 DATA OSCILLATOR
1030 DATA BOTTOM                1280 DATA CASSETTE
1040 DATA SEVERAL               1290 DATA DICTATE
1050 DATA ORANGE                1300 DATA BLANKET
1060 DATA CREAM                 1310 DATA MARBLE
1070 DATA RECEIVER              1320 DATA PAPER
1080 DATA INTEGRATED            1330 DATA TYPEWRITER
1090 DATA PRETZEL               1340 DATA POSSIBLE
1100 DATA VITAMIN               1350 DATA ATLAS
1110 DATA CONTAINER             1360 DATA LINEAR
1120 DATA DEXTROSE              1370 DATA MICROWAVE
1130 DATA FAMILY                1380 DATA HANGMAN
1140 DATA BASIC                 1390 DATA BLINDFOLD
1150 DATA FUNNY                 1400 DATA GALLOWS
1160 DATA EXTREMELY             1410 DATA PLATFORM
1170 DATA EXECUTE               1420 DATA FINANCIAL
                                1430 DATA SECTION
```

YOUR CHEATING COMPUTER
Program Listing

```
10 CLS:RANDOM
20 REM THIS PROGRAM "LEARNS" HOW TO CHEAT
30 REM TO USE IT JUST TYPE RUN
40 PRINT"THIS PROGRAM LETS YOU BE A DETECTIVE.  IT PICKS A LETTER"
50 PRINT"SEQUENCE WHICH YOU MUST GUESS - ONE LETTER AT A TIME."
60 PRINT:PRINT"TO MAKE THIS GAME VERY DIFFICULT, THE COMPUTER CHEATS"
70 PRINT"ON EACH LETTER, WITH THE CHEATING A FUNCTION OF HOW WELL"
80 PRINT"YOU DID ON THE PREVIOUS TRIES.  OBVIOUSLY, THE FIRST TRY"
90 PRINT"WILL BE HONEST."
100 READ A$
110 DATA ABCDEFGHIJKLMNOPQRSTUVWXYZ
120 DIM G$(10)
130 REM GET A SEQUENCE OF TEN RANDOM LETTERS
140 FOR I=1 TO 10
150 K=RND(26)
160 G$(I)=MID$(A$,K,1)
170 NEXT
180 REM SET UP COUNTER FOR LETTER IN PROGRESS
190 C1=0
200 REM SET UP COUNTER FOR ALL LETTERS
210 C2=0
220 REM SET UP POINTER TO LETTER IN QUESTION
230 L=1
240 REM SET UP PROBABILITY
250 P=1
260 PRINT:PRINT"THE SEQUENCE IS SET UP FOR YOU TRIAL.  THE CHANCES"
270 PRINT"THAT I WON'T CHEAT ARE";P*100;"%"
280 PRINT:PRINT"WHAT IS YOUR GUESS";
290 C1=C1+1
300 C2=C2+1
310 INPUT T$
320 IF LEN(T$)>1 THEN 530
330 IF T$<>G$(L) THEN 450
340 CLS:PRINT:PRINT:PRINT"OKAY - YOU GOT THIS LETTER"
350 PRINT"THE SEQUENCE SO FAR IS ";
360 FOR I=1 TO L
370 PRINTG$(I);
380 NEXT
390 PRINT
400 P=P-P*(1/C1)/15
410 C1=0
```

215

```
420 L=L+1
430 IF L>10 THEN 600
440 GOTO 260
450 P1=RND(0)
460 IF P>P1 THEN 480
470 GOTO 580
480 IF T$>G$(L) THEN 510
490 PRINT"NOPE - YOU ARE TOO LOW"
500 GOTO 280
510 PRINT"NOPE - YOU ARE TOO HIGH"
520 GOTO 280
530 PRINT"ONE LETTER AT A TIME - TURKEY"
540 PRINT"THIS TRY MAKES FURTHER EFFORT WORSE. "
550 IF C1<2 THEN 280
560 C1=C1-1
570 GOTO 280
580 IF T$>G$(L) THEN 490
590 GOTO 510
600 IF C2>150 THEN 720
610 IF C2>100 THEN 700
620 IF C2>80 THEN 680
630 IF C2>60 THEN 660
640 PRINT"DA CHAMPION HAS STRUCK AGIN"
650 GOTO 740
660 PRINT"HEY BOSS - THIS GUY IS CHAMPIONSHIP MATERIAL"
670 GOTO 740
680 PRINT"PRACTICE MAKES PERFECT - KEEP GOING"
690 GOTO 740
700 PRINT"NOT BAD FOR A BEGINNER - BUT LOUSY IF YOU PLAYED BEFORE. "
710 GOTO 740
720 PRINT"HAVE YOU THOUGHT OF PLAYING A SIMPLER GAME - LIKE"
730 PRINT"FIND YOUR FINGER?"
740 PRINT
750 PRINT"NUMBER OF TRIES",C2
760 PRINT"PROBABILITY OF CHEATING ON ALL TRIES";P*100;"%"
770 PRINT:PRINT"THE TOTAL SEQUENCE IS ";
780 FOR I = 1 TO 10
790 PRINTG$(I);
800 NEXT
810 PRINT:PRINT:PRINT:PRINT"TRY AGAIN (YES/NO)";
820 INPUT T$
830 IF T$<>"YES" AND T$<>"NO" THEN 810
840 IF T$="YES" THEN 140
850 END
```

216

AUTO RALLYE

Program Listing

```
10 REM THE CAR RALLY
30 CLS:PRINT:PRINT:PRINT:PRINTTAB(15)"T H E    C A R    R A L L Y"
40 PRINT:PRINT:PRINT"THIS IS THE SUPER CAR RALLY, THAT ALL DRIVERS IN"
50 PRINT"THE WORLD WAIT FOR.  THE DRIVING IS TOUGH THIS YEAR,"
60 PRINT"AND WE ALL WISH YOU 'GOOD LUCK'. "
70 FOR I=1TO1500:NEXT
80 CLS:PRINT:PRINT:PRINTTAB(20)"  CHOICE OF CARS":PRINT
90 PRINTTAB(20)"MINI            (1)"
100 PRINTTAB(20)"LOTUS           (2)"
110 PRINTTAB(20)"TRANS-AM        (3)"
120 PRINTTAB(20)"FERRARI         (4)"
200 PRINT:PRINT:PRINT"REMEMBER - THE BETTER THE CAR, THE MORE GAS IT USES. "
210 PRINT:PRINT"ENTER YOUR CHOICE OF CAR (BY NUMBER)";
230 INPUT C1
240 IF C1>4 OR C1<1 THEN PRINT"INVALID CAR NUMBER, TRY AGAIN";:GOTO230
300 CLS:PRINT:PRINT
310 IF N2=1 THEN 350
320 PRINT"NOW CHOOSE WHICH COURSE YOU WANT TO RACE ON.  THE STRAIGTHEST"
330 PRINT"COURSE IS NUMBER 1 (BUT THIS HAS THE MOST HAZARDS).  NUMBER 5"
340 PRINT"CONSISTS MOSTLY OF TURNS AND TWISTS. ":PRINT
350 PRINT"WHICH COURSE DO YOU WANT (ENTER A NUMBER FROM 1 TO 5)";
360 INPUT C2
370 IF C2>5 OR C2<1 THEN PRINT"INVALID COURSE NUMBER, TRY AGAIN. ";:GOTO 360
420 CLS:PRINT:PRINT
430 IF N2=1 THEN 490
440 PRINT"YOU WILL NEED TO TRAVEL 5 MILES WITH .5 GALLONS OF GAS. "
450 PRINT"YOUR STATUS WILL BE SHOWN AT 10 SECOND INTERVALS.  AFTER"
460 PRINT"EACH STATUS CHECK, YOU WILL BE ASKED FOR A NEW RATE OF GAS. "
470 PRINT"A RATE OF 10 IS HARD ACCELERATION, AND -10 IS HARD BRAKING. "
480 PRINT"ANY NUMBER IN BETWEEN IS ALLOWABLE. "
490 FOR I=1 TO C1:READ B,M,S:B=B/10:NEXT
530 A1=.5:M1=0:C1=C1/2:V=0:Z=0
570 PRINT
580 R1=0:T=0:D=0:Q1=0
620 PRINT"PRESENT VELOCITY = ";TAB(35)V
630 PRINT"GALLONS OF FUEL REMAINING =";TAB(35)A1
640 PRINT"MILES TRAVELED =";TAB(35)M1
650 PRINT"TIME PASSED (SECONDS) =";TAB(35)T
660 PRINT:PRINT"WHAT IS YOU NEW RATE OF GAS";
670 INPUT G
680 IF G<-10 OR G>10 THEN PRINT"NOT VALID - TRY AGAIN";:GOTO670
720 IF G<9 THEN 780
730 Z=Z+1
740 IF Z<=4 THEN 790
760 PRINT:PRINT"DUMMY !!  YOU BLEW YOUR ENGINE !!"
```

```
770 GOTO 1270
780 Z=0
790 V=INT(B*G-M*V+V)
800 T=T+10
810 PRINT
820 PRINT"ROAD CONDITIONS - ";
830 IF V>0 THEN 850
840 V=0
850 M1=M1+V/460
860 IF G<0 THEN 890
870 A1=A1-(G*S)/5000
875 IF M1>=5 THEN 1460
880 IF A1<0 THEN 1380
890 IF R1=1 THEN 1050
900 IF Q1=1 THEN 980
910 Q=INT((C2+1)*RND(X))
920 R=INT((3.75-C2)*RND(X))
930 IF R>0 THEN 1290
940 IF Q>0 THEN 1340
950 PRINT"CLEAR AND STRAIGHT"
960 PRINT
970 GOTO 620
980 H=INT(15+35*RND(X))
990 H=H+5*C1
1000 IF V>H THEN 1500
1010 PRINT"THROUGH CURVE"
1020 PRINT
1030 Q1=0
1040 GOTO 620
1050 E=E-(V-D)*3
1060 IF E<0 THEN 1100
1070 PRINT"VEHICLE ";E;" FEET AHEAD"
1080 PRINT
1090 GOTO 620
1100 IF V-D<5 THEN 1180
1110 PRINT"VEHICLE PASSED BY";
1120 D=V-D
1130 PRINTD;"MPH":PRINT
1160 R1=0
1170 GOTO 620
1180 PRINT"VEHICLE BEING PASSED"
1190 D=RND(40)+25:FOR I=1TO500:NEXTI
1200 PRINT:PRINT"GREYHOUND BUS IN THE OTHER LANE DOING";D;"MPH ! ! !"
1250 PRINT:PRINT"CRASH VELOCITY =";V+D;"! ! !"
1260 FOR I=1TO1500:NEXTI:CLS:PRINTCHR$(23):PRINT@530,"CRASH ! !":FOR
     I=1TO1500:NEXT:CLS:PRINT:PRINT
```

218

```
1270 PRINT"WHAT TYPE OF FLOWERS DO YOU WISH, AT YOUR FUNERAL ??"
1280 GOTO 1560
1290 PRINT"VEHICLE AHEAD 1000 FEET"
1300 PRINT
1310 D=RND(35)*C1+25
1320 R1=1
1330 GOTO 620
1340 PRINT"WARNING: CURVE AHEAD"
1350 Q1=1
1360 PRINT:GOTO 620
1380 PRINT"EXCELLENT - BUT WAIT"
1390 PRINT:FOR I=1TO1000:NEXTI
1400 PRINT"TURKEY !!  YOU RAN OUT OF GAS !!"
1410 GOTO 1550
1420 PRINT"DON'T KNOW HOW, BUT YOU MADE IT !!"
1430 PRINT
1440 R1=0
1450 GOTO 620
1460 PRINT"THE FINISH LINE !!"
1470 PRINT
1480 PRINT"YOU ARE LUCKY THIS YEAR !!"
1490 GOTO 1560
1500 PRINT"ARE TERRIBLE"
1510 H=H-5*C1
1520 PRINTH; "WAS THE SPEED THROUGH THE CURVE. "
1530 PRINTV; "WAS YOUR SPEED.   BY THE WAY, "
1540 GOTO 1270
1550 PRINT"YOU LEAD FOOTED #$%!#$%& (EXPLITIVE DELETED)"
1560 PRINT:PRINT"YOU WANT TO TRY AGAIN, RIGHT !!!!"
1570 PRINT"ENTER 'YES' OR 'NO'";
1580 INPUT A$
1590 IF A$="YES" THEN N2=1:GOTO 1640
1600 PRINT:PRINT"CHICKEN !!"
1610 END
1640 RESTORE
1650 GOTO 210
1660 DATA 45,.53,10
1670 DATA 60,.5,10
1680 DATA 70,.41,15
1690 DATA 80,.39,18
```

OTHER PROGRAMS

The following programs included in Section I will run on a TRS-80 with no modifications: *Guess, Math Whiz Kid Quiz, Comp-U-Story.*

To run the program *Guess Again*, change "SUBSTR" to "MOD$" in lines: 400, 410, and 420.

Appendix A
BASIC Statements

BASIC (Beginners' All-purpose Symbolic Instruction Code) was invented and developed between 1963 and 1964 by John Kemeny and Thomas Kurtz of Dartmouth College. Since its first use in 1964, BASIC has steadily gained popularity as a high-level computer language which the user can easily master. The essential vocabulary is below:

Statement	Example	Definition
CHANGE	CHANGE N$ TO N	assigns to the elements of N the ASCII numeric value of the string N$
DATA	DATA 15, -8, 76,...	the DATA statement assigns appropriate values to the variables listed in the READ statement
DEF	DEF FNR (X, Y) = (X 2 + Y 8)	a single line function is defined by the DEF statement
DIM	DIM Z(3, 4)	dimensions the elements of X as a 3 by 4 matrix
END	END	ends program execution
FNEND	FNEND	a multiline DEF statement must end with a FNEND (function end) statement
FOR-TO	FOR X = 2 TO 66	defines the FOR, NEXT loop
GOTO	GOTO 100	transfers execution to line 100
GOSUB	GOSUB 100	transfers program control to a subroutine commencing at 100
IF-THEN	IF A = X THEN 100	transfers program execution to 100 if the relational test is true

INPUT	INPUT X, Y,...	assigns to the variable(s) the values presented by the user from a user defined device
LET	LET A = V	assigns the value of V to A
NEXT	NEXT X	returns control to the beginning of the FOR-TO loop
ON-GO TO	ON M GO TO 10, 20, 30	as M ranges in values from 1 up to 1st, 2nd,...line number is transferred control, as follows to GO TO statement
PRINT	PRINT "LESLIE"	prints the alphanumeric string within quotation marks
RANDOMIZE	RANDOMIZE	assures each call to the RND produces a different order of random numbers
READ	READ L, K,...	reads values from the DATA statement found in the same program
REM	REM AREA	remark is placed in the program to be used only during listing as a debugging aid
RESTORE	RESTORE	restores the data pointer
RETURN	RETURN	returns program execution to the next instruction following the subroutine call
RND	RND	produced a random number
STOP	STOP	stops program execution

Appendix B
Derived Functions

The following functions which are not typical of standard BASIC library functions may be easily implemented by the following formulae:

ARC SIN(X) = ATN(X/SQR(X*X + 1))
ARC COS(X) = ATN(X/SQR(X*X + 1)) + 1.5708
ARC SEC(X) = ATN(SQR(X*X −1)) + (SGN(X) − 1)*1.5708
ARC CSC(X) = ATN(1/SQR(X*X) − 1)) + (SGN(X) − 1)*1.5708
ARC COT(X) = −ATN(X) + 1.5708
ARC SINH(X) = LOG(X + SQR(X*X + 1))
ARC COSH(X) = LOG(X + SQR(X*X − 1))
ARC TANH(X) = LOG((1 + X)/(1 − X))/2
ARC SECH(X) = LOG((SQR(X*X + 1) + 1)/X)
ARC CSCH(X) = LOG((SGN(X)*SQR(X*X + 1) + 1)/ X)
ARC COTH(X) = LOG((X + 1/(X − 1))/2
COT(X) = 1/TAN(X)
CSC(X) = 1/SIN(X)
SEC(X) = 1/COS(X)
COSH(X) = (EXP(X) + EXP(− X))/2
COTH(X) = EXP(−X)/(EXP(X) − EXP(− X))*2 + 1
CSCH(X) = 2/(EXP(X) − EXP(−X))
SECH(X) = 2/EXP(X) + EXP(−X))
SINH(X) = (EXP(X) − EXP(−X))/2
TANH(X) = −EXP(−X)/(EXP(X) + EXP(−X))*2 + 1

DIAGNOSTICS (COMMON)

READ/RESUME, NO DATA: The user has not provided any DATA statements or data but has used either the READ or RESTORE statements.

FOR, NO NEXT: The user has constructed a FOR-TO loop but has not closed it with a NEXT statement.

UNDIMENSIONED: Variables that were being used as matrices were not dimensioned.

VECTOR + ARRAY: The same variable was used both as a vector and an array.

VALUE OUTSIDE RANGE: A value has exceeded the bounds for that particular function.

GOSUB NESTING: The user has used more levels of GOSUB nesting than the version of BASIC used allows.

RETURN: A RETURN statement was executed before a GOSUB statement.

DIVISION BY ZERO: Division by zero was tried.

INVALID EXPONENT: A**B, where A<0 and B< >INT (B).

LOG(−X): The log of a negative number was specified.

SQR(−X): The square root of a negative number was specified.

OUT OF DATA: The set of DATA elements has been exhausted and a READ statement is executed.

ILLEGAL CONSTANT: A string (numeric) data element is read into a numeric (string) variable.

FUNCTION PREVIOUSLY DEFINED: A user defined function (DEF statement) has been defined more than once in one program.

ARRAY PREVIOUSLY DIMENSIONED: An array or a matrix has been defined more than once in one program.

NO SUCH LINE#: A reference has been made to a nonexistent line number.

FOR NESTING (MAX = X): Where the user has exceeded the maximum of nesting (where X is the maximum for that particular version of BASIC).

NESTING SAME INDEX: Where a user has constructed a nested FOR loop with two or more of the FOR-TO statements using the same running variable (index variable).

WRONG NEXT: The matching NEXT statement must follow the corresponding FOR-TO statement.

ILLEGAL NESTING: FOR-TO loops may be nested, but they must not overlap.

OVERFLOW: A numeric constant exceeds the maximum single-precision floating-point value.

UNDERFLOW: A numeric constant is smaller than the minimum single-precision floating-point value.

MEMORY EXCEEDED: The generated object code exceeds the bounds permitted by the computer and/or the version of BASIC being used.

INCREASE PROGRAM SPEED

1) Use GOSUB sparingly.
2) Minimize GOTOs from one section to another section of the program.
3) Check if FOR-NEXT is faster than or slower than IF-THEN loops.
4) For simple integer multiplication such as 2*K,K+K will be faster.
5) Check whether simple code is faster than or slower than complex expressions.

SAVING SPACE

To conserve space and limit the size of programs the following hints may be implemented.

A) Use multiple statements per line number, if the version of BASIC allows. There is an overhead of about 5 bytes associated with each line in a program.
B) Use integer values whenever possible as opposed to real numbers.
C) Delete all unnecessary spaces from program lines.

EXAMPLE:

```
10    PRINT K, J; L
```

Could be entered as

```
10    PRINTK,J;L
```

D) Use as few REM statements as possible.
E) Use variables rather than constants, when the same constant is required more than a few times.
F) A program that is one loop and is ended by either CTRL C or by running out of data usually does not require an END statement.
G) Re-use variables over and over if possible.
H) Use go-subs instead of repeating lines of code.

SPEED

The following programs may be timed to give an indication of processing speed.

```
10    FOR I = 1 TO 1000
20    LET X = X+1
30    NEXT I
40    PRINT X
50    END
```

Instead of line 20 being LET X = X+1, the user may try 20 LET X = 10*X or 20 LET X = X/10. Multiplication and division are fairly complex software routines. Using the above two replacements will give a fair indication of this type of operation speed.

Appendix C
ASCII Code

Hex Code	Meaning	Comments
00	NUL	null
01	SOH	start of heading
02	STX	start text
03	ETX	end text
04	EOT	end of transmission
05	ENQ	enquiry
06	ACK	acknowledgement
07	BEL	bell
08	BS	back space
09	HT	horizontal tab
0A	LF	line feed
0B	VT	vertical tab
0C	FF	form feed
0D	CR	carriage return
0E	SO	shift out
0F	SI	shift in
10	DLE	data link escape
11	DC1	direct control 1
12	DC2	direct control 2
13	DC3	direct control 3
14	DC4	direct control 4
15	NAK	negative acknowledgement
16	SYN	synchronous idle
17	ETB	end of transmission block
18	CAN	cancel
19	EM	end of medium
1A	SUB	substitute
1B	ESC	escape
1C	FS	form separator
1D	GS	group separator
1E	RS	record separator
1F	US	unit separator
20	(special)	–
21	!	–
22	"	–

ASCII

Hex Code	Meaning	Comments
23	#	—
24	$	—
25	%	—
26	&	—
27	'	—
28	(	—
29	)	—
2A	*	—
2B	+	—
2C	,	—
2D	-	—
2E	.	—
2F	/	—
30	0	—
31	1	—
32	2	—
33	3	—
34	4	—
35	5	—
36	6	—
37	7	—
38	8	—
39	9	—
3A	:	—
3B	;	—
3C	>	—
3D	=	—
3E	<	—
3F	?	—
40	@	—
41	A	—
42	B	—
43	C	—
44	D	—
45	E	—
46	F	—
47	G	—
48	H	—
49	I	—
4A	J	—
4B	K	—
4C	L	—
4D	M	—
4E	N	—
4F	O	—
50	P	—
51	Q	—
52	R	—
53	S	—
54	T	—
55	U	—
56	V	—
57	W	—
58	X	—
59	Y	—
5A	Z	—
5B	[	—
5C	\	—

ASCII

Hex Code	Meaning	Comments
5D	]	–
5E	^	–
5F	_	–
60	`	–
61	a	–
62	b	–
63	c	–
64	d	–
65	e	–
66	f	–
67	g	–
68	h	–
69	i	–
6A	j	–
6B	k	–
6C	l	–
6D	m	–
6E	n	–
6F	o	–
70	p	–
71	q	–
72	r	–
73	s	–
74	t	–
75	u	–
76	v	–
77	w	–
78	x	–
79	y	–
7A	z	–
7B	{	–
7C			–
7D	}	–
7E	~	–
7F	DEL	–

Appendix C
Hexadecimal-Decimal Integer Conversion

The following table provides for direct conversions between hexadecimal integers in the range 0—FFF and decimal integers in the range 0—4095. For conversion of larger integers, the table values may be added to the following figures:

Hexadecimal	Decimal	Hexadecimal	Decimal
01 000	4 096	20 000	131 072
02 000	8 192	30 000	196 608
03 000	12 288	40 000	262 144
04 000	16 384	50 000	327 680
05 000	20 480	60 000	393 216
06 000	24 576	70 000	458 752
07 000	28 672	80 000	524 288
08 000	32 768	90 000	589 824
09 000	36 864	A0 000	655 360
0A 000	40 960	B0 000	720 896
0B 000	45 056	C0 000	786 432
0C 000	49 152	D0 000	851 968
0D 000	53 248	E0 000	917 504
0E 000	57 344	F0 000	983 040
0F 000	61 440	100 000	1 048 576
10 000	65 536	200 000	2 097 152
11 000	69 632	300 000	3 145 728
12 000	73 728	400 000	4 194 304
13 000	77 824	500 000	5 242 880
14 000	81 920	600 000	6 291 456
15 000	86 016	700 000	7 340 032
16 000	90 112	800 000	8 388 608
17 000	94 208	900 000	9 437 184
18 000	98 304	A00 000	10 485 760
19 000	102 400	B00 000	11 534 336
1A 000	106 496	C00 000	12 582 912
1B 000	110 592	D00 000	13 631 488
1C 000	114 688	E00 000	14 680 064
1D 000	118 784	F00 000	15 728 640
1E 000	122 880	1 000 000	16 777 216
1F 000	126 976	2 000 000	·33 554 432

	0	1	2	3	4	5	6	7	8	9	A	B	C	D	E	F
000	0000	0001	0002	0003	0004	0005	0006	0007	0008	0009	0010	0011	0012	0013	0014	0015
010	0016	0017	0018	0019	0020	0021	0022	0023	0024	0025	0026	0027	0028	0029	0030	0031
020	0032	0033	0034	0035	0036	0037	0038	0039	0040	0041	0042	0043	0044	0045	0046	0047
030	0048	0049	0050	0051	0052	0053	0054	0055	0056	0057	0058	0059	0060	0061	0062	0063
040	0064	0065	0066	0067	0068	0069	0070	0071	0072	0073	0074	0075	0076	0077	0078	0079
050	0080	0081	0082	0083	0084	0085	0086	0087	0088	0089	0090	0091	0092	0093	0094	0095
060	0096	0097	0098	0099	0100	0101	0102	0103	0104	0105	0106	0107	0108	0109	0110	0111
070	0112	0113	0114	0115	0116	0117	0118	0119	0120	0121	0122	0123	0124	0125	0126	0127
080	0128	0129	0130	0131	0132	0133	0134	0135	0136	0137	0138	0139	0140	0141	0142	0143
090	0144	0145	0146	0147	0148	0149	0150	0151	0152	0153	0154	0155	0156	0157	0158	0159
0A0	0160	0161	0162	0163	0164	0165	0166	0167	0168	0169	0170	0171	0172	0173	0174	0175
0B0	0176	0177	0178	0179	0180	0181	0182	0183	0184	0185	0186	0187	0188	0189	0190	0191
0C0	0192	0193	0194	0195	0196	0197	0198	0199	0200	0201	0202	0203	0204	0205	0206	0207
0D0	0208	0209	0210	0211	0212	0213	0214	0215	0216	0217	0218	0219	0220	0221	0222	0223
0E0	0224	0225	0226	0227	0228	0229	0230	0231	0232	0233	0234	0235	0236	0237	0238	0239
0F0	0240	0241	0242	0243	0244	0245	0246	0247	0248	0249	0250	0251	0252	0253	0254	0255

HEXADECIMAL-DECIMAL INTEGER CONVERSION (continued)

	0	1	2	3	4	5	6	7	8	9	A	B	C	D	E	F
100	0256	0257	0258	0259	0260	0261	0262	0263	0264	0265	0266	0267	0268	0269	0270	0271
110	0272	0273	0274	0275	0276	0277	0278	0279	0280	0281	0282	0283	0284	0285	0286	0287
120	0288	0289	0290	0291	0292	0293	0294	0295	0276	0297	0298	0299	0300	0301	0302	0303
130	0304	0305	0306	0307	0308	0309	0310	0311	0312	0313	0314	0315	0316	0317	0318	0319
140	0320	0321	0322	0323	0324	0325	0326	0327	0328	0329	0330	0331	0332	0333	0334	0335
150	0336	0337	0338	0339	0340	0341	0342	0343	0344	0345	0346	0347	0348	0349	0350	0351
160	0352	0353	0354	0355	0356	0357	0358	0359	0360	0361	0362	0363	0364	0365	0366	0367
170	0368	0369	0370	0371	0372	0373	0374	0375	0376	0377	0378	0379	0380	0381	0382	0383
180	0384	0385	0386	0387	0388	0389	0390	0391	0392	0393	0394	0395	0396	0397	0396	0399
190	0400	0401	0402	0403	0404	0405	0406	0407	0408	0409	0410	0411	0412	0413	0414	0415
1A0	0416	0417	0418	0419	0420	0421	0422	0423	0424	0425	0426	0427	0428	0429	0430	0431
1B0	0432	0433	0434	0435	0436	0437	0438	0439	0440	0441	0442	0443	0444	0445	0446	0447
1C0	0448	0449	0450	0451	0452	0453	0454	0455	0456	0457	0458	0459	0460	0461	0462	0463
1D0	0464	0465	0466	0467	0468	0469	0470	0471	0472	0473	0474	0475	0476	0477	0478	0479
1E0	0480	0481	0482	0483	0484	0485	0486	0487	0488	0489	0490	0491	0492	0493	0494	0495
1F0	0496	0497	0498	0499	0500	0501	0502	0503	0504	0505	0506	0507	0508	0509	0510	0511
200	0512	0513	0514	0515	0516	0517	0518	0519	0520	0521	0522	0523	0524	0525	0526	0527
210	0528	0529	0530	0531	0532	0533	0534	0535	0536	0537	0538	0539	0540	0541	0542	0543
220	0544	0545	0546	0547	0548	0549	0550	0551	0552	0553	0554	0555	0556	0557	0558	0559
230	0560	0561	0562	0563	0564	0565	0566	0567	0568	0569	0570	0571	0572	0573	0574	0575
240	0576	0577	0578	0579	0580	0581	0582	0583	0584	0585	0586	0587	0588	0589	0590	0591
250	0592	0593	0594	0595	0596	0597	0598	0599	0600	0601	0602	0603	0604	0605	0606	0607
260	0608	0609	0610	0611	0612	0613	0614	0615	0616	0617	0618	0619	0620	0621	0622	0623
270	0624	0625	0628	0627	0628	0629	0630	0631	0632	0633	0634	0635	0636	0637	0638	0639

	0640	0641	0642	0643	0644	0645	0646	0647	0648	0649	0650	0651	0652	0653	0654	0655
280	0640	0641	0642	0643	0644	0645	0646	0647	0648	0649	0650	0651	0652	0653	0654	0655
290	0656	0657	0658	0659	0660	0661	0662	0663	0664	0665	0666	0667	0668	0669	0670	0671
2A0	0672	0673	0674	0675	0676	0677	0678	0679	0680	0681	0682	0683	0684	0685	0686	0687
2B0	0688	0689	0690	0691	0692	0693	0694	0695	0696	0697	0698	0699	0700	0701	0702	0703
2C0	0704	0705	0706	0707	0708	0709	0710	0711	0712	0713	0714	0715	0716	0717	0718	0719
2D0	0720	0721	0722	0723	0724	0725	0726	0727	0728	0729	0730	0731	0732	0733	0734	0735
2E0	0736	0737	0738	0739	0740	0741	0742	0743	0744	0745	0746	0747	0748	0749	0750	0751
2F0	0752	0753	0754	0755	0756	0757	0758	0759	0760	0761	0762	0763	0764	0765	0766	0767
300	0768	0769	0770	0771	0772	0773	0774	0775	0776	0777	0778	0779	0780	0781	0782	0783
310	0784	0785	0786	0787	0788	0789	0790	0791	0792	0793	0794	0795	0796	0797	0798	0799
320	0800	0801	0802	0803	0804	0805	0806	0807	0808	0809	0810	0811	0812	0813	0814	0815
330	0816	0817	0818	0819	0820	0821	0822	0823	0824	0825	0826	0827	0828	0829	0830	0831
340	0832	0833	0834	0835	0836	0837	0838	0839	0840	0841	0842	0843	0844	0845	0846	0847
350	0848	0849	0850	0851	0852	0853	0854	0855	0856	0857	0858	0859	0860	0861	0862	0863
360	0864	0865	0866	0867	0868	0869	0870	0871	0872	0873	0874	0875	0876	0877	0878	0879
370	0880	0881	0882	0883	0884	0885	0886	0887	0888	0889	0890	0891	0892	0893	0894	0895
380	0896	0897	0898	0899	0900	0901	0902	0903	0904	0905	0906	0907	0908	0909	0910	0911
390	0912	0913	0914	0915	0916	0917	0918	0919	0920	0921	0922	0923	0924	0925	0926	0927
3A0	0928	0929	0930	0931	0932	0933	0934	0935	0936	0937	0938	0939	0940	0941	0942	0943
3B0	0944	0945	0946	0947	0948	0949	0950	0951	0952	0953	0954	0955	0956	0957	0958	0959
3C0	0960	0961	0962	0963	0964	0965	0966	0967	0968	0969	0970	0971	0972	0973	0974	0975
3D0	0976	0977	0978	0979	0980	0981	0982	0983	0984	0985	0986	0987	0988	0989	0990	0991
3E0	0992	0993	0994	0995	0996	0997	0998	0999	1000	1001	1002	1003	1004	1005	1006	1007
3F0	1008	1009	1010	1011	1012	1013	1014	1015	1016	1017	1018	1019	1020	1021	1022	1023

HEXADECIMAL-DECIMAL INTEGER CONVERSION (continued)

	0	1	2	3	4	5	6	7	8	9	A	B	C	D	E	F
400	1024	1025	1026	1027	1028	1029	1030	1031	1032	1033	1034	1035	1036	1037	1038	1039
410	1040	1041	1042	1043	1044	1045	1046	1047	1048	1049	1050	1051	1052	1053	1054	1055
420	1056	1057	1058	1059	1060	1061	1062	1063	1064	1065	1066	1067	1068	1069	1070	1071
430	1072	1073	1074	1075	1076	1077	1078	1079	1080	1081	1082	1083	1084	1085	1086	1087
440	1088	1089	1090	1091	1092	1093	1094	1095	1096	1097	1098	1099	1100	1101	1102	1103
450	1104	1105	1106	1107	1108	1109	1110	1111	1112	1113	1114	1115	1116	1117	1118	1119
460	1120	1121	1122	1123	1124	1125	1126	1127	1128	1129	1130	1131	1132	1133	1134	1135
470	1136	1137	1138	1139	1140	1141	1142	1143	1144	1145	1146	1147	1148	1149	1150	1151
480	1152	1153	1154	1155	1156	1157	1158	1159	1160	1161	1162	1163	1164	1165	1166	1167
490	1168	1169	1170	1171	1172	1173	1174	1175	1176	1177	1178	1179	1180	1181	1182	1183
4A0	1184	1185	1186	1187	1188	1189	1190	1191	1192	1193	1194	1195	1196	1197	1198	1199
4B0	1200	1201	1202	1203	1204	1205	1206	1207	1208	1209	1210	1211	1212	1213	1214	1215
4C0	1216	1217	1218	1219	1220	1221	1222	1223	1224	1225	1226	1227	1228	1229	1230	1231
4D0	1232	1233	1234	1235	1236	1237	1238	1239	1240	1241	1242	1243	1244	1245	1246	1247
4E0	1248	1249	1250	1251	1252	1253	1254	1255	1256	1257	1258	1259	1260	1261	1262	1263
4F0	1264	1265	1266	1267	1268	1269	1270	1271	1272	1273	1274	1275	1276	1277	1278	1279
500	1280	1281	1282	1283	1284	1285	1286	1287	1288	1289	1290	1291	1292	1293	1294	1295
510	1296	1297	1298	1299	1300	1301	1302	1303	1304	1305	1306	1307	1308	1309	1310	1311
520	1312	1313	1314	1315	1316	1317	1318	1319	1320	1321	1322	1323	1324	1325	1326	1327
530	1328	1329	1330	1331	1332	1333	1334	1335	1336	1337	1338	1339	1340	1341	1342	1343
540	1344	1345	1346	1347	1348	1349	1350	1351	1352	1353	1354	1355	1356	1357	1358	1359
550	1360	1361	1362	1363	1364	1365	1366	1367	1368	1369	1370	1371	1372	1373	1374	1375
560	1376	1377	1378	1379	1380	1381	1382	1383	1384	1385	1386	1387	1388	1389	1390	1391
570	1392	1393	1394	1395	1396	1397	1398	1399	1400	1401	1402	1403	1404	1405	1406	1407

	1408	1409	1410	1411	1412	1413	1414	1415	1416	1417	1418	1419	1420	1421	1422	1423
580	1408	1409	1410	1411	1412	1413	1414	1415	1416	1417	1418	1419	1420	1421	1422	1423
590	1424	1425	1426	1427	1428	1429	1430	1431	1432	1433	1434	1435	1436	1437	1438	1439
5A0	1440	1441	1442	1443	1444	1445	1446	1447	1448	1449	1450	1451	1452	1453	1454	1455
5B0	1456	1457	1458	1459	1460	1461	1462	1463	1464	1465	1466	1467	1468	1469	1470	1471
5C0	1472	1473	1474	1475	1476	1477	1478	1479	1480	1481	1482	1483	1484	1485	1486	1487
5D0	1488	1489	1490	1491	1492	1493	1494	1495	1496	1497	1498	1499	1500	1501	1502	1503
5E0	1504	1505	1506	1507	1508	1509	1510	1511	1512	1513	1514	1515	1516	1517	1518	1519
5F0	1520	1521	1522	1523	1524	1525	1526	1527	1528	1529	1530	1531	1532	1533	1534	1535
600	1536	1537	1538	1539	1540	1541	1542	1543	1544	1545	1546	1547	1548	1549	1550	1551
610	1552	1553	1554	1555	1556	1557	1558	1559	1560	1561	1562	1563	1564	1565	1566	1567
620	1568	1569	1570	1571	1572	1573	1574	1575	1576	1577	1578	1579	1580	1581	1582	1583
630	1584	1585	1586	1587	1588	1589	1590	1591	1592	1593	1594	1595	1596	1597	1598	1599
640	1600	1601	1602	1603	1604	1605	1606	1607	1608	1609	1610	1611	1612	1613	1614	1615
650	1616	1617	1618	1619	1620	1621	1622	1623	1624	1625	1626	1627	1628	1629	1630	1631
660	1632	1633	1634	1635	1636	1637	1638	1639	1640	1641	1642	1643	1644	1645	1646	1647
670	1648	1649	1650	1651	1652	1653	1654	1655	1656	1657	1658	1659	1660	1661	1662	1663
680	1664	1665	1666	1667	1668	1669	1670	1671	1672	1673	1674	1675	1676	1677	1678	1679
690	1680	1681	1682	1683	1684	1685	1686	1687	1688	1689	1690	1691	1692	1693	1694	1695
6A0	1696	1697	1698	1699	1700	1701	1702	1703	1704	1705	1706	1707	1708	1709	1710	1711
6B0	1712	1713	1714	1715	1716	1717	1718	1719	1720	1721	1722	1723	1724	1725	1726	1727
6C0	1728	1729	1730	1731	1732	1733	1734	1735	1736	1737	1738	1739	1740	1741	1742	1743
6D0	1744	1745	1746	1747	1748	1749	1750	1751	1752	1753	1754	1755	1756	1757	1758	1759
6E0	1760	1761	1762	1763	1764	1765	1766	1767	1768	1769	1770	1771	1772	1773	1774	1775
6F0	1776	1777	1778	1779	1780	1781	1782	1783	1784	1785	1786	1787	1788	1789	1790	1791

HEXADECIMAL-DECIMAL INTEGER CONVERSION (continued)

	0	1	2	3	4	5	6	7	8	9	A	B	C	D	E	F
700	1792	1793	1794	1795	1796	1797	1798	1799	1800	1801	1802	1803	1804	1805	1806	1807
710	1808	1809	1810	1811	1812	1813	1814	1815	1816	1817	1818	1819	1820	1821	1822	1823
720	1824	1825	1826	1827	1828	1829	1830	1831	1832	1833	1834	1835	1836	1837	1838	1839
730	1840	1841	1842	1843	1844	1845	1846	1847	1848	1849	1850	1851	1852	1853	1854	1855
740	1856	1857	1858	1859	1860	1861	1862	1863	1864	1865	1866	1867	1868	1869	1870	1871
750	1872	1873	1874	1875	1876	1877	1878	1879	1880	1881	1882	1883	1884	1885	1886	1887
760	1888	1889	1890	1891	1892	1893	1894	1895	1896	1897	1898	1899	1900	1901	1902	1903
770	1904	1905	1906	1907	1908	1909	1910	1911	1912	1913	1914	1915	1916	1917	1918	1919
780	1920	1921	1922	1923	1924	1925	1926	1927	1928	1929	1930	1931	1932	1933	1934	1935
790	1936	1937	1938	1939	1940	1941	1942	1943	1944	1945	1946	1947	1948	1949	1950	1951
7A0	1952	1953	1954	1955	1956	1957	1958	1959	1960	1961	1962	1963	1964	1965	1966	1967
7B0	1968	1969	1970	1971	1972	1973	1974	1975	1976	1977	1978	1979	1980	1981	1982	1983
7C0	1984	1985	1986	1987	1988	1989	1990	1991	1992	1993	1994	1995	1996	1997	1998	1999
7D0	2000	2001	2002	2003	2004	2005	2006	2007	2008	2009	2010	2011	2012	2013	2014	2015
7E0	2016	2017	2018	2019	2020	2021	2022	2023	2024	2025	2026	2027	2028	2029	2030	2031
7F0	2032	2033	2034	2035	2036	2037	2038	2039	2040	2041	2042	2043	2044	2045	2046	2047
800	2048	2049	2050	2051	2052	2053	2054	2055	2056	2057	2058	2059	2060	2061	2062	2063
810	2064	2065	2066	2067	2068	2069	2070	2071	2072	2073	2074	2075	2076	2077	2078	2079
820	2080	2081	2082	2083	2084	2085	2086	2087	2088	2089	2090	2091	2092	2093	2094	2095
830	2096	2097	2098	2099	2100	2101	2102	2103	2104	2105	2106	2107	2108	2109	2110	2111
840	2112	2113	2114	2115	2116	2117	2118	2119	2120	2121	2122	2123	2124	2125	2126	2127
850	2128	2129	2130	2131	2132	2133	2134	2135	2136	2137	2138	2139	2140	2141	2142	2143
860	2144	2145	2146	2147	2148	2149	2150	2151	2152	2153	2154	2155	2156	2157	2158	2159
870	2160	2161	2162	2163	2164	2165	2166	2167	2168	2169	2170	2171	2172	2173	2174	2175

	2176	2177	2178	2179	2180	2181	2182	2183	2184	2185	2186	2187	2188	2189	2190	2191
880	2176	2177	2178	2179	2180	2181	2182	2183	2184	2185	2186	2187	2188	2189	2190	2191
890	2192	2193	2194	2195	2196	2197	2198	2199	2200	2201	2202	2203	2204	2205	2206	2207
8A0	2208	2209	2210	2211	2212	2213	2214	2215	2216	2217	2218	2219	2220	2221	2222	2223
8B0	2224	2225	2226	2227	2228	2229	2230	2231	2232	2233	2234	2235	2236	2237	2238	2239
8C0	2240	2241	2242	2243	2244	2245	2246	2247	2248	2249	2250	2251	2252	2253	2254	2255
8D0	2256	2257	2258	2259	2260	2261	2262	2263	2264	2265	2266	2267	2268	2269	2270	2271
8E0	2272	2273	2274	2275	2276	2277	2278	2279	2280	2281	2282	2283	2284	2285	2286	2287
8F0	2288	2289	2290	2291	2292	2293	2294	2295	2296	2297	2298	2299	2300	2301	2302	2303
900	2304	2305	2306	2307	2308	2309	2310	2311	2312	2313	2314	2315	2316	2317	2318	2319
910	2320	2321	2322	2323	2324	2325	2326	2327	2328	2329	2330	2331	2332	2333	2334	2335
920	2336	2337	2338	2339	2340	2341	2342	2343	2344	2345	2346	2347	2348	2349	2350	2351
930	2352	2353	2354	2355	2356	2357	2358	2359	2360	2361	2362	2363	2364	2365	2366	2367
940	2368	2369	2370	2371	2372	2373	2374	2375	2376	2377	2378	2379	2380	2381	2382	2383
950	2384	2385	2386	2387	2388	2389	2390	2391	2392	2393	2394	2395	2396	2397	2398	2399
960	2400	2401	2402	2403	2404	2405	2406	2407	2408	2409	2410	2411	2412	2413	2414	2415
970	2416	2417	2418	2419	2420	2421	2422	2423	2424	2425	2426	2427	2428	2429	2430	2431
980	2432	2433	2434	2435	2436	2437	2438	2439	2440	2441	2442	2443	2444	2445	2446	2447
990	2448	2449	2450	2451	2452	2453	2454	2455	2456	2457	2458	2459	2460	2461	2462	2463
9A0	2464	2465	2466	2467	2468	2469	2470	2471	2472	2473	2474	2475	2476	2477	2478	2479
9B0	2480	2481	2482	2483	2484	2485	2486	2487	2488	2489	2490	2491	2492	2493	2494	2495
9C0	2496	2497	2498	2499	2500	2501	2502	2503	2504	2505	2506	2507	2508	2509	2510	2511
9D0	2512	2513	2514	2515	2516	2517	2518	2519	2520	2521	2522	2523	2524	2525	2526	2527
9E0	2528	2529	2530	2531	2532	2533	2534	2535	2536	2537	2538	2539	2540	2541	2542	2543
9F0	2544	2545	2546	2547	2548	2549	2550	2551	2552	2553	2554	2555	2556	2557	2558	2559

HEXADECIMAL-DECIMAL INTEGER CONVERSION (continued)

	0	1	2	3	4	5	6	7	8	9	A	B	C	D	E	F
A00	2560	2561	2562	2563	2564	2565	2566	2567	2568	2569	2570	2571	2572	2573	2574	2575
A10	2576	2577	2578	2579	2580	2581	2582	2583	2584	2585	2586	2587	2588	2589	2590	2591
A20	2592	2593	2594	2595	2596	2597	2598	2599	2600	2601	2602	2603	2604	2605	2606	2607
A30	2608	2609	2610	2611	2612	2613	2614	2615	2616	2617	2618	2619	2620	2621	2622	2623
A40	2624	2625	2626	2627	2628	2629	2630	2631	2632	2633	2634	2635	2636	2637	2638	2639
A50	2640	2641	2642	2643	2644	2645	2646	2647	2648	2649	2650	2651	2652	2653	2654	2655
A60	2656	2657	2658	2659	2660	2661	2662	2663	2664	2665	2666	2667	2668	2669	2670	2671
A70	2672	2673	2674	2675	2676	2677	2678	2679	2680	2681	2682	2683	2684	2685	2686	2687
A80	2688	2689	2690	2691	2692	2693	2694	2695	2696	2697	2698	2699	2700	2701	2702	2703
A90	2704	2705	2706	2707	2708	2709	2710	2711	2712	2713	2714	2715	2716	2717	2718	2719
AA0	2720	2721	2722	2723	2724	2725	2726	2727	2728	2729	2730	2731	2732	2733	2734	2735
AB0	2736	2737	2738	2739	2740	2741	2742	2743	2744	2745	2746	2747	2748	2749	2750	2751
AC0	2752	2753	2754	2755	2756	2757	2758	2759	2760	2761	2762	2763	2764	2765	2766	2767
AD0	2768	2769	2770	2771	2772	2773	2774	2775	2776	2777	2778	2779	2780	2781	2782	2783
AE0	2784	2785	2786	2787	2788	2789	2790	2791	2792	2793	2794	2795	2796	2797	2798	2799
AF0	2800	2801	2802	2803	2804	2805	2806	2807	2808	2809	2810	2811	2812	2813	2814	2815
B00	2816	2817	2818	2819	2820	2821	2822	2823	2824	2825	2826	2827	2828	2829	2830	2831
B10	2832	2833	2834	2835	2836	2837	2838	2839	2840	2841	2842	2843	2844	2845	2846	2847
B20	2848	2849	2850	2851	2852	2853	2854	2855	2856	2857	2858	2859	2860	2861	2862	2863
B30	2864	2865	2866	2867	2868	2869	2870	2871	2872	2873	2874	2875	2876	2877	2878	2879
B40	2880	2881	2882	2883	2884	2885	2886	2887	2888	2889	2890	2891	2892	2893	2894	2895
B50	2896	2897	2898	2899	2900	2901	2902	2903	2904	2905	2906	2907	2908	2909	2910	2911
B60	2912	2913	2914	2915	2916	2917	2918	2919	2920	2921	2922	2923	2924	2925	2926	2927
B70	2928	2929	2930	2931	2932	2933	2934	2935	2936	2937	2938	2939	2940	2941	2942	2943

	2944	2945	2946	2947	2948	2949	2950	2951	2952	2953	2954	2955	2956	2957	2958	2959
B80	2944	2945	2946	2947	2948	2949	2950	2951	2952	2953	2954	2955	2956	2957	2958	2959
B90	2960	2961	2962	2963	2964	2965	2966	2967	2968	2969	2970	2971	2972	2973	2974	2975
BA0	2976	2977	2978	2979	2980	2981	2982	2983	2984	2985	2986	2987	2988	2989	2990	2991
BB0	2992	2993	2994	2995	2996	2997	2998	2999	3000	3001	3002	3003	3004	3005	3006	3007
BC0	3008	3009	3010	3011	3012	3013	3014	3015	3016	3017	3018	3019	3020	3021	3022	3023
BD0	3024	3025	3026	3027	3028	3029	3030	3031	3032	3033	3034	3035	3036	3037	3038	3039
BE0	3040	3041	3042	3043	3044	3045	3046	3047	3048	3049	3050	3051	3052	3053	3054	3055
BF0	3056	3057	3058	3059	3060	3061	3062	3063	3064	3065	3066	3067	3068	3069	3070	3071
C00	3072	3073	3074	3075	3076	3077	3078	3079	3080	3081	3082	3083	3084	3085	3086	3087
C10	3088	3089	3090	3091	3092	3093	3094	3095	3096	3097	3098	3099	3100	3101	3102	3103
C20	3104	3105	3106	3107	3108	3109	3110	3111	3112	3113	3114	3115	3116	3117	3118	3119
C30	3120	3121	3122	3123	3124	3125	3126	3127	3128	3129	3130	3131	3132	3133	3134	3135
C40	3136	3137	3138	3139	3140	3141	3142	3143	3144	3145	3146	3147	3148	3149	3150	3151
C50	3152	3153	3154	3155	3156	3157	3158	3159	3160	3161	3162	3163	3164	3165	3166	3167
C60	3168	3169	3170	3171	3172	3173	3174	3175	3176	3177	3178	3179	3180	3181	3182	3183
C70	3184	3185	3186	3187	3188	3189	3190	3191	3192	3193	3194	3195	3196	3197	3198	3199
C80	3200	3201	3202	3203	3204	3205	3206	3207	3208	3209	3210	3211	3212	3213	3214	3215
C90	3216	3217	3218	3219	3220	3221	3222	3223	3224	3225	3226	3227	3228	3229	3230	3231
CA0	3232	3233	3234	3235	3236	3237	3238	3239	3240	3241	3242	3243	3244	3245	3246	3247
CB0	3248	3249	3250	3251	3252	3253	3254	3255	3256	3257	3258	3259	3260	3261	3262	3263
CC0	3264	3265	3266	3267	3268	3269	3270	3271	3272	3273	3274	3275	3276	3277	3278	3279
CD0	3280	3281	3282	3283	3284	3285	3286	3287	3288	3289	3290	3291	3292	3293	3294	3295
CE0	3296	3297	3298	3299	3300	3301	3302	3303	3304	3305	3306	3307	3308	3309	3310	3311
CF0	3312	3313	3314	3315	3316	3317	3318	3319	3320	3321	3322	3323	3324	3325	3326	3327

HEXADECIMAL-DECIMAL INTEGER CONVERSION (continued)

	0	1	2	3	4	5	6	7	8	9	A	B	C	D	E	F
D00	3328	3329	3330	3331	3332	3333	3334	3335	3336	3337	3338	3339	3340	3341	3342	3343
D10	3344	3345	3346	3347	3348	3349	3350	3351	3352	3353	3354	3355	3356	3357	3358	3359
D20	3360	3361	3362	3363	3364	3365	3366	3367	3368	3369	3370	3371	3372	3373	3374	3375
D30	3376	3377	3378	3379	3380	3381	3382	3383	3384	3385	3386	3387	3388	3389	3390	3391
D40	3392	3393	3394	3395	3396	3397	3398	3399	3400	3401	3402	3403	3404	3405	3406	3407
D50	3408	3409	3410	3411	3412	3413	3414	3415	3416	3417	3418	3419	3420	3421	3422	3423
D60	3424	3425	3426	3427	3428	3429	3430	3431	3432	3433	3434	3435	3436	3437	3438	3439
D70	3440	3441	3442	3443	3444	3445	3446	3447	3448	3449	3450	3451	3452	3453	3454	3455
D80	3456	3457	3458	3459	3460	3461	3462	3463	3464	3465	3466	3467	3468	3469	3470	3471
D90	3472	3473	3474	3475	3476	3477	3478	3479	3480	3481	3482	3483	3484	3485	3486	3487
DA0	3488	3489	3490	3491	3492	3493	3494	3495	3496	3497	3498	3499	3500	3501	3502	3503
DB0	3504	3505	3506	3507	3508	3509	3510	3511	3512	3513	3514	3515	3516	3517	3518	3519
DC0	3520	3521	3522	3523	3524	3525	3526	3527	3528	3529	3530	3531	3532	3533	3534	3535
DD0	3536	3537	3538	3539	3540	3541	3542	3543	3544	3545	3546	3547	3548	3549	3550	3551
DE0	3552	3553	3554	3555	3556	3557	3558	3559	3560	3561	3562	3563	3564	3565	3566	3567
DF0	3568	3569	3570	3571	3572	3573	3574	3575	3576	3577	3578	3579	3580	3581	3582	3583
E00	3584	3585	3586	3587	3588	3589	3590	3591	3592	3593	3594	3595	3596	3597	3598	3599
E10	3600	3601	3602	3603	3604	3605	3606	3607	3608	3609	3610	3611	3612	3613	3614	3615
E20	3616	3617	3618	3619	3620	3621	3622	3623	3624	3625	3626	3627	3628	3629	3630	3631
E30	3632	3633	3634	3635	3636	3637	3638	3639	3640	3641	3642	3643	3644	3645	3646	3647
E40	3648	3649	3650	3651	3652	3653	3654	3655	3656	3657	3658	3659	3660	3661	3662	3663
E50	3664	3665	3666	3667	3668	3669	3670	3671	3672	3673	3674	3675	3676	3677	3678	3679
E60	3680	3681	3682	3683	3684	3685	3686	3687	3688	3689	3690	3691	3692	3693	3694	3695
E70	3696	3697	3698	3699	3700	3701	3702	3703	3704	3705	3706	3707	3708	3709	3710	3711

	0	1	2	3	4	5	6	7	8	9	A	B	C	D	E	F
E80	3712	3713	3714	3715	3716	3717	3718	3719	3720	3721	3722	3723	3724	3725	3726	3727
E90	3728	3729	3730	3731	3732	3733	3734	3735	3736	3737	3738	3739	3740	3741	3742	3743
EA0	3744	3745	3746	3747	3748	3749	3750	3751	3752	3753	3754	3755	3756	3757	3758	3759
EB0	3760	3761	3762	3763	3764	3765	3766	3767	3768	3769	3770	3771	3772	3773	3774	3775
EC0	3776	3777	3778	3779	3780	3781	3782	3783	3784	3785	3786	3787	3788	3789	3790	3791
ED0	3792	3793	3794	3795	3796	3797	3798	3799	3800	3801	3802	3803	3804	3805	3806	3807
EE0	3808	3809	3810	3811	3812	3813	3814	3815	3816	3817	3818	3819	3820	3821	3822	3823
EF0	3824	3825	3826	3827	3828	3829	3830	3831	3832	3833	3834	3835	3836	3837	3838	3839
F00	3840	3841	3842	3843	3844	3845	3846	3847	3848	3849	3850	3851	3852	3853	3854	3855
F10	3856	3857	3858	3859	3860	3861	3862	3863	3864	3865	3866	3867	3868	3869	3870	3871
F20	3872	3873	3874	3875	3876	3877	3878	3879	3880	3881	3882	3883	3884	3885	3886	3887
F30	3888	3889	3890	3891	3892	3893	3894	3895	3896	3897	3898	3899	3900	3901	3902	3903
F40	3904	3905	3906	3907	3908	3909	3910	3911	3912	3913	3914	3915	3916	3917	3918	3919
F50	3920	3921	3922	3923	3924	3925	3926	3927	3928	3929	3930	3931	3932	3933	3934	3935
F60	3936	3937	3938	3939	3940	3941	3942	3943	3944	3945	3946	3947	3948	3949	3950	3951
F70	3952	3953	3954	3955	3956	3957	3958	3959	3960	3961	3962	3963	3964	3965	3966	3967
F80	3968	3969	3970	3971	3972	3973	3974	3975	3976	3977	3978	3979	3980	3981	3982	3983
F90	3984	3985	3986	3987	3988	3989	3990	3991	3992	3993	3994	3995	3996	3997	3998	3999
FA0	4000	4001	4002	4003	4004	4005	4006	4007	4008	4009	4010	4011	4012	4013	4014	4015
FB0	4016	4017	4018	4019	4020	4021	4022	4023	4024	4025	4026	4027	4028	4029	4030	4031
FC0	4032	4033	4034	4035	4036	4037	4038	4039	4040	4041	4042	4043	4044	4045	4046	4047
FD0	4048	4049	4050	4051	4052	4053	4054	4055	4056	4057	4058	4059	4060	4061	4062	4063
FE0	4064	4065	4066	4067	4068	4069	4070	4071	4072	4073	4074	4075	4076	4077	4078	4079
FF0	4080	4081	4082	4083	4084	4085	4086	4087	4088	4089	4090	4091	4092	4093	4094	4095

Appendix E
Standard Logic Symbols

POSITIVE OR

A
B
C
D

Boolean logic:

$$D = A + B + C$$

Truth table:

A	B	C	D
0	0	0	0
1	0	0	1
0	1	0	1
1	1	0	1
0	0	1	1
1	0	1	1
0	1	1	1
1	1	1	1

NEGATIVE OR

A
B
C
D

Boolean logic:

$$D = A + B + C$$

Truth table:

A	B	C	D
0	0	0	0
1	0	0	0
0	1	0	0
1	1	0	0
0	0	1	0
1	0	1	0
0	1	1	0
1	1	1	1

POSITIVE EXCLUSIVE OR

A
B
C
D

Boolean logic:

$$D = A\bar{B}\bar{C} + \bar{A}B\bar{C} + \bar{A}\bar{B}C$$

Truth table:

A	B	C	D
0	0	0	1
1	0	0	0
0	1	0	0
1	1	0	1
0	0	1	0
1	0	1	1
0	1	1	1
1	1	1	1

NEGATIVE EXCLUSIVE OR

A
B
C
D

Boolean logic:

$$D = A\bar{B}\bar{C} + \bar{A}B\bar{C} + \bar{A}\bar{B}C$$

Truth table:

A	B	C	D
0	0	0	1
1	0	0	1
0	1	0	1
1	1	0	0
0	0	1	1
1	0	1	0
0	1	1	0
1	1	1	1

POSITIVE NOR

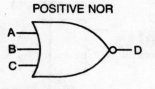

Boolean logic:

$$D = \overline{A + B + C}$$

Truth table:

A	B	C	D
0	0	0	1
1	0	0	0
0	1	0	0
1	1	0	0
0	0	1	0
1	0	1	0
0	1	1	0
1	1	1	0

NEGATIVE NOR

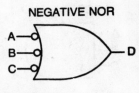

Boolean logic:

$$D = \overline{\overline{A} + \overline{B} + \overline{C}}$$

Truth table:

A	B	C	D
0	0	0	1
1	0	0	1
0	1	0	1
1	1	0	1
0	0	1	1
1	0	1	1
0	1	1	1
1	1	1	0

POSITIVE EXCLUSIVE NOR

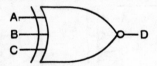

Boolean logic:

$$D = \overline{A}\overline{B}\overline{C} + AB\overline{C} +$$
$$A\overline{B}C + \overline{A}BC + ABC$$
$$(\overline{A}\overline{B}\overline{C} + AB + AC + BC)$$

Truth table:

A	B	C	D
0	0	0	1
1	0	0	0
0	1	0	0
1	1	0	1
0	0	1	0
1	0	1	1
0	1	1	1
1	1	1	1

NEGATIVE EXCLUSIVE NOR

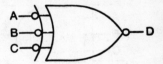

Boolean logic:

$$D = \overline{A}\overline{B}\overline{C} + AB\overline{C} +$$
$$A\overline{B}C + \overline{A}BC + ABC$$
$$(\overline{A}\overline{B}\overline{C} + AB + AC + BC)$$

Truth table:

A	B	C	D
0	0	0	0
1	0	0	0
0	1	0	0
1	1	0	1
0	0	1	0
1	0	1	1
0	1	1	1
1	1	1	0

POSITIVE AND

Boolean logic:

D = ABC

Truth table:

A	B	C	D
0	0	0	0
1	0	0	0
0	1	0	0
1	1	0	0
0	0	1	0
1	0	1	0
0	1	1	0
1	1	1	0

NEGATIVE AND

Boolean logic:

$D = \overline{ABC}$

Truth table:

A	B	C	D
0	0	0	0
1	0	0	1
0	1	0	1
1	1	0	1
1	0	1	1
0	0	1	1
1	0	1	1
0	1	1	1
1	1	1	1

POSITIVE INCLUSIVE AND

Boolean logic:

$D = \overline{A}\overline{B}\overline{C} + A\overline{B}\overline{C} +$
$\overline{A}B\overline{C} + \overline{A}\overline{B}C + ABC$

$(ABC + \overline{A}\overline{B} + \overline{A}\overline{C} + \overline{B}\overline{C})$

Truth table:

A	B	C	D
0	0	0	1
1	0	0	1
0	1	0	1
1	1	0	0
0	0	1	1
1	0	1	0
0	1	1	0
1	1	1	1

NEGATIVE INCLUSIVE AND

Boolean logic:

$D = \overline{A}\overline{B}\overline{C} + A\overline{B}\overline{C} +$
$\overline{A}B\overline{C} + \overline{A}\overline{B}C + ABC$

$(ABC + \overline{A}\overline{B} + \overline{A}\overline{C} + \overline{B}\overline{C})$

Truth table:

A	B	C	D
0	0	0	0
1	0	0	1
0	1	0	1
1	1	0	0
0	0	1	1
1	0	1	0
0	1	1	0
1	1	1	0

POSITIVE NAND

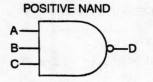

Boolean logic:

$D = \overline{ABC}$

Truth table:

A	B	C	D
0	0	0	1
1	0	0	1
0	1	0	1
1	1	0	1
0	0	1	0
1	0	1	1
0	1	1	1
1	1	1	0

NEGATIVE NAND

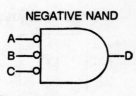

Boolean logic:

$D = \overline{\overline{A}\overline{B}\overline{C}}$

Truth table:

A	B	C	D
0	0	0	1
1	0	0	0
0	1	0	0
1	1	0	0
0	0	1	0
1	0	1	0
0	1	1	0
1	1	1	0

POSITIVE INCLUSIVE NAND

Boolean logic:

$D = AB\overline{C} + A\overline{B}C + \overline{A}BC$

Truth table:

A	B	C	D
0	0	0	0
1	0	0	0
0	1	0	0
1	1	0	1
0	0	1	0
1	0	1	1
0	1	1	1
1	1	1	0

NEGATIVE INCLUSIVE NAND

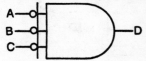

Boolean logic:

$D = AB\overline{C} + A\overline{B}C + \overline{A}BC$

Truth table:

A	B	C	D
0	0	0	1
1	0	0	0
0	1	0	0
1	1	0	1
0	0	1	0
1	0	1	1
0	1	1	1
1	1	1	1

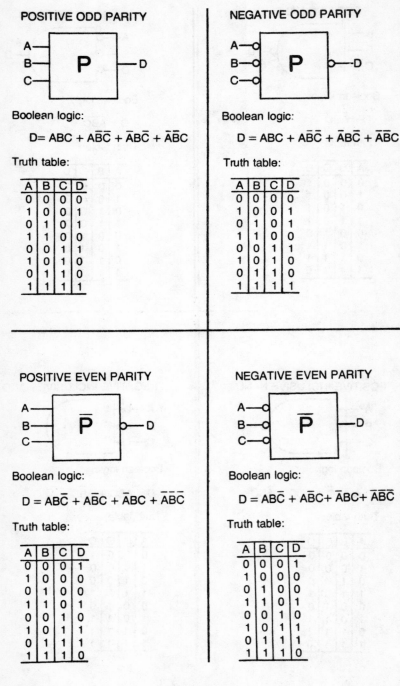

POSITIVE ODD PARITY

Boolean logic:

$$D = ABC + A\overline{B}\overline{C} + \overline{A}B\overline{C} + \overline{A}\overline{B}C$$

Truth table:

A	B	C	D
0	0	0	0
1	0	0	1
0	1	0	1
1	1	0	0
0	0	1	1
1	0	1	0
0	1	1	0
1	1	1	1

NEGATIVE ODD PARITY

Boolean logic:

$$D = ABC + A\overline{B}\overline{C} + \overline{A}B\overline{C} + \overline{A}\overline{B}C$$

Truth table:

A	B	C	D
0	0	0	0
1	0	0	1
0	1	0	1
1	1	0	0
0	0	1	1
1	0	1	0
0	1	1	0
1	1	1	1

POSITIVE EVEN PARITY

Boolean logic:

$$D = AB\overline{C} + A\overline{B}C + \overline{A}BC + \overline{A}\overline{B}\overline{C}$$

Truth table:

A	B	C	D
0	0	0	1
1	0	0	0
0	1	0	0
1	1	0	1
0	0	1	0
1	0	1	1
0	1	1	1
1	1	1	0

NEGATIVE EVEN PARITY

Boolean logic:

$$D = AB\overline{C} + A\overline{B}C + \overline{A}BC + \overline{A}\overline{B}\overline{C}$$

Truth table:

A	B	C	D
0	0	0	1
1	0	0	0
0	1	0	0
1	1	0	1
0	0	1	0
1	0	1	1
0	1	1	1
1	1	1	0

POSITIVE MAJORITY

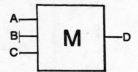

Boolean logic:

$$D = AB + AC + BC$$

Truth table:

A	B	C	D
0	0	0	0
1	0	0	0
0	1	0	0
1	1	0	1
0	0	1	0
1	0	1	1
0	1	1	1
1	1	1	1

NEGATIVE MINORITY

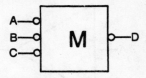

Boolean logic:

$$D = AB + AC + BC$$

Truth table:

A	B	C	D
0	0	0	0
1	0	0	0
0	1	0	0
1	1	0	1
0	0	1	0
1	0	1	1
0	1	1	1
1	1	1	1

POSITIVE NOT MAJORITY

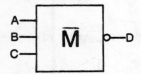

Boolean logic:

$$D = \overline{AB + AC + BC}$$

Truth table:

A	B	C	D
0	0	0	1
1	0	0	1
0	1	0	1
1	1	0	0
0	0	1	1
1	0	1	0
0	1	1	0
1	1	1	0

NEGATIVE NOT MINORITY

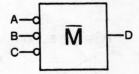

Boolean logic:

$$D = \overline{AB + AC + BC}$$

Truth table:

A	B	C	D
0	0	0	1
1	0	0	1
0	1	0	1
1	1	0	0
0	0	1	1
1	0	1	0
0	1	1	0
1	1	1	0

247

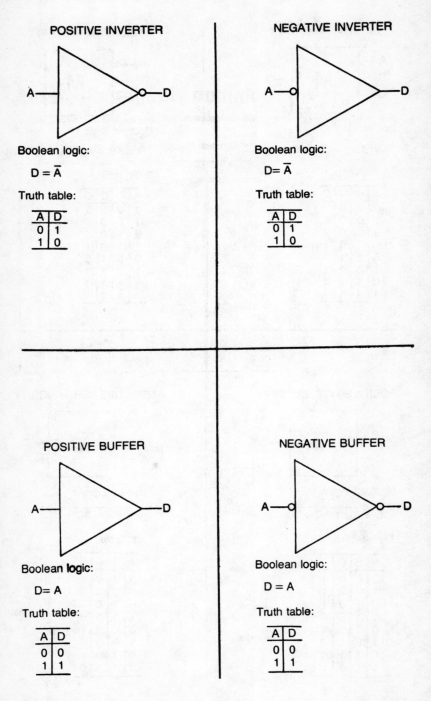

POSITIVE INVERTER

A ————▷o— D

Boolean logic:

$D = \overline{A}$

Truth table:

A	D
0	1
1	0

NEGATIVE INVERTER

A —o◁————— D

Boolean logic:

$D = \overline{A}$

Truth table:

A	D
0	1
1	0

POSITIVE BUFFER

A ————▷— D

Boolean logic:

$D = A$

Truth table:

A	D
0	0
1	1

NEGATIVE BUFFER

A —o◁————o— D

Boolean logic:

$D = A$

Truth table:

A	D
0	0
1	1

Appendix F
Common Number Systems

Common Number Systems.

Decimal	Binary	BCD		Octal	Excess-3 BCD		Hexadecimal
0	00000	0000		0	0011		0
1	00001	0001		1	0100		1
2	00010	0010		2	0101		2
3	00011	0011		3	0110		3
4	00100	0100		4	0111		4
5	00101	0101		5	1000		5
6	00110	0110		6	1001		6
7	00111	0111		7	1010		7
8	01000	1000		10	1011		8
9	01001	1001		11	1100		9
10	01010	0001	0000	12	0001	0011	A
11	01011	0001	0001	13	0001	0100	B
12	01100	0001	0010	14	0001	0101	C
13	01101	0001	0011	15	0001	0110	D
14	01110	0001	0100	16	0001	0111	E
15	01111	0001	0101	17	0001	1000	F
16	10000	0001	0110	20	0001	1100	10